Student Study Guide

CHILDREN

JOHN W. SANTROCK

Y0-ABY-309

Student Study Guide

CHILDREN
JOHN W. SANTROCK

Debra E. Clark
The Neurologic Center of Cortland

Melvyn B. King
State University of New York at Cortland

A Gift from the Estate of
Michael Hart
www.gutenberg.org

wcb
Wm. C. Brown Publishers
Dubuque, Iowa

Cover photo courtesy of Northern Telecom. Photographer JoAnn Carney.

Copyright © 1988 by Wm. C. Brown Publishers. All rights reserved

ISBN 0–697–01281–6

No part of this publication may be reproduced, stored in a
retrieval system, or transmitted, in any form or by any means,
electronic, mechanical, photocopying, recording, or otherwise,
without the prior written permission of the publishers.

Printed in the United States of America by Wm. C. Brown Publishers
2460 Kerper Boulevard, Dubuque, IA 52001

10 9 8 7 6 5 4

To Our Parents
    Gwendolyn and Paris
    and
    Susan and Joseph

Contents

To the Student

This study guide is designed to help you master the material in *Children* by John W. Santrock. The emphasis is on reading, reviewing with active learning, and evaluating your mastery of the text.

Each study guide chapter has seven sections designed to help you learn the textbook material. The sections are:

1. **Learning Objectives**

   This list provides an outline for mastery of the chapter material. Notice that each objective is phrased in behavioral terms, such as *list, name, describe,* and *explain,* so that you can determine whether or not you have mastered the item. Each learning objective is accompanied by a textbook reference that highlights the text pages that cover the learning objective material.

2. **Chapter Summary**

   The chapter summary provides a brief overview of the major concepts of the text chapter. Although you may find the summary helpful for a quick review before exams or classes, it cannot be used as a substitute for reading the chapter itself, since detailed information is not included. If you read the summary before you read the text chapter, you will have a general, overall picture of the material that will help you to make sense of the more specific details.

3. **Guided Review**

   The guided review consists of fill-in-the-blank items that guide you through your reading of the chapter. You may want to look at the answers to the "Guided Review" statements as you read, or you may want to use the exercise as a form of self-test by covering up the answers below the statements with a sheet of paper and not consulting them until you have attempted to fill in the blanks of each statement.

4. **Key Terms Matching Exercise**

   The key terms matching exercise asks you to match each important chapter term with its definition. Completing this exercise will test your knowledge of key terms and concepts. Once the answers have been filled in, this section will function as a chapter glossary for study and review. Check your work against the answers given at the end of the exercise. Each term is accompanied by a learning objective reference and a reference to the text page on which the term is found.

5. **Self-Tests**

   In recognition of the widespread use of multiple-choice questions for testing, the study guide provides you with two 20-question multiple-choice tests. Both tests cover the same material with different questions. These questions are of the same type that your instructor is likely to use on an examination. There is a mix of difficult and easy questions, and they evenly sample the material in the chapters. Each question is accompanied by a learning objective number and the number of the text page on which the answer is found. The answers are presented immediately after each test.

6. **Questions to Stimulate Thought**

   These questions are designed to prompt you to think about integrating sections of the chapter and even sections from different chapters. No answers are provided because there are no "correct" answers, or more properly, there is no single correct answer for each question. There are many ways to integrate these materials; hence, the hope is that these questions will stimulate thought and discussion among class members. These items also are similar to essay questions, and you can treat them as such in your review.

7. **Research Project**

   Each chapter is provided with a research project of some sort. Many of them are short observation studies; several are like little experiments. Each of them is safe. These exercises allow you to practice psychology in a small way, to discover some of the joys and frustrations of actually going out into the world to learn something about children. If performed, these projects can make the study of child development come alive for you.

The study guide was written from the textbook and is designed to facilitate the learning of the text material. The study guide alone, however, is very unlikely to provide you any benefit.

Using the Study Guide

Read the learning objectives before picking up the textbook to read the chapter. This will focus your attention on the important topics covered in each chapter. Try to think about information you will be required to learn for each chapter. How would you respond to each objective? Do you have information from a previous course that bears on the objective? Can you relate that information to the current material? You can use the learning objectives as a preview to the chapter so that, when you read the chapter, you will know what to expect and what is important to understand and remember. The more active you make your learning, the better that learning will be.

After studying the learning objectives, read the chapter through. Think about the learning objectives as you read, but do not become bogged down in detail. You should try to get a general idea of what the chapter is about. Mark those sections that seem particularly difficult to understand for special attention later.

After reading the chapter, do the "Guided Review." The items in the "Guided Review" are fill-in items designed to give you practice in understanding and recall. For this practice to provide benefit, you must try to answer each question, struggling to recall a term or concept, if necessary, before reading the answer. The first time through the "Guided Review," you should write your responses in the margin. This will allow you to go through the exercise a second time if there are many questions that you do not answer correctly, or during your review for an examination.

After completing the "Guided Review," go back over the portions of the chapter covering the items you missed. If there are many such items, reread the chapter carefully, with special attention to the troublesome material, and go through the "Guided Review" again, covering up the margins with your first answers. Remember, to be effective, the learning should be active, not passive. Think about the material in novel ways and become part of the learning process.

Next, do the "Key Terms Matching Exercise." Check your answers. Each term is cross-referenced to a learning objective and to the page in the chapter where the term is introduced and discussed. If you answer incorrectly, or if you do not understand a definition, review the appropriate learning objective, then go to the textbook page and reread the relevant material. Make sure you understand the meaning of the term. If necessary, rewrite the definition in your own words.

Do Self-Test A. When you have completed the self-test, grade it. Give yourself five points for each correct answer. This should give you an estimate of how ready you are to take an exam. Remember, to be effective, the learning should be active, not passive. Struggle to recall the information; practice your retrieval skills.

Each question is cross-indexed to the section in the textbook from which it came and to the relevant learning objective. This allows you to go back to the text and study the material you missed.

After studying these sections again, take Self-Test B. If you write your answers in the margin, you can use Self-Test B again during your review for an examination. Your performance on Self-Test B should be better than on Self-Test A, if you used the results of Self-Test A to indicate the material you had not yet mastered.

Write short answers to the "Questions to Stimulate Thought," perhaps a paragraph or two on each. Then go to the relevant sections of the text and evaluate your responses. You might also want to use the questions to start a discussion with some of your friends from the class. If the discussion is active, you may be forced to think about the material in a way you had not before and to remember things about the topic you might otherwise not remember.

There are two kinds of research projects presented in this study guide. The first kind involves the public behavior of children and uses naturalistic observation. You go to public places, such as neighborhood playgrounds, grocery stores, and shopping malls, and unobtrusively observe some specified behavior of a child in that context. These projects can be done on your own, perhaps with the aid of a partner from class.

The second kind of research project requires specific testing of one or more children on a particular task. These projects may require the informed consent of the parents of the children and also may require approval by the Human Subjects Review Committee at your school. The projects that fall into this category should not be done without the direction of your instructor. If there is any doubt at all, consult your instructor for guidance.

The section that follows describes ethical practices used for doing research with human subjects. You should read this section before doing any of the research projects.

Debra E. Clark
Melvyn B. King

Ethical Practices in Research with Human Subjects*

There are four issues of major importance in conducting research with human subjects. They are (1) consent, (2) deception and risk, (3) coercion, and (4) privacy and confidentiality.

1. Informed consent is required from the subject prior to any psychological testing. In doing research with children, written consent of the parents is required. Informed consent means that the purpose of the research and the procedures involved have been explained to the parents and that they understand what is involved and agree to allow their child to participate in the study. The procedures should then be explained to the child at the child's level of understanding, the child's cooperation should be enlisted, and an attempt should be made to maintain the child's interest during his or her participation in the project. Parents must be informed that both they and their child have the right to withdraw from participation at any time for any reason.
2. A Human Subjects Review Committee, by that or some similar name, exists at all institutions that do research with human subjects to evaluate the research projects and to safeguard the rights and the safety of potential subjects. Determinations of such review committees are usually based, in part, upon the possible use of deception and any potential risk to subjects. The concept of informed consent assumes that the real purpose of the experiment has been revealed to subjects and that the subjects are competent to decide whether or not to participate. This condition is violated when the experiment requires deception of the subject. None of the projects in this study guide require deception of the subjects. The second problem is possible risk to subjects. None of the projects presented here involves risk to the subjects. However, they do not provide positive benefits to the subjects either. They are neutral along this dimension.
3. The requirement for informed consent is violated when coercion is used on subjects because, when coercion is used, subjects are not free to refuse to participate. This freedom to refuse must be guaranteed to the subjects. When working with children as subjects, it is necessary to make the study as playful and gamelike as possible to enlist the interest of the children. However, their rights to refuse to participate and to not be coerced must also be respected and protected.
4. Privacy and confidentiality must be guaranteed. It is important to inform the parents that, in any report of the information gained, their child will not be reported by name but only by averages or by identifiers that cannot be traced to the individual child. The child's privacy will be protected. This requires that, when you present data in class, you report the data only by age and sex of the child, never by name.

Human Subjects Information

Your school should have forms available to use for the submission of research studies to the Human Subjects Review Committee on your campus. The kind of information generally required on these forms includes:

1. A description of the purpose of the research and a detailed description of the procedures used, including potential hazards and benefits to the subjects
2. A copy of the informed consent form that subjects will sign, along with a description of the way in which their consent will be elicited
3. A description of any possible harm—physical, emotional, or psychological—that might come from participation in the project
4. A description of the subjects to be seen, including number, age, and other characteristics

It is also possible that your school allows, as some do, for entire study guides such as this one to be submitted for consideration so that all the research exercises can be considered at once. This is a great convenience. Ask your instructor if your school has such a policy.

---

*M. A. Carroll, H. G. Schneider, and G. R. Wesley, *Ethics in the Practice of Psychology* (Englewood Cliffs, N.J.: Prentice-Hall, 1985).

Informed Consent Form

The informed consent form that the parents sign should include several kinds of information:

1. A description of the procedures and the purpose of the study.
2. A statement of the rights of the subject to refuse to participate and to withdraw from participation at any time.
3. A statement guaranteeing the privacy and confidentiality of the results of the study. This usually involves a statement saying that results will not be reported by name and that any identifying information will be omitted from the report.
4. A description of any possible risks or discomforts that the subject might experience.
5. A description of any possible benefits to be expected for the subject. In the exercises presented in this study guide, the benefits tend to simply be enjoyment from playing some of the games.

It is very likely that your school has such a form already prepared for use by faculty researchers. You can use the same form.

1 History, Issues, and Methods

Learning Objectives

After studying this chapter, you should be able to:

1. Briefly describe the concerns in child development regarding divorce, working mothers, latchkey children, computers and children, hurried children, Type A behavior, and children's health. (pp. 7–9)
2. Describe the prevailing views of children and child development in ancient times. (pp. 9–10)
3. Describe the prevailing views of children and child development during the Middle Ages. (p. 10)
4. Describe the prevailing views of children and child development during the Renaissance. (p. 11)
5. List and explain the assumptions made by those who espouse the philosophies of original sin, *tabula rasa,* and innate goodness views, respectively. (pp. 10–11)
6. Describe the prevailing views of children and child development in recent (late 19th century) and contemporary times. (pp. 11–13)
7. Define the following terms: *prenatal period, infancy, early childhood, middle and late childhood,* and *adolescence.* (pp. 15–17)
8. Describe the major processes that shape child development—biological, physical, cognitive, social, and personality processes—and how they relate to each other. (pp. 17–19)
9. Compare and contrast qualitative versus quantitative changes in development. (p. 19)
10. Explain how stages of development fit into an understanding of child development. (pp. 19–20)
11. Describe and explain continuity versus discontinuity in child development. (p. 20)
12. Explain the role of individual differences in understanding child development. (pp. 20, 22)
13. Explain the issues surrounding the relative roles of genetics or heredity versus social and environmental factors in child development. (pp. 22–23)
14. Describe systematic observation, naturalistic observation, the interview, the survey/questionnaire, and the standardized test, and give one strength and weakness of each. (pp. 23–30)
15. Describe the experimental, quasi-experimental, and correlational strategies for studying child development and give one strength and weakness of each. (pp. 30–32)
16. Describe cross-sectional, longitudinal, and sequential designs and give one strength and weakness of each. (pp. 32–34)
17. Describe the cohort effect and specify the design that eliminates it. (p. 34)
18. List four important elements in the American Psychological Association and the Society for Research in Child Development's code of ethics for working with children and specify what each means. (p. 34)

Summary

Three areas are of contemporary concern in child development. First, the family is changing, and the current quality of child care that children receive in either single-parent families or families in which both parents work may be a problem. Second, young children are now exposed to computers, and it is necessary to understand the possible effect that computers may have on children's social and intellectual development. Third, children today are exposed to stress early and are pressured to live up to extraordinarily high standards.

The view of children and child development has changed throughout history. Aries used samples of art to conclude that, historically, childhood has consisted of only two phases—infancy and adulthood—but his conclusions have been called into question. In ancient Greece and Rome, infanticide, sexual abuse, and abandonment of children occurred, although children were sometimes treated with special rules. During the Middle Ages, both the Church and the medical profession worked at developing children's physical and psychological (spiritual) well-being. The Magna Carta gave children the legal right to inheritance and specified that children with major disabilities should receive special treatment by society. During the Renaissance, schooling became available for many more children, and pediatric medicine arose.

The three philosophical views of the child were the original sin view, which appeared during the Middle Ages, and the *tabula rasa* and innate goodness views, which appeared during the Renaissance. The original sin view reflected the philosophical perspective that children were inherently evil and that societal constraints and salvation were necessary for children to become mature adults. Locke's *tabula rasa* view saw the child as a blank slate upon which experience would write. Rousseau's innate goodness view conceived of the child as basically good and stressed that the child should be allowed to grow naturally, without constraints from parents or society.

More scientific approaches to studying children developed during the 19th and 20th centuries. In the late 19th century, Darwin made the scientific study of children respectable. Hall, in the early 20th century, was strongly influenced by Darwin and viewed adolescence as a period of storm and stress. Freud also saw child development as based in conflict. Watson's theory of behaviorism emphasized the role of experience and supported the scientific study of children's behavior. Gesell also promoted the scientific study of children, proposing a biological, maturational view.

Political realities influence research in child development. Research has flourished when there has been national activity on behalf of children and families. Childhood is now considered a unique time in life that is characterized by growth and change, in part as a result of experience.

The periods of childhood development are the prenatal period (conception to birth), infancy (birth to 18 to 24 months), early childhood (the preschool years), middle and late childhood (the elementary school years), and adolescence (puberty to 18 to 21 years). Different developmental tasks are important at each of these stages, ranging from the physical structures that appear during the prenatal period to the formation of logical reasoning and abstract thought during adolescence.

Processes are the explanations that child developmentalists use to explain the nature of development. There are five processes in development. The biological and physical processes include evolution, ethology, genetics, neurological development, and physical growth. Cognitive processes include thought, perception, memory, attention, problem solving, and language. Cognitive activities are seen as causal influences on behavior. Experience alone does not determine the child's behavior but is tempered by how the child's cognitive processes interpret it. Social and personality processes include interactions with other individuals in the environment and properties of the individual child, such as self, sex roles, and morality.

An important issue in child development is that of qualitative change. Piaget argued that there were qualitative changes in intelligence. He viewed the development of thinking as a shift from one kind of thinking to another, not just an accumulation of mental power. Another issue in child development is the question of stages of development. The concept of developmental stages includes the notion of qualitative change, as well as order or sequence. Two other notions—abruptness of transition from one stage to the next and the simultaneous appearance of multiple behaviors or competencies that characterize a stage—are thought to be necessary to the stage idea. The issue of continuity versus discontinuity in development involves the extent to which later development is dependent on earlier development.

Individual differences may exist in intraindividual change. Although research reports group means, individual children may not behave in ways that reflect the group of which they are members. Biological and social forces both influence the developing child.

Common to all described methods for collecting information about children is the emphasis on systematic observation under controlled conditions. Laboratory settings allow the most control. However, field studies or naturalistic observation also provide important information, although with less control. Interviews and surveys/questionnaires are two ways of getting information. Problems with these methods include the possibility of the subject wishing to appear a certain way and thus distorting the responses. Standardized tests are used to compare an individual's characteristics relative to a large group of similar individuals.

The most important research strategy for determining causal relations between variables is the experiment. In an experiment, the independent variable is manipulated, and the dependent variable is measured. Subjects are randomly assigned to receive a given level of the independent variable; one group gets a certain level, while another group gets the zero level. Both groups are then measured on the dependent variable. Differences between the groups on the dependent variable are attributed to the differences in the level of the independent variable, and causal statements can be made. In the quasi-experimental strategy, subjects are not randomly assigned to levels of the independent variable—they come into the study with this already assigned. Correlational strategy involves measuring the degree of relation between two variables on subjects, such as height and weight. Causal statements cannot be made from either quasi-experimental or correlational studies.

Cross-sectional, longitudinal, and sequential designs examine the effects of age on behavior. In a cross-sectional study, groups of children in different age ranges are compared at the same point in time. This is easy and time efficient. However, differences that appear may be due to cohort effects (that is, generation differences) rather than to age. In a longitudinal study, a group of same-age children are examined at two or more points in time. While this design is more time consuming, changes within the individual can be observed. Sequential designs have at least two cohorts, two age groups, and two times of measurement. This design shows whether the same pattern of development is produced by each research strategy.

Ethical standards are important in child development research. There are four separate issues: (1) Informed consent must be obtained from parents or guardians who have a complete description of what will be done with their children. (2) Children have the right to refuse to participate, and the experimenter has an obligation to calm the child if any upset occurs during the procedure. (3) The benefits of the experience for the child must outweigh any chance of harm, and the psychologist must convince a peer review board of this. (4) Children should be treated courteously and respectfully.

Guided Review

You may want to look at the answers to the "Guided Review" statements as you read, or you may want to use the exercise as a form of self-test by covering up the answers below the statements with a sheet of paper and not consulting them until you have attempted to fill in the blanks of each statement.

1. According to Santrock, the increase in _____ and the tendency of modern women to have _____ are having a major impact on the structure of the modern family. Two effects have been the increase in _____ families and the increase in the number of so-called _____ children.

   divorce, careers or jobs, stepparent, latchkey

2. Our modern time has been called the _____ age. Part of the responsibility for this development is attributable to advances in _____ science. Computers may now be used by children as young as _____ years old.

   information, computer, four

3. Elkind has asserted that American parents try to move their children through development too _____ . The observation of _____ _____ behavior in children may be evidence that this assertion is well-founded.

   fast, Type A

4. The area of psychology that has recently developed to consider such effects as those that might be produced by too much stress on children is called _____ psychology.

   health

5. Aries presented the view that most societies divided development into two periods: _____ and _____ . However, this view may have been based on the work of _____ , and recent work casts doubt on its validity.

   infancy, adulthood, artists

6. One of the problems of children in ancient times was _____ _____ . However, in some classical writings, children are portrayed as _____ .

   child abuse, special

7. _____ had a pervasive influence on the lives of children during the Middle Ages. However, in England, some rights were given to children by the _____ _____ .

   Christianity, Magna Carta

8. During the Middle Ages, it was generally believed that children were born filled with evil. This is known as the _____ _____ view. During this time, the goal of child rearing was _____ .

   original sin, salvation

9. During the Renaissance, two other views about the nature of the child appeared. At the end of the 17th century, John Locke developed the view that the child is born with a mind that is a _____ _____ . He proposed that the adult mind is constructed from _____ .

   tabula rasa, experience

10. During the 18th century, Rousseau stressed that children are innately _____ . He suggested that parents impose no _____ on their children but rather allow the children to grow _____ .

    good, constraints, naturally

11. The essence of the argument among the proponents of these three views of development is now known as the _____-_____ controversy (or debate).

    nature-nurture

12. Toward the end of the 19th century, _____ _____ made the scientific study of children respectable when he developed a _____ _____ . This was the first _____ strategy for the study of child development. Psychologist _____ _____ _____ incorporated Darwin's ideas about _____ into his views of development. He thought that development unfolded in a pattern of _____ that mimicked the natural evolutionary course. He also thought that adolescence was a time of terrific _____ and _____ .

    Charles Darwin, baby journal, systematic, G. Stanley Hall, evolution, stages, storm, stress

13. _____ proposed a theory of personality formation with a strong child developmental component. The weakness of Freud's theory of development, which was compatible with _____'s ideas, was that it could not generate _____ . _____ _____ proposed a theory that was based on ideas similar to those of _____ , that is, that society (or experience) shaped the child. Watson's view is called _____ and carries a strong commitment to research.

    Freud, Hall, research, John Watson, Locke, behaviorism

14. Between 1920 and 1950, _____ _____ charted the development of children. His perspective was largely _____ and was described by him as _____ . Gesell believed that a _____ blueprint guided development. He also believed that the environment was the _____ , not the _____ of development.

    Arnold Gesell, biological, maturational, genetic, setting, cause

15. During the current century, the _____ has emerged as a potent force in the lives of children, both because of its regulations and programs and its sponsorship of research.

    government

16. Today, we think of childhood as an important and eventful time during which the child requires _____ and _____ .

    protection, training

17. The prenatal period extends from _____ to _____ . Infancy begins at _____ and extends through the _____ or _____ month. The period from the end of infancy to about _____ or _____ years of age is called early childhood. The elementary school years are divided into _____ childhood and _____ childhood. The range

of ages for the former is _____ to _____ years and for the latter is _____ to _____ years. Adolescence is the period of transition from _____ to early _____ . It begins at about _____ to _____ years of age and ends by about _____ to _____ years of age.

conception, birth, birth, 18th, 24th, five, six, middle, late, 6, 8, 9, 11, childhood, adulthood, 11, 13, 18, 21

18. The explanations that child developmentalists use to explain the nature of development are called _____ . The type of process that stems from the genetic composition of the individual is called a _____ process. The process that involves thinking is called a _____ process. The process involving interaction with other individuals is called a _____ process, and the process related to the last but more reflecting of individual characteristics is called a _____ process. The overall pattern of movement or change that is characteristic of the entire life span is called _____ .

processes, biological, cognitive, social, personality, development

19. According to _____ , the child's intelligence or cognitive functioning is not simply less than that of the adult, it is _____ . One bit of evidence for this is that, during the first two years of life, the _____ _____ develops.

Piaget, different, object concept

20. Piaget proposed that there are identifiable _____ of intellectual development in childhood and that, for each individual child, the _____ of the stages is always the same. According to Piaget, the difference between stages is _____ .

stages, sequence, qualitative

21. A part of the continuity-discontinuity controversy is the issue of the extent to which later development is dependent upon _____ _____ . The view that early experience is the primary determinant of development later in life is a strong form of the continuity argument and was proposed by _____ theorists.

earlier development, Freudian

22. Those psychologists who believe that early experience does not have irreversible effects take a _____ stance. This increases the importance of _____ experiences.

discontinuity, later

23. Work in _____ has indicated that _____ supplements during the first _____ years of life can increase _____ and decrease _____ . A study in San Diego found that the children of mothers who were _____ during pregnancy interacted less with their _____ .

Guatemala, nutritional, four, activity, anxiety, undernourished, peers

24. Everyone is not the same. This statement reflects the existence of _____ _____ among people. Often, the research results reported are for _____ differences. This hides the individual _____ that compose _____ _____ .

individual differences, group, variations, individual differences

25. The process of _____ _____ involves knowing _____ we are looking for, _____ we are going to observe, _____ and _____ we are going to observe, _____ the observations are going to be made, and in what form the observations are going to be _____ .

systematic observation, what, whom, when, where, how, recorded

26. Observations made in the laboratory setting facilitate the control of other _____ that might influence development. At the other end of the continuum from the laboratory setting is the totally nonintrusive _____ observation or _____ _____ .

factors or variables, naturalistic, field study

27. The set of questions put to someone and the responses the person makes is called an _____ . A _____ is similar to a structured interview, but the subject reads the questions and marks the answers on a prepared sheet.

interview, questionnaire

28. Bryant developed a special interviewing technique for children. It involves a _____ through the child's _____ . She studied _____ development by asking the children to tell about the people who lived in the familiar _____ .

walk, neighborhood, social, homes

29. A critical problem facing users of the structured interview is the tendency of respondents to replace the truth with what is _____ _____ . This is called the set of _____ _____ .

socially acceptable, social desirability

30. Standardized tests provide a _____ of one child's performance with a large group; that is, they provide information about _____ _____ among children. The test score is frequently presented as a _____ .

comparison, individual differences, percentile

31. The most important advantage of the experimental strategy is that it allows for the determination of a _____ relationship between two variables.

causal or cause-and-effect

32. In an experiment, the variable manipulated by the experimenter so that two or more groups are exposed to different levels of it is the _____ _____ . The experimenter measures the _____ _____ , usually a measure of behavior, that is being examined for change resulting from the influence of the independent variable.

independent variable, dependent variable

33. A method used to assure that experimental groups initially do not differ in any systematic way is called _____ selection. The _____ group is arbitrarily and randomly chosen to be exposed to some of the independent variable. The group that is exposed to none of the independent variable is called the _____ group.

random, experimental, control

34. If the degree of prior control that may be exercised over the independent variable is less than that for a true experiment, the procedure is called a _____ - _____ . _____ cannot be inferred from quasi-experiments.

quasi-experiment, Causality

35. A procedure used to reduce the differences between the groups in a quasi-experiment involves _____ the groups on relevant variables.

matching

36. The correlation coefficient is a statistic that measures the strength of the _____ between any two variables. A correlation cannot be used to support the argument that a change in one variable _____ the effect in another.

association or relationship, caused

37. A cross-sectional study compares children of _____ _____ . A longitudinal study examines effects related to age by testing a child at least _____ .

different ages, twice

38. A difficulty arises in interpreting cross-sectional studies because they cannot control for _____ effects. Longitudinal studies allow the tracking of changes in an individual over time, but they are difficult to do because they may require a _____ _____ to complete.

cohort, long time

39. Sequential research designs combine the important factors in the _____ - _____ and _____ designs by including at least _____ age groups, _____ cohorts, and _____ times of measurement.

cross-sectional, longitudinal, two, two, two

40. The code of ethics of the American Psychological Association and the Society for Research in Child Development requires that, before research is carried out on children, their parents or guardians provide _____ _____ . The researcher must also have the consent of the _____ . It is essential that the researcher weigh the (potential) _____ to the child against the potential benefit. The researcher must also adhere to accepted _____ of _____ .

informed consent, child, risk or harm, standards, practice

Key Terms Matching Exercise

Match the Key Term on the left with the correct definition on the right.

_____ 1. latchkey children (LO–1, p. 7)
_____ 2. original sin view (LO–5, p. 10)
_____ 3. *tabula rasa* view (LO–5, p. 11)
_____ 4. innate goodness view (LO–5, p. 11)
_____ 5. periods (LO–7, p. 15)

a. Philosophical view that children are born basically good and should be permitted to grow naturally, without constraints from parents

b. Children who live a portion of their day unmonitored by adults

c. Time frames that characterize a particular segment of development

d. Philosophical view that children are basically evil and that only through the constraints of their upbringing will they become mature adults

e. Philosophical view that the child's mind is a blank slate at birth, with experience determining the kind of adult the child becomes

___ 6. prenatal period (LO–7, p. 15)
___ 7. infancy (LO–7, p. 15)
___ 8. early childhood (LO–7, p. 15)
___ 9. middle and late childhood (LO–7, p. 15)
___ 10. adolescence (LO–7, p. 15)

a. Period of transition from childhood to early adulthood
b. Period that roughly corresponds to the elementary school years
c. Period from conception to birth
d. Period from birth to about 18 or 24 months of age
e. Corresponds to the preschool years

___ 11. early adolescence (LO–7, p.17)
___ 12. late adolescence (LO–7, p. 17)
___ 13. processes (LO–8, p. 17)
___ 14. biological processes (LO–8, p. 17)
___ 15. physical development (LO–8, p. 18)

a. Processes that include neurological development and growth
b. Time period corresponding to the junior high school years
c. Examples are evolution, heredity (genetics), and ethology
d. Period that includes the late teenage years and early 20s
e. Explanations used to explain the nature of development

___ 16. cognitive processes (LO–8, p. 18)
___ 17. social processes (LO–8, p. 18)
___ 18. personality processes (LO–8, p. 18)
___ 19. development (LO–9, p. 19)
___ 20. qualitative change (LO–9, p. 19)

a. Changes in kind, not just amount; for example, the child does not simply have less intelligence than an adult but simply thinks differently
b. A pattern of movement or change that begins at conception and continues through the entire life span
c. Mental activities, such as perception, attention, thought, problem solving, memory, and language
d. Properties of the individual child, such as the self, sex roles, gender identity, and morality
e. The child's interactions with other individuals in the environment

___ 21. stages (LO–10, p. 20)
___ 22. continuity-discontinuity (LO–11, p. 20)
___ 23. systematic observation (LO–14, p. 25)
___ 24. laboratory (LO–14, p. 26)
___ 25. naturalistic observations (field studies) (LO–14, p. 26)

a. Observations made according to a specific set of rules
b. A controlled setting in which many complex factors existing in the real world have been removed
c. Research conducted in real-world settings
d. Qualitative changes in development must occur in a certain sequence; may also include the constraint that the change is abrupt and that many new behaviors or competencies appear together
e. The extent to which early dimensions of the child and his or her life are connected to what the child is like at a later point in development

_____ 26. interview (LO–14, p. 27)

_____ 27. survey/questionnaire (LO–14, p. 27)

_____ 28. social desirability (LO–14, p. 27)

_____ 29. standardized tests (LO–14, p. 27)

_____ 30. experiment (LO–15, p. 31)

a. A highly structured interview on paper, in which the subject reads the question and then marks the answer on a sheet of paper

b. A set of questions put to an individual along with the responses the person makes

c. A controlled context in which the factors that are believed to influence the mind or behavior are controlled or manipulated; causation can be concluded from the results

d. A tendency to respond to a question in a way one thinks is acceptable, rather than in the way one really feels

e. Tests developed to identify an individual's characteristics or abilities relative to those of a large group of similar individuals

---

_____ 31. independent variable (LO–15, p. 30)

_____ 32. dependent variable (LO–15, p. 30)

_____ 33. experimental group (LO–15, p. 31)

_____ 34. control group (LO–15, p. 31)

_____ 35. quasi-experiment (LO–15, p. 31)

a. The variable in an experiment that is measured

b. The group of subjects in an experiment that gets the independent variable or receives the treatment condition

c. The variable in an experiment that is manipulated by the experimenter

d. A technique that resembles an experiment except that the independent variable cannot be randomly assigned to the subjects; that is, the subjects come into the situation already selected into the group; age and sex are two variables that are good examples

e. The group of subjects in an experiment that receives zero level of the independent variable; also, the comparison group in an experiment

---

_____ 36. correlation (LO–15, p. 32)

_____ 37. correlation coefficient (LO–15, p. 32)

_____ 38. cross-sectional design (LO–16, p. 33)

_____ 39. longitudinal design (LO–16, p. 33)

_____ 40. sequential design (LO–16, p. 33)

_____ 41. cohort effect (LO–17, p. 34)

a. A design that incorporates both a longitudinal and a cross-sectional component; has at least two cohorts, two age groups, and two times of measurement

b. A quasi-experimental design that tests a single group of individuals of the same age at two or more separate times, and, thus, at two or more ages

c. A quasi-experimental design that compares groups of different children in different age ranges at the same time

d. A mathematical measure of the strength of the relationship between two measured variables; may range from -1.00 to +1.00

e. The effects in a developmental study due to a subject's time of birth or generation rather than age

f. A measure of the association between two variables

Answers to Key Terms Matching Exercise

1. b	8. e	15. a	22. e	29. e	36. f
2. d	9. b	16. c	23. a	30. c	37. d
3. e	10. a	17. e	24. b	31. c	38. c
4. a	11. b	18. d	25. c	32. a	39. b
5. c	12. d	19. b	26. b	33. b	40. a
6. c	13. e	20. a	27. a	34. e	41. e
7. d	14. c	21. d	28. d	35. d	

Self-Test A

Choose the best alternative.

1. Children who are unsupervised by adults for part of their day (LO–1, p. 8)
    a. are more likely to be competent than other children.
    b. are more likely to be in trouble than other children.
    c. are of current interest to child development researchers.
    d. are more prone to illness than other children.

2. Infanticide was common in (LO–2, p. 10)
    a. ancient Greece and Rome.
    b. the Middle Ages.
    c. the Renaissance.
    d. 17th-century England.

3. The assumption that the child is basically evil and that parental constraints are necessary for the child to become a mature adult is characteristic of which view of the nature of the child? (LO–4, p. 10)
    a. innate goodness view
    b. *tabula rasa* view
    c. original sin view
    d. cognitive view

4. The assumption that the child should be allowed to grow naturally, without constraints from the parents, is characteristic of which view of the nature of the child? (LO–4, p. 11)
    a. innate goodness view
    b. *tabula rasa* view
    c. original sin view
    d. social learning view

5. The individual who provided the first systematic strategy for obtaining data about child development was (LO–5, p. 11)
    a. John Watson.
    b. Sigmund Freud.
    c. G. Stanley Hall.
    d. Charles Darwin.

6. The period of development that is characterized by physical changes in cells and the development of new physical structures is (LO–6, p. 15)
    a. the prenatal period.
    b. infancy.
    c. early childhood.
    d. adolescence.

7. Sarah is learning how to identify numbers and how to dress herself. Which period of development is most characteristic of her current behavior? (LO–6, p. 16)
   a. the prenatal period
   b. infancy
   c. early childhood
   d. middle childhood

8. Ethology is considered a part of which process of development? (LO–7, p. 17)
   a. biological/physical
   b. cognitive
   c. social
   d. personality

9. The development of the concept of self is part of which process of development? (LO–7, p. 18)
   a. biological/physical
   b. cognitive
   c. social
   d. personality

10. Piaget argued that a child's intelligence is not simply less than an adult's but that it is intelligence of a different kind as well. This illustrates an argument for (LO–8, p. 19)
    a. quantitative changes.
    b. qualitative changes.
    c. stages.
    d. continuity.

11. According to Flavell, the concept of stages in development requires all of the following except (LO–9, p. 20)
    a. qualitative changes in development.
    b. a specific sequence in the appearance of stages.
    c. gradual change in the transition from one stage to another.
    d. the concurrent appearance of many behaviors or abilities that characterize a stage.

12. The purpose of a standardized test is to (LO–13, p. 27)
    a. gather information it would be unethical to get experimentally.
    b. determine an individual's standing relative to a large group.
    c. provide an unstructured environment in which the child can set the pace.
    d. remove the possibility of receiving socially desirable responses.

13. An important advantage of the correlation strategy is that (LO–14, p. 32)
    a. causal statements can be made.
    b. variables that are unethical to manipulate can be studied.
    c. only one variable needs to be measured.
    d. the independent variable can be chosen by the researcher.

14. Dr. Jones, a researcher, is interested in physical development. In the fall of 1986, she measured the height of boys and girls in the first, third, and fifth grades in Smith Elementary School in upstate New York. She found that the oldest children were the tallest group and that the youngest children were the shortest group. She concluded that children get taller as they get older. This study is an example of which research strategy? (LO–14, p. 31)
    a. experimental
    b. longitudinal
    c. quasi-experimental
    d. case study

15. Dr. Jones, a researcher, is interested in physical development. In the fall of 1986, she measured the height of boys and girls in the first, third, and fifth grades in Smith Elementary School in upstate New York. She found that the oldest children were the tallest group and that the youngest children were the shortest group. She concluded that children get taller as they get older. The independent variable was (LO–14, p. 30)
    a. age.
    b. sex.
    c. height.
    d. socioeconomic status.

16. Dr. Jones, a researcher, is interested in physical development. In the fall of 1986, she measured the height of boys and girls in the first, third, and fifth grades in Smith Elementary School in upstate New York. She found that the oldest children were the tallest group and that the youngest children were the shortest group. She concluded that children get taller as they get older. The dependent variable was (LO–14, p. 30)
    a. age.
    b. sex.
    c. height.
    d. socioeconomic status.

17. Dr. Jones, a researcher, is interested in physical development. In the fall of 1986, she measured the height of boys and girls in the first, third, and fifth grades in Smith Elementary School in upstate New York. She found that the oldest children were the tallest group and that the youngest children were the shortest group. She concluded that children get taller as they get older. This study is an example of what type of research design? (LO–15, p. 33)
    a. cross-sectional
    b. sequential
    c. longitudinal
    d. survey

18. One of the advantages of the cross-sectional research design is that (LO–15, p. 33)
    a. true developmental changes can be seen.
    b. cohort effects can be dismissed.
    c. it is relatively easy to do.
    d. causal statements can be made.

19. The longitudinal design differs from the sequential design in what way? (LO–16, p. 33)
    a. The longitudinal design tests one cohort, the sequential design at least two.
    b. The longitudinal design tests one age, the sequential design at least two.
    c. The longitudinal design tests at one time, the sequential design at least at two times.
    d. The longitudinal design tests different children, the sequential design the same children.

20. The ethical standards for working with children in psychological research include all of the following except (LO-17, p. 34)
    a. the parents or guardian must give their consent.
    b. a peer review board must approve the project.
    c. the child must participate if the parents give their consent.
    d. the child should be treated with courtesy and respect.

Answers to Self-Test A

1. c	6. a	11. c	16. c
2. a	7. c	12. b	17. a
3. c	8. a	13. b	18. c
4. a	9. d	14. c	19. a
5. d	10. b	15. a	20. c

Self-Test B

Choose the best alternative.

21. Child abuse was common in (LO–2, p. 10)
    a. ancient Greece and Rome.
    b. the Middle Ages.
    c. the Renaissance.
    d. 17th-century England.

22. The assumption that the child is a blank slate that is affected by experience is characteristic of which view of development? (LO–4, p. 11)
    a. innate goodness view
    b. *tabula rasa* view
    c. original sin view
    d. cognitive view

23. The assumption that nature is important in development is characteristic of which view of development? (LO–4, p. 11)
    a. innate goodness view
    b. *tabula rasa* view
    c. social view
    d. learning view

24. The psychologist who made careful observations of children's behavior and who developed the maturational theory of development was (LO–5, p. 12)
    a. Freud.
    b. Watson.
    c. Hall.
    d. Gesell.

25. The time of development during which sensorimotor coordination is a primary task is (LO–6, p. 15)
    a. the prenatal period.
    b. infancy.
    c. early childhood.
    d. early adolescence.

26. Attention is considered a part of which process of development? (LO–7, p. 18)
    a. biological/physical
    b. cognitive
    c. social
    d. personality

27. Interactions with other people is part of which process of development? (LO–7, p. 18)
    a. biological/physical
    b. cognitive
    c. social
    d. personality

28. Which issue focuses on the extent to which early experiences influence what an individual is like in later life? (LO–11, p. 20)
    a. qualitative versus quantitative changes
    b. stages
    c. continuity versus discontinuity in development
    d. individual differences in development

29. The question of what children bring to a situation when they are being studied by psychologists is of interest to researchers studying (LO–11, p. 22)
    a. individual differences.
    b. universal stages.
    c. qualitative changes in development.
    d. quantitative changes in development.

30. The question of how much of development is due to heredity and how much is due to the environment is a component of which of the following issues? (LO–13, p. 23)
    a. whether or not there are stages in development
    b. the nature/nurture controversy
    c. the continuity/discontinuity issue
    d. whether qualitative change occurs in development

31. Systematic observation of children involves all of the following except (LO–13, p. 25)
    a. changing what we observe from one moment to the next.
    b. knowing who we are to observe.
    c. knowing when and where we are to observe.
    d. knowing how we will record our observations.

32. The purpose of an experiment is to (LO–14, p. 30)
    a. gather information it would be unethical to get with systematic observation.
    b. determine an individual's standing relative to a large group.
    c. provide an unstructured environment in which the child can set the pace.
    d. allow the determination of causal relations between variables.

33. An important advantage of the quasi-experimental strategy is that (LO–14, p. 31)
    a. causal statements can be made.
    b. variables that cannot be manipulated can be studied.
    c. several different variables can be measured.
    d. the independent variable is assigned by the researcher.

34. Dr. Robin, a researcher, was interested in language development. In the fall of 1985, he measured the vocabulary of 12 two-year-olds (both boys and girls) in a small town in upstate New York. He measured their vocabulary again in the fall of 1986, when they were three. He found that the vocabulary of all of the children had more than doubled in size. He concluded that the children learned many words during their third year. His study was an example of which research strategy? (LO–14, p. 31)
    a. experimental
    b. quasi-experimental
    c. cross-sectional
    d. case study

35. Dr. Robin, a researcher, was interested in language development. In the fall of 1985, he measured the vocabulary of 12 two-year-olds (both boys and girls) in a small town in upstate New York. He measured their vocabulary again in the fall of 1986, when they were three. He found that the vocabulary of all of the children had more than doubled in size. He concluded that the children learned many words during their third year. The independent variable in this study was (LO–14, p. 30)
    a. age.
    b. sex.
    c. vocabulary.
    d. socioeconomic status.

36. Dr. Robin, a researcher, was interested in language development. In the fall of 1985, he measured the vocabulary of 12 two-year-olds (both boys and girls) in a small town in upstate New York. He measured their vocabulary again in the fall of 1986, when they were three. He found that the vocabulary of all of the children had more than doubled in size. He concluded that the children learned many words during their third year. The dependent variable in this study was (LO–14, pp. 30–31)
    a. age.
    b. sex.
    c. vocabulary.
    d. socioeconomic status.

37. Dr. Robin, a researcher, was interested in language development. In the fall of 1985, he measured the vocabulary of 12 two-year-olds (both boys and girls) in a small town in upstate New York. He measured their vocabulary again in the fall of 1986, when they were three. He found that the vocabulary of all of the children had more than doubled in size. He concluded that the children learned many words during their third year. His study is an example of what design? (LO–15, p. 33)
    a. cross-sectional
    b. longitudinal
    c. sequential
    d. naturalistic observation

38. One of the advantages of the longitudinal method is that (LO–15, p. 33)
    a. true developmental changes can be seen.
    b. cohort differences can be explained.
    c. it is efficient.
    d. causal statements can be made.

39. The cross-sectional design differs from the sequential design in what way? (LO–15, pp. 33–34)
    a. The cross-sectional design tests one cohort, the sequential design at least two.
    b. The cross-sectional design tests one age, the sequential design at least two.
    c. The cross-sectional design tests at one time, the sequential design at least two.
    d. The cross-sectional design tests different children, the sequential design the same children.

40. The ethical standards for working with children in psychological research include which of the following? (LO–17, p. 34)
    a. The parents or guardian must give their consent.
    b. If the research question is important, it should be done, regardless of the potential harm to the child.
    c. The child must participate if his or her parents give consent.
    d. Psychologists are not required to present their research to a peer review board.

Answers to Self-Test B

21. a	26. b	31. a	36. c
22. b	27. c	32. d	37. b
23. a	28. c	33. b	38. a
24. d	29. a	34. b	39. c
25. b	30. b	35. a	40. a

Questions to Stimulate Thought

1. What would childhood be like today if we were to adopt the views of those in (a) ancient times, (b) the Middle Ages, or (c) the Renaissance?
2. What kinds of changes take place during development? Are they gradual or stagelike?
3. Is what we see as development the result of changes in the environment or heredity? What issues are involved in this question?

4. What differences in educational systems might arise from the three different philosophies of Rousseau, Locke, and the original sin view?
5. What is science? In what ways does the science of child development differ from the ordinary, everyday experiences we have with children?
6. Compare and contrast the cross-sectional, longitudinal, and sequential designs. What are the advantages and disadvantages of each? What does each tell us about development?
7. What is the difference between an experiment and a quasi-experiment? When would a correlational strategy be employed in place of an experiment?
8. Why are ethical considerations important for psychologists? What might happen without ethical guidelines?

Research Project

This exercise has two purposes: (1) it teaches you to observe children, and (2) it introduces you to the process of systematic observation.

Go to a local playground or park with a classmate. Choose two children of the same sex (that is, either two girls or two boys). The first child should be three or four years old; the second child should be eight or nine years old. One of you should observe each child for five minutes while the other records the observations.

Observe the amount of social interaction in which the children engage. For each 30 seconds of the five minutes, record whether or not the child you are observing interacted with another person and whether that person was a child (C) or an adult (A). Use the data sheet to record your observations. Then answer the questions that follow.

Data Sheet

Time	Child 1 (Three to Four Years Old) Sex ____ Age ____			Child 2 (Eight to Nine Years Old) Sex ____ Age ____		
0–30 Seconds	O	C	A	O	C	A
31–60 Seconds	O	C	A	O	C	A
61–90 Seconds	O	C	A	O	C	A
91–120 Seconds	O	C	A	O	C	A
121–150 Seconds	O	C	A	O	C	A
151–180 Seconds	O	C	A	O	C	A
181–210 Seconds	O	C	A	O	C	A
211–240 Seconds	O	C	A	O	C	A
241–270 Seconds	O	C	A	O	C	A
271–300 Seconds	O	C	A	O	C	A

Circle: O = No Social Interaction
C = Interacts with Child
A = Interacts with Adult

Questions

1. During how many time slots (from 0 to 10) did Child 1 (age three to four) interact with only a child? With only an adult? With both a child and an adult? With neither a child nor an adult?
2. During how many time slots (from 0 to 10) did Child 2 (age eight to nine) interact with only a child? With only an adult? With both a child and an adult? With neither a child nor an adult?
3. Are there any differences between the total number of intervals in which social interaction occurred for Child 1 and Child 2? What is the nature of this difference (that is, who interacted more)?

4. Which child interacted more often with other children? Which child interacted more often with adults? Which child interacted more overall? (Your comparisons should be based only on the number of intervals in which an interaction occurred, not on your memory of the length of the interaction, which was not directly measured.)
5. What do you think is the explanation for the differences you found? Could any factors other than age account for the differences? Why were you instructed to observe two children of the same sex?

---

2 Theories

Learning Objectives

After studying this chapter, you should be able to:

1. Describe Freud's theory of personality formation and explain its relationship to current thinking on child development. (pp. 42–50)
2. Describe Erikson's theory of development and explain its relationship to Freud's. (pp. 50–53)
3. List some strengths and weaknesses of the psychoanalytic approach. (pp. 52–53)
4. Describe Piaget's theory of cognitive development. (pp. 53–60)
5. Describe the information processing perspective, including both Broadbent's and Klatsky's approaches. (pp. 60–63)
6. List some strengths and weaknesses of the cognitive approach. (pp. 63–64)
7. Describe Skinner's behavioral approach to child development. (pp. 65–66)
8. Describe the cognitive social learning approach and compare it to the behavioral approach. (pp. 66–68)
9. List some strengths and weaknesses of the behavioral/social learning approaches. (pp. 68–69)
10. Describe the ethological approach to child development. (pp. 70–73)
11. List some strengths and weaknesses of the ethological views. (p. 73)
12. Explain why an eclectic view is most likely to successfully explain child development at this point in history. (p. 74)

Summary

Psychoanalytic theory is a view of personality that emphasizes biological forces, the symbolic transformation of experience, and the private, unconscious aspects of a person's mind. Freud proposed a division of personality into three structures. The id, the source of psychic energy, is composed of unconscious sexual and aggressive instincts. It operates according to the pleasure principle and primary process thought. The ego is concerned with reality and operates according to the reality principle, which attempts to satisfy the pleasure needs of the id within the boundaries of reality. It is also seen as the source of reason and logical thinking. The superego is the moral branch of the personality that arises through interactions with parents. Conflicts arise when the ego must balance the demands of the id and the requirements of the superego.

The ego reduces conflicts with the id through the use of defense mechanisms, which express the desires of the id in disguised fashions. Defense mechanisms include repression, reaction formation, regression, and projection. Anna Freud and Peter Blos have reported that the use of defense mechanisms in adolescence is necessary for adjustment at this time.

Psychoanalysis is a stage theory, with different areas of the body the source of pleasure at different stages of development. In the oral stage, the mouth is the region of maximum pleasure. In the anal stage, the anus is the focus of attention. During the phallic stage, the child focuses on the genital region and experiences feelings of desire for the opposite-sexed parent. During the latency stage, the child represses sexual feelings. The final psychosexual stage begins with the onset of puberty and is called the genital stage. During this period, sexual interest is reawakened.

Freud's theory has been criticized on the grounds that not all motivation is unconscious and sexual tension does not underlie all efforts to achieve competence. Freudian revisionists have suggested that (1) sex is not the underlying force behind all personality; (2) experience past the first five years of life does influence personality; (3) social factors influence personality development; and (4) the ego and conscious thought processes develop separately from the id and have an important role in personality development.

Erikson's stage theory incorporates aspects of Freud's theory but sees development as psychosocial, rather than psychosexual, and continuous throughout the life span. Erikson's stages of development are trust versus mistrust, autonomy versus shame and doubt, initiative versus guilt, industry versus inferiority, identity versus identity confusion (diffusion), intimacy versus isolation, generativity versus stagnation, and ego integrity versus despair.

Strengths of the psychoanalytic approach include: (1) emphasis on the role of the past, (2) discussion of the developmental course of personality, (3) the role of mental representation of the environment, (4) the role of the unconscious mind, (5) the emphasis on conflict, and (6) its influence on developmental psychology as a discipline. Weaknesses of the model include: (1) the difficulty of testing the concepts, (2) the lack of an empirical data base and the reliance on self-reports of the past, (3) the overemphasis on the unconscious mind and sexuality, (4) a negative and pessimistic view of human nature, and (5) too much emphasis on early experience.

Jean Piaget was interested in zoology and later in philosophy and psychology. His theorizing about the development of thought in children had a basis in biology, was broad in scope, and has changed developmental psychology.

Cognitive developmental theory focuses on the rational thinking of the developing child. It emphasizes biological maturation and how this maturation underlies the child's stage of cognitive development. Cognition is seen as the central focus of development and as causing the child's behavior.

There are several important concepts in Piaget's theory. Adaptation is subdivided into the dual processes of assimilation and accommodation. Assimilation occurs when a current cognitive structure is used to understand some aspect of the world. Accommodation occurs when a new feature of the environment is incorporated into a structure by modifying the structure. A second important concept in Piaget's theory is organization. Existing structures are grouped into higher-order systems. Development involves the continual reorganization of existing structures into more complex, abstract, and more smoothly functioning systems. Development proceeds to achieve equilibration, a more lasting state of balance between the world and the child's understanding of the world.

Piaget's theory stresses four stages of cognitive development. Infancy comprises the sensorimotor stage, when thought is characterized by sensory and perceptual processes and action. Thought is not symbolic. By the end of this stage, however, the ability to use simple symbols develops. During Piaget's preoperational stage, stable concepts are formed, mental reasoning emerges, magical belief systems are constructed, and egocentrism is perceptually based. Piaget's concrete operational stage extends from about seven years of age to the beginning of adolescence. During this period, thought is characterized as reversible and decentered but is limited to reasoning about the concrete world as it is. Thought is made up of operations that are mental actions or representations that are reversible. The last stage of Piaget's theory is called formal operational thought, which appears in adolescents and adults. It is characterized by abstractness, hypothetical-deductive reasoning, contrary-to-fact reasoning, idealism, and understanding of metaphor. Thought is no longer limited to the real and concrete but can be applied to the possible and to abstract propositions.

The information processing perspective is concerned with how people process information about their world. Information processing psychologists use a computer metaphor to attempt to understand human cognition. They consider memory and attention to be limited processes. Different levels of processing determine the extent or depth to which information is processed. Automatic processes require less capacity than do controlled processes. One possible developmental difference is that more processes become automatic as children develop. Another possibility is that capacity increases.

Both Piaget's theory and the information processing perspective have a number of strengths. Piaget made four major contributions: (1) brilliant observations of children (his observations have been replicated repeatedly), (2) ideas about what to look for in development, (3) a focus on the qualitative nature of changes in mental development, and (4) imaginative ideas about how change occurs, such as assimilation and accommodation. The information processing perspective provides a strong research orientation for studying children's cognition and a precision in conceptualizing children's thought.

Several aspects of cognitive theory have been criticized: (1) stages do not seem to exist empirically in the behavior of the child as they are discussed in Piaget's theory; (2) some of the concepts in Piaget's theory, while apparently powerful, are difficult to tie down operationally (for example, assimilation); (3) the information processing model has not produced an overall perspective on development; and (4) both views underestimate the role of experience in the environment.

Skinner was a major proponent of operant conditioning. According to Skinner, behavior is based on consequences experienced in the environment. Experiences that increase the frequency of a behavior are called reinforcement; consequences that reduce the frequency of a behavior are called punishment. Behavior modification is a therapeutic program based on the principles of operant conditioning and used to change the behavior of individuals in classroom or institutional settings. Bandura and Mischel developed cognitive social learning theory, which proposes that learning occurs through imitation and modeling, as well as through reinforcement, and that attention and memory are important components in learning as well.

Strengths of the behavioral/social learning theories are: (1) the emphasis on specific behaviors and environmental stimuli, (2) the contribution of the observational method in learning about development, (3) the application of a rigorous experimental approach to development, (4) the highlighting of the tremendous importance of information processing in mediating the relation between behavior and environmental stimuli, and (5) the emphasis on the context in development. Weaknesses of these perspectives include: (1) the assumption that processes determining development are the same at all ages; (2) not enough focus on biological processes in development; (3) too strong a focus on a micro-level of analysis, perhaps missing the big picture; and (4) for the behavioral view, a suggestion that cognitive processes are irrelevant for understanding development.

Ethologists focus on the biological determinants of behavior. Lorenz studied imprinting in greylag geese, and Tinbergen observed mating and territorial behavior in the stickleback fish. They developed the concept of critical periods in development, times in development during which an organism *must* encounter specific experiences for certain behaviors to develop. Ethologists consider the development of behavior in terms of the ultimate developmental course and the function of the behavior at the time it appears. Modern ethologists suggest that sensitive periods may be a more accurate way to describe development than critical periods. Strengths of ethological theory include: (1) its emphasis on the evolutionary basis of behavior, (2) the use of observation in naturalistic surroundings, (3) the belief that development involves some long sensitive periods, and (4) an emphasis on the functional importance of behavior. Weaknesses include: (1) an overemphasis on sensitive periods, (2) a lack of sufficient consideration of the interaction between biology and environment, and (3) the difficulty in testing ideas generated from the theory.

The eclectic orientation proposed in this book emphasizes the complexity of the developing human. It proposes that there is no single theoretical orientation that explains all of development and advocates that one should be familiar with multiple perspectives and use information that is useful from each.

Guided Review

You may want to look at the answers to the "Guided Review" statements as you read, or you may want to use the exercise as a form of self-test by covering up the answers below the statements with a sheet of paper and not consulting them until you have attempted to fill in the blanks of each statement.

1. A _____ is a set of assumptions to explain something.
   theory

2. _____ is a view of personality that emphasizes the private, unconscious aspects of a person's mind. It is a theory in which _____ forces are very important.
   Psychoanalysis, biological

3. According to Freud, the only personality structure present at birth is a mass of sexual and aggressive instincts called the _____ . Freud took the philosophical position that people born into the world are basically _____ .
   id, bad or evil

4. According to Freud, the id works according to the _____ principle, uses _____ _____ thought, and is devoid of _____ .
   pleasure, primary process, morality

5. According to Freud, the part of the personality that develops to deal with reality is the _____ . Its functioning obeys the _____ _____ . The ego houses the _____ mental functions.
   ego, reality principle, higher

6. According to Freud, the part of the personality that deals with moral issues (right and wrong) is the
    _____ . It develops through interactions with the _____ .
    superego, parents

7. The part of the superego in which moral inhibitions are reflected is the _____ . The part
    that holds the image of perfect behavior and thinking is called the _____ _____ . Freud
    believed that moral behavior is largely the result of feelings of _____ instilled by punitive parents.
    conscience, ego ideal, guilt

8. According to Freud, _____ is a dominant theme in the functioning of the personality. One way in
    which the ego reduces conflict is by using _____ _____ .
    conflict, defense mechanisms

9. According to Freud, the most powerful defense mechanism is _____ .
    repression

10. The process by which repressed thoughts appear in the conscious part of the child's mind as mirror opposites of
    the repressed thoughts is called _____ _____ . According to Freud,
    if the ego forces the person back to an earlier stage of development, this is called _____ .
    If one person attributes to another an unpleasant characteristic that correctly belongs to the first person, this is a
    case of _____ .
    reaction formation, regression, projection

11. Freud's theory of personality development is a _____ theory.
    stage

12. The Freudian stage during which all activity centers around pleasures of the mouth is called the _____
    stage. The Freudian stage during which all pleasure comes from control of eliminative functions is called the
    _____ stage.
    oral, anal

13. During Freud's phallic stage, the focus is on the child's _____ . One of the major themes during
    the phallic stage is that the child _____ with the same-sex parent.
    genitals, identifies

14. During Freud's phallic stage, boys experience a sexual desire for the mother and rivalrous feelings toward the
    father. This is called the _____ complex. Girls, however, experience a sexual desire for the father
    and rivalrous feelings toward the mother. This is called the _____ complex. Unresolved aspects of
    the Oedipus and Electra complexes are repressed, and this repression marks the beginning of the
    _____ stage.
    Oedipus, Electra, latency

15. Puberty marks the beginning of the _____ stage. Peter Blos considers _____
    by an adolescent to be a normal part of puberty, rather than a defense mechanism. According to Anna Freud,
    adolescent _____ _____ are used to ward off intrusions into the
    consciousness of incompletely repressed feelings of attachment to infantile love objects.
    genital, regression, defense mechanisms

16. Neo-Freudians do not see _____ as the all-pervasive underlying force behind personality that
    Freud believed it to be. Further, the neo-Freudians _____ the importance of the first five years of
    life in personality formation.
    sexuality, reduce or deemphasize

17. Erikson believes that Freud did not give enough weight to the importance of _____ in determining personality.

culture

18. According to Erikson, the infant who learns that the world is predictable and that caregivers are reliable develops a feeling of _____ . When these qualities are lacking, the infant develops a sense of _____ .

trust, mistrust

19. The second stage in Erikson's theory is _____ versus _____ and _____ . It corresponds to Freud's _____ stage.

autonomy, shame, doubt, anal

20. According to Erikson, if the child discovers ways of coping with feelings of helplessness, he or she will develop the healthy feeling of being the _____ of action. Otherwise, a sense of _____ may develop. This corresponds to Freud's _____ stage.

initiator, guilt, phallic

21. According to Erikson, the feeling that the child develops from a positive comparison of self with social peers is called _____ . If the comparison is not favorable, feelings of _____ may develop. This stage corresponds to the _____ period of psychoanalysis.

industry, inferiority, latency

22. The positive resolution of developing a stable self-image results in the formation of an _____ . Failure to do so results in _____ _____ . This stage in Erikson's theory corresponds to the _____ stage of psychoanalysis.

identity, identity confusion, genital

23. Erikson's first post-Freudian stage, _____ versus _____ , reflects the young adult's formation of an intimate _____ relationship.

intimacy, isolation, heterosexual

24. The central issue of _____ is the feeling of helping to shape the next generation. The feeling of having done nothing for the next generation leads to the outcome of _____ .

generativity, stagnation

25. The older person who has resolved each of Erikson's previous seven crises in a positive way will be satisfied with his or her life. According to Erikson, this leads to feelings of _____ _____ . If one or more of Erikson's crises have been resolved in a negative way, the older person may have feelings of _____ .

ego integrity, despair

26. Psychoanalysis directed attention to the _____ as an important influence on current thought and behavior. Freud's interest in the stages of personality formation indicated a _____ perspective. Psychoanalysis introduced the concept that experiences can be _____ transformed. Psychoanalysis also developed the concept of the _____ , a part of the mind not accessible to ordinary thought. Psychoanalytic theory has promoted the view that _____ is an important ingredient in adjustment.

past, developmental, mentally, unconscious, conflict

27. However, psychoanalytic concepts have been difficult to _____ scientifically, and there is an overreliance on the patient's _____ for the empirical base.

test, memory

28. The leader in the field of cognitive development is _____ _____ .
Jean Piaget

29. Cognitive developmental theory focuses on the development of _____ thinking in stages of development that are _____ and _____ .
rational, ordered, uniform

30. The newborn is in Piaget's _____ stage. During the sensorimotor period, the infant develops the ability to organize and coordinate his or her _____ and _____ .
sensorimotor, sensations, actions

31. Piaget's preoperational period lasts from _____ to _____ years of age. During this time, the child's _____ system expands, as does his or her use of _____ . The child sees things only from his or her _____ . The child gets stuck or _____ in static stages and is unable to _____ situations mentally.
two, seven, symbol, language, perspective, centered, reverse

32. The concrete operational period lasts from _____ to _____ years of age, cutting across the _____ _____ years. The child's system of thinking matures because of a shift from _____ to _____ . The child also becomes able to operate _____ in a series of actions. The concrete operational thinker is restricted to reasoning about things that are _____ .
seven, eleven, middle school, egocentrism, relativism, mentally, perceivable

33. Formal operational thinkers can think in more _____ terms. They tend to be more interested in _____ and _____ . Their thinking becomes more _____ , and they can generate testable _____ .
abstract, ideals, possibilities, systematic, hypotheses

34. In _____ , the child tries to incorporate features of the environment into existing schemes or modes of thinking about them. If incorporation of new features of the environment requires a slight modification of existing schemes or modes of thought, the process of cognitive change is called _____ . Both of these processes are components of what Piaget called _____ .

assimilation, accommodation, adaptation

35. Pretending that a cup in the bathtub is a boat is _____ . Understanding that the thing described by the word *cup* may have many different shapes is an example of _____ .
assimilation, accommodation

36. The mind's grouping of isolated behaviors and thoughts into a higher-order system is called _____ . This is achieved as thought becomes more _____ and _____ .

organization, logical, abstract

37. The goal of adaptation and organization is to reach a more lasting state of balance in thought called _____ . The condition that forces accommodation/growth is _____ .

equilibration, cognitive conflict

38. The information processing approach compares the human mind to a _____ .
computer

39. Broadbent's information processing model emphasizes the importance of three different types of
_____ .

memory

40. According to Broadbent, the sensory store is capable of _____ processing. Short-term memory has limited capacity. It acts as a _____ to serve the function of selective _____ .

parallel, filter, attention

41. Consider your last experience at a party as an example of the filtering capabilities of short-term memory. You were able to shift _____ from one conversation to another without moving any part of your body.

attention

42. The memory store that holds all of our permanent knowledge is called _____ - _____ memory in Broadbent's system.

long-term

43. A more recent model of information processing that reflects the current view that the human mind is a more complex and flexible processor of information than is reflected in the Broadbent model has been proposed by
_____ _____ .

Roberta Klatzky

44. In Klatzky's model, there is a continuum of levels along which information is processed. The first of these is the sensory analysis of stimuli. This is a _____ level of processing. The second level of information processing in Klatzky's model is the deeper process of _____ and _____ of stimuli. The deepest level of processing in Klatzky's model is that of _____ and making _____ about stimuli. The memory traces left by the deeper levels of processing support _____ long-term memory.

shallow, categorization, naming, thinking, inferences, better

45. One of the strengths of the information processing approach is that its theoretical _____ allows the generation of testable hypotheses.

precision

46. The information processing approach raises the question of processing speed. Processing speed appears to be _____ in younger than in older children.

slower

47. Information processing capacity can be conceptualized as a form of _____ _____ , of which there is a limited amount. _____ processes are assumed to be a heavy drain on information processing capacity. Controlled processes are _____ , in addition to being effortful. _____ processes are more difficult to control once initiated.

mental energy, Controlled, intentional, Automatic

48. Some evidence suggests that developmental differences in cognitive functioning often involve _____ processes.

controlled

49. Piaget's theory directed research at children's _____ processes. The information processing approach provided a _____ -oriented atmosphere for the study of children's cognition. In addition, the concepts of information processing were _____ .

thought, research, precise

50. However, there is skepticism about the pureness of the Piagetian _____ . Some of Piaget's concepts are _____ defined, and information processing has not yet produced an overall perspective on development. Both may have underestimated the importance of the _____ and the _____ _____ in determining behavior.

stages, poorly or loosely, environment, unconscious mind

51. The behavioral perspective emphasizes the influence of the _____ . The child's behavior is viewed as _____ . This orientation stresses the _____ - _____ analysis of the child's behavior. _____ _____ and/or _____ _____ are believed to be outside the realm of scientific study.

environment, learned, fine-grained, Mental events, cognitive processes

52. One of the most important figures in the development of modern behaviorism is _____ _____ _____ . He argues that all people are under the control of _____ _____ .

B. F. Skinner, positive reinforcement

53. Skinner's type of learning is called _____ conditioning or _____ conditioning. For him, behavior is determined by environmental _____ . A positive consequence is called _____ . A negative consequence is called _____ .

operant, instrumental, consequences, reinforcement, punishment

54. The application of operant conditioning techniques to human problems is called _____ _____ .

behavior modification

55. In Bandura's view of learning theory, the consequences of behavior may be _____ - _____ . Bandura believes social behavior to be _____ determined. He also believes that people can learn by observation, a process he called _____ _____ .

self-produced, reciprocally, observational learning

56. In Mischel's view, learning theory should be more _____ .

cognitive

57. Both the behavioral and social learning approaches have highlighted the importance of the _____ in the determination of behavior. They have emphasized the use of the _____ as a method of inquiry. The social learning approach has underscored the importance of _____ _____ , and both the behavioral and social learning perspectives have stressed the changing _____ of behavior.

environment, experiment, information processing, contexts

58. Ethologists believe that behavior is determined _____ . They emphasize the importance of _____ in the understanding of the survival value of a particular behavior.

biologically, evolution

59. Lorenz showed that the following response of greylag goslings was determined by _____ _____ rather than innate. This phenomenon is called _____ .

early experience, imprinting

60. A fixed time period during development during which a behavior must emerge is called a _____ _____ .

critical period

61. According to the ethological perspective, both _____ _____ and _____ _____ must be carefully described and classified. Second, the _____ must be examined for important _____ influences. These must be coordinated with present _____ . Third, the ethologist attempts to understand the meaning of the behavior in question with reference to _____ .
behavioral events, antecedent conditions, past, environmental, contexts, evolution

62. Ethologists emphasize the importance of careful _____ as a key to understanding development. However, they prefer to work in a _____ _____ rather than in a _____ .
observation, natural setting, laboratory

63. Ethologists argue that we should try to understand a behavior in terms of its _____ for the stage of development in which it is found.
function or importance

64. Another ethological issue involves the extent to which a behavior is under the control of _____ (biological) influences as opposed to _____ ones. Ethologists are interested in the _____ origin of the behavior in question.
hereditary, environmental, evolutionary

65. Hinde made a distinction between _____ periods and _____ ones. He and other ethologists now believe that the former may be too rigid and that the sensitive period is a time in development during which a particular effect can be produced _____ _____ .
critical, sensitive, more easily

66. Hinde's view of social behavior emphasizes that _____ with others form an important part of the child's environment. Hinde also believes that we must study the interaction between relationships and the _____ of the participants.
relationships, personalities

67. The ethological view has emphasized the _____ basis of behavior and the use of _____ _____ in naturalistic surroundings. It has also indicated the importance of considering long _____ periods during development and the _____ importance of behavior. Hinde, in particular, has highlighted the importance of _____ in development.
biological, careful observations, sensitive, functional, relationships

68. Some believe that even sensitive periods are too _____ a concept. The emphasis of ethological theories may tilt too strongly toward a _____ - _____ explanation of behavior rather than a biological-environmental mix. The theory has been _____ in generating testable ideas and seems to work best _____ .
rigid, biological-evolutionary, slow, retrospectively

69. An _____ position is a combination of the best of several other perspectives.
eclectic

Key Terms Matching Exercise

Match the Key Term on the left with the correct definition on the right.

_____ 1. theory (LO–1, p. 42)
_____ 2. psychoanalytic theory (LO–1, p. 42)
_____ 3. Oedipus complex (LO–1, p. 42)
_____ 4. id (LO–1, p. 42)
_____ 5. pleasure principle (LO–1, p. 43)

a. Complex that exists during the phallic stage and involves a young boy's sexual desires for his mother and his rivalrous feelings toward his father

b. Bundle of sexual and aggressive instincts or drives that are primarily unconscious

c. Involves always seeking pleasure and avoiding pain, regardless of the impact such behavior has on life in the real world

d. View of personality developed by Freud that emphasizes the private, unconscious aspects of a person's mind as the dominant feature of personality; it also stresses biological forces and the symbolic transformation of experience

e. A set of assumptions used to explain something

_____ 6. primary process thinking (LO–1, p. 43)
_____ 7. ego (LO–1, p. 44)
_____ 8. reality principle (LO–1, p. 44)
_____ 9. superego (LO–1, p. 44)
_____ 10. conscience (LO–1, p. 44)

a. Involves the ego seeking to satisfy the wants and needs of the id within the bounds of reality

b. Part of the superego formed by parents' punishments, reflecting moral inhibitions

c. Effort on the part of the id to satisfy wants and needs by forming a mental image of the desired object

d. Freudian element of the personality that considers the demands of reality

e. Freudian part of the personality that is the moral branch of personality

_____ 11. ego ideal (LO–1, p. 44)
_____ 12. defense mechanisms (LO–1, p. 44)
_____ 13. repression (LO–1, p. 45)
_____ 14. reaction formation (LO–1, p. 45)
_____ 15. regression (LO–1, p. 45)

a. Ego defense mechanism that is reflected in the tendency to return to an earlier stage of development

b. Ego defense mechanism in which repressed thoughts appear in the conscious part of the mind as mirror opposites of the repressed thoughts

c. Part of the superego consisting of standards of perfection that result from parents' reward of good behavior

d. Ego defense mechanism that pushes anxiety-producing information into the unconscious

e. Ego processes for transforming the desires of the id so that they are expressed in a disguised manner; reduces conflict between the id and the ego

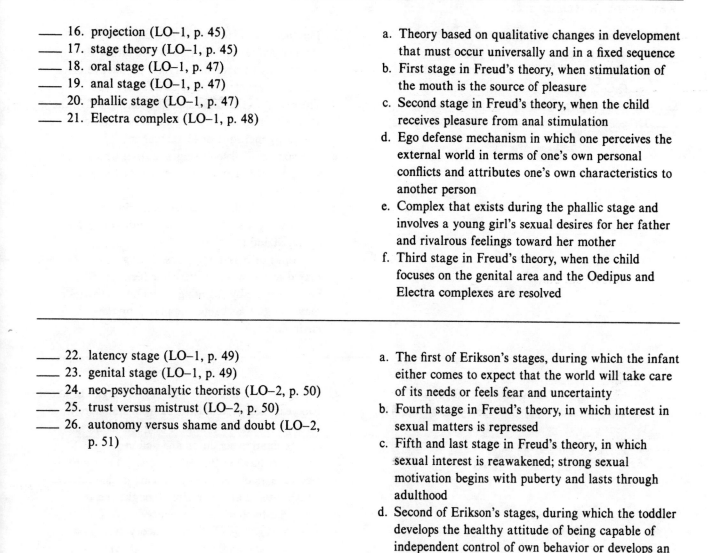

_____ 16. projection (LO–1, p. 45)
_____ 17. stage theory (LO–1, p. 45)
_____ 18. oral stage (LO–1, p. 47)
_____ 19. anal stage (LO–1, p. 47)
_____ 20. phallic stage (LO–1, p. 47)
_____ 21. Electra complex (LO–1, p. 48)

a. Theory based on qualitative changes in development that must occur universally and in a fixed sequence

b. First stage in Freud's theory, when stimulation of the mouth is the source of pleasure

c. Second stage in Freud's theory, when the child receives pleasure from anal stimulation

d. Ego defense mechanism in which one perceives the external world in terms of one's own personal conflicts and attributes one's own characteristics to another person

e. Complex that exists during the phallic stage and involves a young girl's sexual desires for her father and rivalrous feelings toward her mother

f. Third stage in Freud's theory, when the child focuses on the genital area and the Oedipus and Electra complexes are resolved

_____ 22. latency stage (LO–1, p. 49)
_____ 23. genital stage (LO–1, p. 49)
_____ 24. neo-psychoanalytic theorists (LO–2, p. 50)
_____ 25. trust versus mistrust (LO–2, p. 50)
_____ 26. autonomy versus shame and doubt (LO–2, p. 51)

a. The first of Erikson's stages, during which the infant either comes to expect that the world will take care of its needs or feels fear and uncertainty

b. Fourth stage in Freud's theory, in which interest in sexual matters is repressed

c. Fifth and last stage in Freud's theory, in which sexual interest is reawakened; strong sexual motivation begins with puberty and lasts through adulthood

d. Second of Erikson's stages, during which the toddler develops the healthy attitude of being capable of independent control of own behavior or develops an unhealthy attitude because he or she is incapable of control

e. The theorists who offered revised versions of psychoanalytic theory

_____ 27. initiative versus guilt (LO–2, p. 51)
_____ 28. industry versus inferiority (LO–2, p. 51)
_____ 29. identity versus identity confusion (diffusion) (LO-2, p. 52)
_____ 30. intimacy versus isolation (LO–2, p. 52)
_____ 31. generativity versus stagnation (LO–2, p. 52)

a. The fourth of Erikson's stages, during which the child compares self with peers and either views self as basically competent and feels productive or views self as incompetent and feels inferior
b. The seventh of Erikson's stages, during which the adult either feels like he or she is helping to shape the next generation or feels stagnant
c. The sixth of Erikson's stages, during which the young adult either forms friendships with others and a pair-bond or feels alone
d. The fifth of Erikson's stages, centering on establishing a stable personal identity or feeling confused and troubled
e. The third of Erikson's stages, during which the child may discover ways to overcome feelings of powerlessness by engaging in various activities or may feel guilt at being dominated by the environment

_____ 32. ego integrity versus despair (LO–2, p. 53)
_____ 33. cognitive developmental theory (LO–4, p. 53)
_____ 34. sensorimotor stage (LO–4, p. 55)
_____ 35. preoperational stage (LO–4, p. 55)
_____ 36. concrete operational stage (LO–4, p. 56)

a. The first stage in Piaget's theory, lasting until about two years of age, and extends from simple reflexes through the use of primitive symbols as the means of coordinating sensation and action
b. The third stage of Piaget's theory, from seven to eleven years of age, when thinking is characterized by decentered and reversible thought and is restricted to concrete experience
c. The second stage of Piaget's theory, from two to seven years of age, when thought is symbolic (not yet logical), egocentric, and magical
d. The eighth of Erikson's stages, when the person reflecting on his or her life either feels satisfied or feels doubt and despair
e. Theory proposed by Piaget that focuses on the rational thinking of the child and on how thought unfolds in a stagelike sequence; emphasizes biological maturation of the child and how such maturation underlies the child's cognitive stage of development

_____ 37. formal operational stage (LO–4, p. 57)
_____ 38. adaptation (LO–4, p. 57)
_____ 39. assimilation (LO–4, p. 57)
_____ 40. accommodation (LO–4, p. 57)
_____ 41. organization (LO–4, p. 59)

a. The tendency of isolated behaviors or thoughts to be grouped into higher-order and more smoothly functioning systems

b. The final stage of thought in Piaget's theory, when thought is characterized by abstractness, hypothetical-deductive reasoning, idealism, and an understanding of metaphor

c. Incorporating new features of the environment into one's thinking by slightly modifying existing modes of thought (schemes)

d. Effective interaction of an organism with its environment

e. Incorporating features of the environment into already existing ways of thinking about them (schemes)

_____ 42. equilibration (LO–4, p. 59)
_____ 43. information processing perspective (LO–5, p. 60)
_____ 44. controlled processes (LO–5, p. 62)
_____ 45. automatic processes (LO–5, p. 63)
_____ 46. operant conditioning (instrumental conditioning) (LO–7, p. 65)

a. Processes that are assumed to be both intentional and to draw heavily on information processing capacity

b. Learning that occurs as a function of the consequences that follow an organism's actions; the consequences serve either to strengthen or weaken a behavior

c. Processes that are not under conscious control and that do not draw substantially on information processing capacity

d. A view concerned with how people attend, code, retrieve, and reason about information

e. A balance in thought that is the goal of better organization

_____ 47. reinforcement (LO–7, p. 66)
_____ 48. punishment (LO–7, p. 66)
_____ 49. behavior modification (LO–7, p. 66)
_____ 50. cognitive social learning theory (LO–7, p. 66)
_____ 51. reciprocal determinism (LO–7, p. 67)

a. The use of learning principles to change behavior; most often used in therapeutic and educational settings

b. A coercive process in which two people attempt to control each other's behavior

c. A consequence to a behavior that leads to an increase in the performance of that behavior

d. The presentation of consequences to behavior that decrease the frequency of that behavior

e. The view that both cognitive processes and experiences determine one's personality

____ 52. imitation (modeling, observational learning) (LO–7, p. 68)

____ 53. classical ethological theory (LO–10, p. 70)

____ 54. imprinting (LO–10, p. 70)

____ 55. sign stimulus (LO–10, p. 70)

____ 56. critical period (LO–10, p. 71)

____ 57. sensitive period (LO–10, p. 72)

____ 58. eclectic orientation (LO–12, p. 74)

a. A following response in ducks and geese to the first moving object they see after hatching

b. A time in development when a given effect can be produced more easily than earlier or later

c. The view that behavior is biologically determined and that evolution plays a key role

d. The belief that a fixed time period very early in development exists for the emergence of a behavior

e. The perspective that multiple theoretical orientations are necessary for understanding child development

f. A naturally occurring stimulus that triggers the release of an unlearned behavior universal to a species

g. Learning by watching and listening to a model and subsequently imitating the behavior seen

Answers to Key Terms Matching Exercise

1. e	10. b	19. c	27. e	35. c	43. d	51. b
2. d	11. c	20. f	28. a	36. b	44. a	52. g
3. a	12. e	21. e	29. d	37. b	45. c	53. c
4. b	13. d	22. b	30. c	38. d	46. b	54. a
5. c	14. b	23. c	31. b	39. e	47. c	55. f
6. c	15. a	24. e	32. d	40. c	48. d	56. d
7. d	16. d	25. a	33. e	41. a	49. a	57. b
8. a	17. a	26. d	34. a	42. e	50. e	58. e
9. e	18. b					

Self-Test A

Choose the best alternative.

1. According to Freud's theory, which part of the personality is responsible for interactions with reality? (LO–1, p. 44)
   a. id
   b. ego
   c. superego
   d. Oedipus complex

2. Jimmy tells lies all the time. Jimmy claims that Johnny, who does not lie, always lies. Which defense mechanism is Jimmy using? (LO–1, p. 45)
   a. projection
   b. repression
   c. rationalization
   d. displacement

3. Melissa derives much pleasure from biting and sucking on objects. Freud would place Melissa in which stage of development? (LO–1, p. 47)
   a. genital
   b. phallic
   c. anal
   d. oral

4. Which of the following is not a difference between Freud and his revisionists? (LO–1, pp. 50, 52–53)
   a. The revisionists do not see sexuality as the underlying force behind personality.
   b. The revisionists deemphasize the first five years of life as determinants in shaping personality.
   c. The revisionists provide concepts more easily tested than the ideas proposed by Freud.
   d. The revisionists give the ego more strength in personality.

5. Kevin has been comparing himself to his friends and has decided that he is good at doing things. He decides that he enjoys engaging in productive activities. Kevin has just successfully completed which of Erikson's stages? (LO–2, p. 51)
   a. autonomy versus shame and doubt
   b. initiative versus guilt
   c. industry versus inferiority
   d. identity versus identity confusion

6. Betty has just fallen in love with a man and is forming a very close, open relationship with him. Betty is in which of Erikson's stages? (LO–2, p. 52)
   a. initiative versus guilt
   b. industry versus inferiority
   c. identity versus identity confusion
   d. intimacy versus isolation

7. Which of the following is not a strength of the psychoanalytic position? (LO–3, pp. 52–53)
   a. the belief that personality develops
   b. the emphasis on an empirical data base for making conclusions
   c. the belief that some behaviors are unconsciously motivated
   d. the belief that the past influences our current behavior

8. The primary focus of Piaget's theory is (LO–4, p. 53)
   a. emotional development.
   b. social development.
   c. cognitive development.
   d. biological development.

9. Which of the following is the purest example of assimilation? (LO–4, pp. 57–59)
   a. cooking a pancake on an imaginary stove
   b. building a tower of blocks
   c. riding a bicycle
   d. imitating a man shaving

10. Which of the following is the purest example of accommodation? (LO–4, pp. 57–59)
    a. cooking a pancake on an imaginary stove
    b. building a tower of blocks
    c. riding a bicycle
    d. imitating a man shaving

11. Which of the following is the purest example of adaptation, where assimilation and accommodation are in balance? (LO–4, pp. 57–59)
    a. cooking a pancake on an imaginary stove
    b. feeding a cookie to a doll at a tea party
    c. riding a bicycle
    d. imitating a man shaving

12. A very young person picks up a rattle, looks at it intently, waves it in front of his eyes, and sticks it into his mouth to chew on it and explore it. This person is most likely in which of Piaget's stages? (LO–4, p. 55)
    a. sensorimotor
    b. preoperational
    c. concrete operational
    d. formal operational

13. A child is asked to classify a set of shapes into groups that go together. She first puts a square down, then a circle on top of the square for a head. Next, she chooses two triangles for the legs and two rectangles for the arms. This child is most likely in which of Piaget's stages? (LO–4, p. 55)
    a. sensorimotor
    b. preoperational
    c. concrete operational
    d. formal operational

14. A child is asked to classify a set of shapes into groups that go together. He puts all the circles together, all the squares together, and all the triangles together. This child is in at least which of Piaget's stages? (LO–4, pp. 56–57)
    a. sensorimotor
    b. preoperational
    c. concrete operational
    d. formal operational

15. A child is asked to generate all possible combinations for the order in which five people might be chosen to play in a game. He systematically plans a way to generate all possible orders without repetition. He is in which of Piaget's stages of cognitive development? (LO–4, p. 57)
    a. sensorimotor
    b. preoperational
    c. concrete operational
    d. formal operational

16. After much trial and error, a young child manages to ride down the sidewalk on a two-wheeled bicycle without falling down and skinning her knees. Of what kind of learning is this an example? (LO–7, p. 65)
    a. classical conditioning
    b. operant conditioning
    c. observational learning
    d. cognitive behavior modification

17. After much trial and error, a young child manages to ride down the sidewalk on a two-wheeled bicycle without falling down and skinning her knees. What is the positive reinforcer? (LO–7, p. 66)
    a. not falling down
    b. not skinning her knees
    c. both not falling down and not skinning her knees
    d. being able to ride down the sidewalk

18. John is in a classroom where he receives a star every time he completes an assignment in the time allowed. He is then able to trade the stars in to buy free time to do with as he likes. John's classroom is based upon which of the following? (LO–7, p. 66)
    a. classical conditioning
    b. behavior modification
    c. observational learning
    d. insight learning

19. Concern with the evolutionary origin of behavior is the province of which theoretical perspective? (LO–10, p. 70)
    a. psychoanalytic
    b. behavioral
    c. cognitive
    d. ethological

20. The view that the social behavior of a three-year-old child has an adaptive value at that time in the child's life is most compatible with which theoretical perspective? (LO–10, pp. 72–73)
    a. psychoanalytic
    b. behavioral
    c. cognitive
    d. ethological

Answers to Self-Test A

1. b	6. d	11. c	16. b
2. a	7. b	12. a	17. d
3. d	8. c	13. b	18. b
4. c	9. a	14. c	19. d
5. c	10. d	15. d	20. d

Self-Test B

Choose the best alternative.

21. Teddy is sleeping and has to go to the bathroom. He then dreams that he gets up, goes to the bathroom, and returns to his bed. According to Freud, what part of the personality is likely to be controlling Teddy's behavior? (LO–1, p. 43)
    a. id
    b. ego
    c. superego
    d. reality principle

22. Lori does not play with her brother's kite, even though she wants to, because she believes that it is wrong to use someone else's things without their permission. If this is Lori's real reason for not playing with the kite, what is controlling her behavior, according to Freud? (LO–1, p. 44)
    a. id
    b. ego
    c. reality principle
    d. superego

23. Nick is a ten-year-old boy. He is afraid of dogs. If he sees a dog coming down the street, he buries his head on his mother's shoulder. This is an example of (LO–1, p. 45)
    a. repression.
    b. suppression.
    c. regression.
    d. displacement.

24. The stage in Freud's theory that lasts from about 18 months to three years of age is called (LO–1, p. 47)
    a. oral.
    b. anal.
    c. phallic.
    d. latency.

25. Nancy is learning how to feed herself and how to dress herself. She is feeling like she is capable of controlling her actions. In which of Erikson's stages is Nancy? (LO–2, p. 51)
    a. trust versus mistrust
    b. autonomy versus shame and doubt
    c. initiative versus guilt
    d. industry versus inferiority

26. Olin's mother feeds him when she thinks he should be hungry, not when he cries and is hungry. Olin is becoming quite fearful as a consequence. In which of Erikson's stages is Olin? (LO–2, pp. 50–51)
    a. trust versus mistrust
    b. autonomy versus shame and doubt
    c. initiative versus guilt
    d. industry versus inferiority

27. Each of the following has been suggested as a weakness of Freud's psychoanalytic position except (LO–3, p. 53)
    a. the difficulty of testing the concepts.
    b. the lack of an empirical data base.
    c. too much emphasis on early experience.
    d. a developmental perspective to personality.

28. Piaget's theory claims that cognitive development depends greatly upon (LO–4, p. 55)
    a. emotional development.
    b. social development.
    c. biological maturation.
    d. history of reinforcement.

29. Which of the following is the purest example of assimilation? (LO–4, p. 57)
    a. eating an imaginary hamburger
    b. bouncing a ball
    c. washing dishes
    d. imitating a dancer dancing

30. Which of the following is the purest example of accommodation? (LO–4, pp. 57, 59)
    a. eating an imaginary hamburger
    b. bouncing a ball
    c. washing dishes
    d. imitating a dancer dancing

31. Which of the following is the purest example of adaptation, with assimilation and accommodation in balance? (LO–4, pp. 57, 59)
    a. eating an imaginary hamburger
    b. bouncing a ball
    c. stirring in a pretend bowl, making a cake
    d. imitating a dancer dancing

32. Which of the following is characteristic of sensorimotor thought? (LO–4, p. 55)
    a. symbolic functioning
    b. reversible thought
    c. coordination between action and perception
    d. decentration

33. Which of the following characterizes preoperational thought? (LO–4, p. 55)
    a. reversible thought
    b. coordination between action and perception
    c. decentration
    d. symbolic functioning

34. A child is given the conservation of liquid task. The child argues that the liquid in the two containers is the same because, although one container is taller, the other is fatter. This child is in at least which of Piaget's stages? (LO–4, p. 57)
   a. sensorimotor
   b. preoperational
   c. concrete operational
   d. formal operational

35. A child says to himself, "I think the way to get a good grade on a test is to study hard. Therefore, if I study hard for my next exam, then I will get a good grade." This child is in which of Piaget's stages? (LO–4, p. 57)
   a. sensorimotor thought
   b. preoperational thought
   c. concrete operational thought
   d. formal operational thought

36. A psychologist is interested in teaching an infant to press a panel. The psychologist makes a light go on every time the infant presses a panel. This is referred to as (LO–7, p. 65)
   a. classical conditioning.
   b. operant conditioning.
   c. observational learning.
   d. insight learning.

37. A very tired child wants to go to sleep. Her mother makes her pick up her toys and put them away before she goes to sleep. In this situation, going to sleep is (LO–7, p. 66)
   a. a reinforcer.
   b. adaptation.
   c. a punishment.
   d. an intervention.

38. The application of learning principles to change maladaptive behavior is called (LO–7, p. 66)
   a. classical conditioning.
   b. operant conditioning.
   c. behavior modification.
   d. cognitive behavior modification.

39. A child sees her friend turn a bowl of oatmeal upside down and spill it on the floor. The next day, the child turns her own bowl of oatmeal upside down and spills it. This is an example of (LO–8, p. 68)
   a. classical conditioning.
   b. operant conditioning.
   c. behavior modification.
   d. observational learning.

40. The concept of sensitive periods in development comes from which framework? (LO–10, p. 72)
   a. ethological
   b. cognitive
   c. behavioral
   d. psychoanalytic

Answers to Self-Test B

21. a	26. a	31. b	36. b
22. d	27. d	32. c	37. a
23. c	28. c	33. d	38. c
24. b	29. a	34. c	39. d
25. b	30. d	35. d	40. a

Questions to Stimulate Thought

1. Identify the similarities and reconcile the differences among the comparable stages in the developmental theories of Freud, Erikson, and Piaget.
2. What contributions have Freud's work made to the progress of developmental psychology?
3. What contributions have Erikson's theory made to the progress of developmental psychology?
4. Explain Freud's and Erikson's theories in behavioral terms; that is, explain how the same behaviors might have been learned.
5. Explain Freud's and Erikson's theories in social behavioral terms; that is, show how the same effects might have been acquired according to social learning.
6. Do the concepts adaptation, assimilation, accommodation, organization, and equilibration bear any similarities to any concepts in learning? If so, what and how? If not, why?
7. In what ways does sensorimotor thought provide a foundation for what follows?
8. Can all other perspectives be explained in behavioral (or social behavioral) terms?
9. What are the limitations of learning as a means of explaining child development?
10. How do ethologists view social development in children? Is there any role for experience in the ethological view of development?

Research Project

In this project, you observe a parent-child interaction and evaluate it according to a Freudian analysis, a behavioral learning analysis, and a cognitive developmental analysis. Go to a local supermarket and watch a mother or father shop with a two- to four-year-old child. Describe the interaction you see, including the child's demands, verbal exchanges between the parent and child, and ways in which the parent responds to the child's demands, and record your observations on the data sheet. Then refer to your observations to answer the questions that follow.

Data Sheet

_____

Description: Child   Age _____ Sex _____

_____

Questions

1. What would Freud focus on in this interaction? How would he explain the sequence of events observed?
2. How would a behavioral psychologist analyze the situation? What reinforcements or punishments characterized the interaction? Did specific things occur that would make a behavior more likely to occur in the future? Less likely to occur?
3. What would a cognitive developmental theorist focus on in this situation? An information processing theorist?
4. What is the child learning in this situation? What does the child already know?

3 The Evolutionary Perspective, Genetics, Prenatal Development, and the Birth Process

Learning Objectives

After studying this chapter, you should be able to:

1. Explain how evolution works. (pp. 85–86)
2. Explain the role of heredity (genetics) in development, including defining chromosomes, genes, DNA, and the concepts of genotype and phenotype. (pp. 86–87)
3. Describe the genetic principles of gene dominance, sex-linked characteristics, polygenic inheritance, reaction range, and canalization, and explain how they relate to genotype and phenotype. (pp. 87–89)
4. Describe the role in behavior genetics of selective breeding, inbreeding, twin studies, family-of-twin studies, kinship studies, and adoption studies. (pp. 89–90)
5. Define heritability and describe the role of heredity and environment in determining intelligence and temperament. (pp. 90–91)
6. Explain a current view about the interaction between heredity and the environment with regard to development. (pp. 91–92)
7. Describe the process of conception, the production of spermatozoa and ova, in-vitro fertilization, and the cell that results from the union of sperm and ovum. (pp. 92–95)
8. Describe the formation and structure of the blastula and its implantation. (p. 95)
9. Describe the differentiation of the embryo into the endoderm, mesoderm, and ectoderm and the appearance of the parts of the body. (pp. 96–97)
10. Describe the changes that occur during the fetal period and define the age of viability. (pp. 97–98)
11. List and explain at least four possible environmental influences on prenatal development and define teratology. (pp. 100–106)
12. Describe different childbirth strategies, the stages of birth, and possible delivery complications. (pp. 106–11)
13. Explain the concepts of short-gestation, low-birth-weight, and high-risk as applied to infants. (pp. 111–13)
14. Describe how improved technology/medicine and social class differences affect the survivability of short-gestation or low-birth-weight infants. (pp. 114–15)
15. Describe the use of the Apgar and Brazelton scales. (p. 114)
16. Define bonding and describe its current status. (pp. 115–17)

Summary

When studying development, it is important to keep in mind that humans are biological beings. Darwin observed extensive variability in individuals of a species. He argued that some variations are more advantageous for survival than others and that, over time, organisms with favorable characteristics comprise a greater proportion of the population, resulting in the modification of the species. This process is called natural selection.

Genes are the building blocks of chromosomes, which provide the blueprint for the development of the organism. Each human cell has 46 chromosomes. Genes are transmitted from parents to offspring by gametes—the ovum or egg from the female and sperm from the male. The process of meiosis produces the gametes. In humans, each gamete has 23 chromosomes. Conception occurs when a sperm fertilizes an ovum, producing a zygote. The genetic structure that is made possible is called the genotype. The actual characteristics observed in an individual are called phenotypes.

Some genes are dominant: They are always expressed when present. Others are recessive: They are expressed only when paired with another recessive gene on the other chromosome. Some characteristics are sex-linked. If a recessive characteristic is carried on the X chromosome, it will always show up in the male with that gene, but not in the female if she also has the dominant gene on her other X chromosome. Thus, some characteristics are more common in males than females.

Some characteristics are determined by the interaction of many different genes. This is referred to as polygenic inheritance. Reaction range refers to the range of phenotypes that could be expressed, given a genotype. The genetic codes set broad limits on the range of possible outcomes, which are then affected by the environment. Canalization refers to the extent to which certain genotypes might be immune to changes in environmental events.

The field of behavior genetics is concerned with the degree and nature of the hereditary basis of behavior. Twin studies compare identical and fraternal twins for the degree of similarity. Family-of-twins designs compare monozygotic twins, siblings, half-siblings, and parents and offspring. Kinship studies examine the role of heredity in behavior by including other family members, such as uncles, cousins, and grandparents. Adoption studies compare the adopted child with both biological and adoptive parents.

Heritability is a mathematical estimate that compares the amount of variation in genetic material in a population to the total amount of variation among people. It can range from 0 to 1.00. Three limitations are important when evaluating a heritability index: (1) the narrower the range of environmental differences represented in the sample, the higher the heritability quotient; (2) the reliability and validity of the measure of the characteristic must be kept in mind; and (3) the heritability quotient assumes that inheritance and environmental influences are additive.

Prenatal development includes conception and the zygote, germinal, embryonic, and fetal periods. Conception usually occurs when a sperm cell unites with an ovum in the female's fallopian tube. Modern technology has made possible a new form of conception called in-vitro fertilization. An ovum is surgically removed, fertilized in a laboratory medium, and implanted back in the woman's uterus. This allows women who could not otherwise conceive to bear their own children.

The first four days of gestation are called the zygote period. The first two weeks of gestation are called the germinal period, during which the blastula, a round structure of 100 to 150 cells, forms. The inner layer of the blastula is the blastocyst, which later develops into the embryo. The outer layer of the blastula is the trophoblast, which later develops into the placenta. The implantation of the blastula marks the beginning of the embryonic period.

During the next six weeks, the blastocyst differentiates into an outer layer (ectoderm), a middle layer (mesoderm), and an inner layer (endoderm). From the ectoderm develops the hair, skin, nails, nervous system, and sensory receptors. The mesoderm becomes the muscles, bones, circulatory, excretory, and reproductive systems. The endoderm develops into the digestive and respiratory systems. During the embryonic period, a primitive human form takes shape, and the basic parts of the body can be identified. The placenta and umbilical cord form. The embryonic period ends at about eight weeks after conception.

The remaining seven months until birth are called the fetal period. During this time, fetal size increases, the organs start functioning, reflexes appear, and there is sexual differentiation.

Environmental influences can act on the developing zygote, embryo, and fetus. Birth defects and/or developmental problems can be caused by maternal diseases and infections, the mother's age, malnutrition, diet, the mother's emotional state and stress, and drugs, such as thalidomide, alcohol, and cigarettes.

Expectant parents can choose from a number of childbirth strategies, including standard childbirth, the Leboyer method, and the Lamaze method. The birth process has been divided into three stages. In the first stage, uterine contractions dilate the woman's cervix so that the baby can move from the uterus to the birth canal. The second birth stage begins when the baby's head starts to move through the birth canal and ends when the baby is born. The third birth stage, called afterbirth, involves the detachment and expelling of the placenta. A number of complications, such as a precipitate or breech delivery, can accompany the baby's arrival.

Normal gestation is 37 to 40 weeks. Infants born earlier than that are called short-gestation babies. Full-term infants born after normal gestation but who weigh less than 5.5 pounds are called low-birth-weight or high-risk infants. Four important conclusions about preterm infants are: (1) advances in intensive-care technology have reduced the likelihood of serious consequences for preterm infants; (2) outcomes for infants born with an identified problem are likely to be worse than for those born without a recognizable problem; (3) more favorable outcomes for preterm infants are associated with higher socioeconomic status; and (4) preterm infants do not generally encounter difficulty in school several years later.

The Apgar Scale is a quick screen of infant status that assesses heart rate, respiratory effort, muscle tone, body color, and reflex irritability at one and five minutes after birth. The Brazelton Neonatal Behavioral Assessment Scale is a more detailed evaluation, typically given on the third day of life. It evaluates 20 reflexes and the infant's reactions to 26 different circumstances involving both physical and social stimulation.

There are differences in the parent-child relationships for preterm infants, perhaps because of feelings of inadequacy in the mothers or perhaps because the mothers do not have early interaction with their infants. There also may be differences in the infants themselves that elicit different behaviors from parents.

Bonding is the development of an emotional tie between parents and infant. In recent years, a critical period hypothesis has been advanced, suggesting that bonding *must* occur within the first few days of life. Although the exact time period has been questioned, this view has led to a revision of hospital procedures, allowing mothers and fathers more access to their infants in hospitals than was previously permitted.

Guided Review

You may want to look at the answers to the "Guided Review" statements as you read, or you may want to use the exercise as a form of self-test by covering up the answers below the statements with a sheet of paper and not consulting them until you have attempted to fill in the blanks of each statement.

1. _____ _____ is credited with the development of the theory of evolution upon which current concepts are based. His observations of extensive variability among individuals in a species were the basis for his theory of _____ .
   Charles Darwin, evolution

2. Some of the variations among individuals in a species result in characteristics that are advantageous, and individuals with these characteristics are more likely to _____ and to _____ . This is called _____ _____ .
   survive, reproduce, natural selection

3. As a result of genetic diversity and differential _____ , a species will _____ to an environment over time. This is called _____ .
   survival, adapt, evolution

4. The physical basis of heredity is called a _____ . There are _____ pairs of chromosomes in each human cell. The _____ are small parts of the chromosome that may carry the basis for individual traits.
   chromosome, 23, genes

5. The chromosomes are composed of _____ _____ , a double-stranded molecule that looks like a long ladder twisted into a helix.
   deoxyribonucleic acid

6. The cells in which chromosomes are transmitted to offspring are called _____ . They are created in the _____ of males and the _____ of females through a process of cell division called _____ .
   gametes, testes, ovaries, meiosis

7. The zygote is formed by the union of an ovum and a sperm cell. The process that accomplishes this is called _____ .
   conception or fertilization

8. The hypothetical hereditary basis of each individual is called the _____ . The observable and measurable characteristics of the individual are called the _____ .
   genotype, phenotype

9. When Gregor Mendel bred round and wrinkled pea plants, he found that all the offspring were round. This means that the gene for round was _____ to the gene for wrinkled. The gene for wrinkled was _____ . The only time that the effect of a _____ gene shows is when it is carried on both chromosomes.

dominant, recessive, recessive

10. Characteristics carried only on the 23rd chromosome are referred to as _____ - _____ . In humans, it is likely that most phenotypic characteristics are _____ determined.

sex-linked, polygenetically

11. Given a particular genotype, there is a _____ of phenotypes that can be expressed, with a limit on how much the _____ can change characteristics, such as personality and intelligence. A term that embodies this concept is _____ _____ . Canalization refers to a _____ range of possible outcomes for a particular interaction between the genotype and the environment.

range, environment, reaction range, narrower

12. Monozygotic and dizygotic (identical and fraternal) twins come from _____ and _____ ova, respectively. Twin, family-of-twins, kinship, and adoption studies compare _____ and _____ similarities.

one, two, genetic, behavioral

13. Heritability is a _____ estimate of the degree to which a phenotypic characteristic is determined by heredity.

statistical or mathematical

14. Heritability estimates are sensitive to the variation in the environments in the sample tested. A narrow range of environments results in a _____ heritability index. When considering heritability estimates, there is always a question of the _____ and _____ of the measures of the underlying characteristic. The use of the heritability quotient assumes that we can separate and add up the influence of inheritance and the environment. It is more likely that these two factors _____ .

higher, reliability, validity, interact

15. The female reproductive cell is called an _____ . The male reproductive cell is called a _____ . _____ occurs when one sperm cell unites with an ovum.

ovum, sperm, Conception

16. The cell formed by the union of sperm cell and ovum is called the _____ . It immediately begins to undergo _____ divisions. The period of time during which this is taking place is about _____ to _____ days long and is called the _____ period.

zygote, cleavage, three, four, zygote

17. A recently developed procedure for achieving conception outside the body is called _____ - _____ .

in-vitro fertilization

18. The two weeks immediately after conception are called the _____ period. During this period, rapid cell division results in the formation of a _____ .

germinal, blastula

19. The inner layer of the blastula is called the _____ . The outer layer develops into tissues that provide nutrition and protection for the embryo and is called the _____ . During the second week, the blastula becomes attached to the inner lining of the uterine wall in a process called

    _____ .

    blastocyst, trophoblast, implantation

20. Following the germinal period of prenatal development is the _____ period. During this time, the blastocyst differentiates into three tissue layers: the _____ , _____ , and

    _____ .

    embryonic, ectoderm, mesoderm, endoderm

21. The _____ gives rise to the digestive and respiratory systems. The _____ gives rise to the nervous system, skin, and sensory receptors. The _____ gives rise to the muscles, bones, circulatory system, excretory system, and reproductive system.

    endoderm, ectoderm, mesoderm

22. The part of the embryo attached to the uterine wall becomes the _____ . The _____ houses the arteries and veins that pass very small molecules between the mother and the embryo. The pouch that holds the embryo suspended in a clear fluid is called the _____ .

    placenta, umbilical cord, amnion

23. The first two months of prenatal development have been called _____ because of the formation of many of the body's organ systems.

    organogenesis

24. The last part of the gestation period is called the _____ period.

    fetal

25. By three months after conception, the fetus is about _____ inches long and weighs _____ ounce. Most physical features are differentiated, and _____ can be identified.

    3, 1, gender

26. By the end of the fourth month after conception, fetal _____ become stronger. The fetus is about _____ inches long and weighs _____ to _____ ounces.

    reflexes, 6, 4, 7

27. By the end of the fifth month after conception, the infant displays a preference for a particular _____ in the womb. The fetus is about _____ inches long and weighs about _____ ounces.

    position, 12, 16

28. By the end of the sixth month after conception, there is evidence of both _____ movements and a _____ reflex. The fetus is about _____ inches long and weighs approximately _____ pounds.

    breathing, grasping, 14, 2

29. By the end of the seventh month after conception, the fetus is about _____ inches long and weighs approximately _____ pounds. If born, the fetus's chances of survival are _____ .

    16, 3, good

30. The final two months of the fetal period are devoted mainly to overall _____ . The fetus grows to an average of _____ inches in length and a weight of _____ pounds.

    growth, 20, 7

31. Such factors as maternal disease, blood disorders, age, and emotional well-being of the mother have been associated with the _____ of the newborn.

health

32. An agent that can cause a birth defect is called a _____ . Sensitivity to the effects of a teratogen depends in part on the _____ during gestation at which the mother is exposed. The _____ is most vulnerable to teratogens between 15 and 25 days after conception, the _____ between 24 and 40 days, the _____ between 20 and 40 days, and the _____ between 24 and 36 days.

teratogen, time, brain, eye, heart, legs

33. An outbreak of _____ caused large numbers of birth defects in the mid-1960s. Rubella is also called _____ _____ . The greatest damage seems to occur when mothers contract rubella in the _____ and _____ weeks of pregnancy. _____ , a venereal disease, has damaging effects later in prenatal development and after birth.

rubella, German measles, third, fourth, Syphilis

34. Both CMV or _____ and HVH or _____ _____ _____ are members of the _____ _____ family of viruses. They can infect the baby at _____ . When they do, the death of the infant is very possible. If the exposed infant does not die, very serious problems may result, ranging from _____ _____ to _____ .

cytomegalovirus, herpes virus hominis, herpes simplex, birth, brain damage, blindness

35. The mortality rate of infants born to adolescent mothers is _____ times that of infants born to mothers over 20 years of age. Much of this effect may be due to lack of _____ _____ , but some may result from an immature _____ system.

two, prenatal care, reproductive

36. Mothers over the age of _____ are more likely to give birth to babies with _____ _____ . Older women are also less likely to _____ _____ .

30, Down's syndrome, get pregnant

37. The developing fetus gets its food from its _____ . Malnutrition can result in infants that are _____ , that have less _____ , and that are most likely to _____ .

mother, smaller, vitality, die

38. The mother's emotional state can affect the _____ of contractions during the birth process. One study found that the babies of anxious mothers _____ more and were more _____ .

regularity, cried, active

39. During the 1960s, the tranquilizer _____ was found to produce birth defects (missing arms and legs) when taken by pregnant women.

thalidomide

40. Consumption of _____ by the expectant mother can adversely affect fetal health. A cluster of characteristics known as _____ _____ _____ includes such defects as microencephaly and mental retardation. Moderate drinking has been linked to _____ birth weight of infants.

alcohol, fetal alcohol syndrome, lower

41. Cigarette smoking has been associated with _____ prematurity rates, _____ birth weights, and _____ problems in infancy. _____ problems are also more common in the offspring of smokers.

higher, lower, sleep, Respiratory

42. The gestation period ends with _____ . The method that eases the transition of birth for the infant is the _____ method. The method that uses special exercises to help women deal with the discomfort of childbirth is the _____ method.

birth, Leboyer, Lamaze

43. During the first stage of labor, uterine contractions _____ in _____ and _____ and become more regular. This phase ends when the _____ dilates to a diameter of about _____ inches.

increase, frequency, intensity, cervix, 4

44. The second stage of labor involves the _____ of the baby. It ends when the baby is _____ .

birth, born

45. The _____ is delivered during the third stage of labor. This is accompanied by the _____ _____ and other _____ .

placenta, umbilical cord, membranes

46. A too-fast delivery is called _____ . It can disturb the normal flow of _____ in the infant. A very long delivery can result in _____ , or lack of _____ in the infant. Another complication of birth involves the position of the baby in the uterus. Some babies come with their buttocks first, which is referred to as the _____ position. Some breech positions may require a _____ delivery.

precipitate, blood, anoxia, oxygen, breech, cesarean

47. Drugs used during delivery can cross the _____ barrier and affect the _____ . A drug that has been used to speed delivery is _____ . Its use is controversial since it may precipitate more _____ .

placental, infant, oxytocin, complications

48. Babies born before their estimated time of delivery are now referred to as _____ - _____ babies. Babies who weigh less than 5.5 pounds at birth are referred to as _____ - _____ - _____ or _____ - _____ babies. _____ has improved the prospects for the short-gestation and high-risk newborn.

short-gestation, low-birth-weight, high-risk, Technology

49. The _____ Scale is a short screening procedure for evaluating the health of the newborn minutes after birth. The _____ Neonatal Behavioral Assessment Scale is a more complete evaluation of the newborn that includes an evaluation of the infant's reaction to _____ . _____ training may be recommended for socially sluggish infants.

Apgar, Brazelton, people, Brazelton

50. Improvements in _____ have reduced the incidence of serious consequences associated with preterm births. Preterm infants with an identifiable problem have a poorer _____ than babies born without a recognizable problem. _____ _____ is associated with better outcomes for the preterm infant. As a rule, preterm babies do not seem to be more at _____ for cognitive problems than the average newborn.

technology, prognosis, Social class, risk

51. _____ is a controversial concept that implies that there is a critical period in the development of a close emotional attachment between the mother and the infant. The evidence _____ (does or does not) support strong conclusions at this time.

Bonding, does not

Key Terms Matching Exercise

Match the Key Term on the left with the correct definition on the right.

____ 1. amniocentesis (LO–1, p. 84)
____ 2. chorionic villus test (LO–1, p. 84)
____ 3. natural selection (LO–1, p. 85)
____ 4. chromosomes (LO–2, p. 86)
____ 5. DNA (LO–2, p. 86)

a. When organisms with characteristics more favorable for survival come to comprise a larger proportion of the population because they have a reproductive advantage, which changes the characteristics of the whole population

b. Long molecule that runs along the length of each chromosome; the key chemical substance in an individual's genetic makeup

c. Test that detects genetic defects in the fetus; fluid is extracted through a needle inserted into the pregnant woman's abdomen, and fetal cells are grown in the laboratory for two to four weeks to be examined for abnormalities

d. Test that detects genetic defects in the fetus; a small sample of the placenta is removed between the ninth and tenth weeks

e. Helical structures that are paired in the cells; they are the biochemical bases of heredity (23 pairs in humans)

____ 6. gene (LO–2, p. 86)
____ 7. gametes (LO–2, p. 86)
____ 8. meiosis (LO–2, p. 86)
____ 9. reproduction (LO–2, p. 86)
____ 10. zygote (LO–2, p. 87)

a. Sex cells that are created in the testes of males and ovaries of females; they each have 23 unpaired chromosomes

b. Process that occurs when a female gamete (ovum) is fertilized by a male gamete (sperm) to create a single cell with 46 chromosomes

c. Single-celled entity with 23 pairs of chromosomes formed by the union of a sperm cell with an ovum

d. Biochemical agent that is the basic building block of heredity; part of a chromosome

e. Process of cell division that produces cells with 23 unpaired chromosomes (gametes)

_____ 11. genotype (LO–2, p. 87)
_____ 12. phenotype (LO–2, p. 87)
_____ 13. dominant-recessive genes (LO–3, p. 87)
_____ 14. sex-linked genes (LO–3, p. 88)
_____ 15. polygenic inheritance (LO–3, p. 88)

a. Includes genes that determine the observed characteristics whenever present in the organism and genes that only determine the observed characteristics when paired with other identical genes
b. Hypothetical sum of the potential characteristics that our genetic structure makes possible
c. Genes that are carried on the 23rd chromosome pair
d. Phenotypic characteristic of the organism determined by the interaction of many different genes
e. Observable and measurable characteristics of an individual

_____ 16. reaction range (LO–3, p. 89)
_____ 17. canalization (LO–3, p. 89)
_____ 18. behavior genetics (LO–4, p. 89)
_____ 19. twin study (LO–4, p. 90)
_____ 20. monozygotic (LO–4, p. 90)

a. Studies that involve the comparison between identical and fraternal twins
b. Term that describes twins that come from the same egg
c. Narrow path or track that marks the development of some characteristics; these characteristics are those that seem immune to vast changes in environmental events
d. Field of study concerned with the degree and nature of the hereditary basis of behavior
e. Range within which the environment can modify the expression of the genetic potential

_____ 21. dizygotic (LO–4, p. 90)
_____ 22. family-of-twins design (LO–4, p. 90)
_____ 23. kinship studies (LO–4, p. 90)
_____ 24. adoption studies (LO–4, p. 90)
_____ 25. heritability (LO–5, p. 90)

a. Research design that compares monozygotic twins, siblings, half-siblings, parents, and offspring
b. Mathematical estimate of the amount of variation in genetic material compared to the total amount of variation among people for a population; estimates the degree to which a behavioral characteristic is determined by heredity
c. Twins that come from two different eggs
d. Research design that assesses the role of heredity in behavior by comparing the genetic relationship between family members, including uncles, cousins, and grandparents, as well as other more distant relatives.
e. Research design that compares the characteristics of an adopted child to those of both the biological and adoptive parents

____ 26. conception (LO–7, p. 92)
____ 27. cleavage divisions (LO–7, p. 94)
____ 28. zygote period (LO–7, p. 94)
____ 29. in-vitro fertilization (LO–7, p. 94)
____ 30. germinal period (LO–8, p. 95)

a. The two weeks after conception that ends with completed implantation
b. When a single sperm cell from the male unites with the ovum in the female's fallopian tube
c. When the ovum is surgically removed from the mother, fertilized in a laboratory medium with live sperm, stored in a solution that substitutes for the uterine environment, and then implanted back in the mother's uterus
d. The first three to four days after conception, including the journey of the zygote to the uterus
e. The early process of cell divisions

____ 31. blastula (LO–8, p. 95)
____ 32. blastocyst (LO–8, p. 95)
____ 33. trophoblast (LO–8, p. 95)
____ 34. implantation (LO–8, p. 95)
____ 35. embryonic period (LO–9, p. 96)

a. Developmental period lasting from about two to eight weeks after conception; begins after implantation
b. Outer layer of the blastula that develops into the placenta and amniotic sac
c. Inner layer of the blastula that develops into the embryo
d. Spherical structure of about 100 to 150 cells that is formed within one week after conception
e. The blastula's firm attachment to the wall of the uterus

____ 36. endoderm (LO–9, p. 96)
____ 37. ectoderm (LO–9, p. 96)
____ 38. mesoderm (LO–9, p. 96)
____ 39. placenta (LO–9, p. 96)
____ 40. umbilical cord (LO–9, p. 96)

a. Meeting ground for the circulatory systems of the embryo and mother; oxygen and nutrients, but not blood, pass through to the embryo
b. Middle layer of the blastocyst that later becomes the muscles and bones, circulatory system, excretory system, and reproductive system
c. Contains the artery that transports waste material from the embryo to the placental barrier; also contains the vein that transports oxygen and nutrients from the placenta to the embryo
d. Outer layer of the blastocyst that later becomes the hair, skin, and nervous system
e. Inner layer of the blastocyst that later becomes the digestive system, lungs, pancreas, and liver

_____ 41. amnion (LO–9, p. 96)
_____ 42. organogenesis (LO–9, p. 97)
_____ 43. fetal period (LO–10, p. 97)
_____ 44. teratology (LO–11, p. 100)
_____ 45. teratogen (LO–11, p. 100)

a. Field of study that focuses on birth defects
b. Any agent that causes birth defects
c. Bag of clear fluid in which the developing embryo floats
d. Lasts from about eight weeks to birth
e. First two months of prenatal development, during which time organ systems form and are sensitive to influence from environmental events

_____ 46. CMV (cytomegalovirus) (LO–11, p. 102)
_____ 47. HVH (herpes virus hominis) (LO–11, p. 102)
_____ 48. thalidomide (LO–11, p. 104)
_____ 49. fetal alcohol syndrome (FAS) (LO–11, p. 104)
_____ 50. sudden infant death syndrome (SIDS) (LO–11, p. 105)

a. Unexplained death of a child in the first year of life, usually when the baby just stops breathing
b. Disease in the genitalia of the mother that can cause damage to the sensory parts of the nervous system in children born to these mothers
c. Characterized by small heads and defective limbs, joints, face, and heart; may affect the offspring of mothers who consumed alcoholic beverages during pregnancy
d. Venereal disease in women that may infect their infants, possibly causing death, brain damage, or blindness
e. Tranquilizer prescribed to pregnant women that resulted in birth defects in their infants, many involving limb deformities

_____ 51. Leboyer method (LO–12, p. 108)
_____ 52. Lamaze method (LO–12, p. 108)
_____ 53. afterbirth (LO–12, p. 108)
_____ 54. precipitate (LO–12, p. 108)
_____ 55. anoxia (LO–12, p. 108)

a. Form of prepared childbirth; designed to help the pregnant woman to cope with the pain of childbirth and avoid medication
b. Delivery in which the baby moves too rapidly through the birth canal
c. When insufficient oxygen is available to the infant during delivery, possibly causing brain damage
d. Expelling of the placenta, umbilical cord, and other membranes
e. Technique designed to make the birth experience less stressful for the infant; includes placing the infant on the mother's stomach immediately after birth

_____ 56. breech position (LO–12, p. 108)
_____ 57. oxytocin (LO–12, p. 108)
_____ 58. premature birth (LO–13, p. 111)
_____ 59. short-gestation babies (LO–13, p. 111)
_____ 60. gestation (LO–13, p. 111)

a. Length of time between conception and birth; for humans, it is normally 37 to 40 weeks
b. Outdated term for when infants are born after fewer than 37 weeks in the womb
c. Current term for infants born after a briefer than usual time period in the womb
d. Terminology describing infants born buttocks first
e. Hormone that stimulates uterine contractions

_____ 61. low-birth-weight babies (high-risk babies) (LO–13, p. 113)
_____ 62. Apgar Scale (LO–15, p. 114)
_____ 63. Brazelton Neonatal Behavioral Assessment Scale (LO-15, p. 114)
_____ 64. Brazelton training (LO–15, p. 114)
_____ 65. bonding (LO–16, p. 115)

a. Assessment of a newborn's neurological integrity; measures 20 reflexes and reactions to 26 circumstances, such as physical and social stimulation
b. An infant weighing less than 5.5 pounds at birth with a normal-length gestation period
c. Method used to assess the health of the newborn that measures heart rate, respiratory effort, muscle tone, body color, and reflex irritability
d. Occurrence of an emotional tie between neonate and mother
e. Use of the Brazelton scale to show parents how their newborn responds to people

Answers to Key Terms Matching Exercise

1. c	10. c	18. d	26. b	34. e	42. e	50. a	58. b
2. d	11. b	19. a	27. e	35. a	43. d	51. e	59. c
3. a	12. e	20. b	28. d	36. e	44. a	52. a	60. a
4. e	13. a	21. c	29. c	37. d	45. b	53. d	61. b
5. b	14. c	22. a	30. a	38. b	46. b	54. b	62. c
6. d	15. d	23. d	31. d	39. a	47. d	55. c	63. a
7. a	16. e	24. e	32. c	40. c	48. e	56. d	64. e
8. e	17. c	25. b	33. b	41. c	49. c	57. e	65. d
9. b							

Self-Test A

Choose the best alternative.

1. For natural selection to occur, there must be (LO–1, p. 85)
   a. rapid evolution.
   b. a large, similar group.
   c. genetic diversity.
   d. a constant environment.

2. Human cells consist of (LO–2, p. 86)
   a. 23 chromosomes.
   b. 23 pairs of chromosomes.
   c. 46 pairs of chromosomes.
   d. 47 pairs of chromosomes.

3. Genotype is to phenotype as _____ is to _____ . (LO–2, p. 87)
   a. capacity/behavior
   b. behavior/environment
   c. reality/fantasy
   d. measurement/gene

4. Eye color is an example of a trait that is controlled by (LO-3, p. 87)
   a. polygenic inheritance.
   b. sex-linked genes.
   c. reaction range.
   d. dominant/recessive genes.

5. Which of the following is not used by behavior geneticists? (LO–4, pp. 89–90)
   a. selective breeding
   b. kinship studies
   c. forward reference
   d. adoption studies

6. Which of the following is a twin study? (LO–4, p. 90)
   a. Twins, parents, and other siblings are compared.
   b. Fraternal and identical twins are compared.
   c. Twins, parents, other siblings, aunts, uncles, and cousins are compared.
   d. Children are compared with adoptive and biological parents.

7. Which of the following is not a limitation of the heritability index? (LO–5, pp. 90–91)
   a. the range of environmental differences represented
   b. the reliability and validity of the measure
   c. the political arguments made from heritability data
   d. the assumption that the influence of genes and the environment is additive

8. Where does fertilization occur? (LO–7, p. 92)
   a. in the fallopian tube
   b. in the uterus
   c. in the ovary
   d. in the vagina

9. What is the span of the zygote period? (LO–7, p. 94)
   a. conception to birth
   b. conception through the journey to the uterus
   c. conception to implantation
   d. implantation to beginning of cleavage divisions

10. What is the span of the germinal period? (LO–8, p. 95)
    a. implantation to birth
    b. conception to beginning of cleavage divisions
    c. conception to implantation
    d. implantation to beginning of cleavage divisions

11. The blastocyst is to the trophoblast as the _____ is to the _____ .
    (LO–8, pp. 95–96)
    a. blastula/embryo
    b. endoderm/ectoderm
    c. mesoderm/ectoderm
    d. endoderm/mesoderm

12. Which structure gives rise to the skin and nervous system? (LO–9, p. 96)
    a. trophoblast
    b. endoderm
    c. mesoderm
    d. ectoderm

13. What event signals the start of the embryonic period? (LO–9, p. 96)
    a. implantation on the uterine wall
    b. birth
    c. conception
    d. cleavage divisions

14. What event signals the end of the fetal period? (LO–10, pp. 97–98)
    a. implantation of the fetus on the uterine wall
    b. birth
    c. the differentiation of the blastula
    d. cleavage divisions

15. A mother who has CMV is most likely to cause which of the following in her newborn? (LO–11, p.102)
    a. death
    b. brain damage
    c. sensory problems
    d. mental retardation

16. A child is born with a small head, defective limbs and joints, and a defective heart. She also is hyperactive and has seizures. Her mother most likely used which of the following substances during pregnancy? (LO–11, p. 104)
    a. alcohol
    b. nicotine
    c. caffeine
    d. heroin

17. A high-risk infant is an infant who (LO–13, p. 113)
    a. is born before a gestation period of 37 weeks.
    b. is both born early and weighs less than 5.5 pounds.
    c. is born after a normal gestation period but weighs less than 5.5 pounds.
    d. is born with a birth defect.

18. Which high-risk infant has the greatest chance of a good outcome? (LO–14, pp. 114–15)
    a. upper social class, no identified problem
    b. lower social class, no identified problem
    c. upper social class, lung problem
    d. lower social class, lung problem

19. The Apgar Scale measures all of the following except (LO–15, p. 114)
    a. heart rate.
    b. body color.
    c. social reactions.
    d. reflex irritability.

20. What is the status of the critical period argument for bonding? (LO–16, p. 117)
    a. It is widely accepted.
    b. It has been disproved.
    c. It is a controversial issue.
    d. It is believed that the infant should be kept in a newborn nursery so that the mother doesn't expose it to germs.

Answers to Self-Test A

1. c	6. b	11. b	16. a
2. b	7. c	12. d	17. c
3. a	8. a	13. a	18. a
4. d	9. b	14. b	19. c
5. c	10. c	15. c	20. c

Self-Test B

Choose the best alternative.

21. In natural selection, what is being selected? (LO–1, p. 85)
    a. the individual organism
    b. a population
    c. a particular environment
    d. a certain characteristic

22. Gene is to chromosome as _____ is to _____ . (LO–2, p. 86)
    a. meiosis/gamete
    b. DNA/heredity
    c. chromosome/DNA
    d. chromosome/gamete

23. The process that produces gametes is called (LO–2, p. 86)
    a. reproduction.
    b. meiosis.
    c. differentiation.
    d. mitosis.

24. Color blindness is an example of a trait that is controlled by (LO–3, p. 88)
    a. polygenic inheritance.
    b. sex-linked genes.
    c. reaction range.
    d. dominant/recessive genes.

25. Twin studies involve (LO–4, p. 90)
    a. comparing identical and fraternal twins.
    b. doing two identical studies with two different families.
    c. comparing offspring of siblings.
    d. comparing twins with their parents.

26. Which of the following is a kinship study? (LO–4, p. 90)
    a. Twins, parents, and other siblings are compared.
    b. Fraternal and identical twins are compared.
    c. Twins, parents, other siblings, aunts, uncles, and cousins are compared.
    d. Children are compared with adoptive and biological parents.

27. Heritability refers to (LO–5, p. 90)
    a. the degree to which a particular characteristic is genetically determined.
    b. a measure of environmental similarity.
    c. a measure of environmental variability.
    d. a measure of genetic similarity in a population of inbred animals.

28. The blastocyst later becomes the (LO–8, p. 95)
   a. placenta.
   b. uterus.
   c. embryo.
   d. blastula.

29. The trophoblast later becomes the (LO–8, p. 95)
   a. placenta.
   b. uterus.
   c. embryo.
   d. blastula.

30. The muscles and skeletal system arise from which structure(s)? (LO–9, p. 96)
   a. ectoderm
   b. mesoderm
   c. endoderm
   d. mesoderm and ectoderm, respectively

31. The ectoderm gives rise to which systems? (LO–9, p. 96)
   a. muscle and skeletal systems
   b. heart, lungs, and internal organs
   c. hair, skin, sensory receptors, and nervous system
   d. gastrointestinal tract

32. What does not appear during the embryonic period? (LO–9, pp. 96–97)
   a. the arms and legs
   b. the heartbeat
   c. the eyes and ears
   d. the genitalia

33. What does not first appear during the fetal period? (LO–10, pp. 97–98)
   a. the arms and legs
   b. reflexes
   c. hair on the body
   d. the genitalia

34. The genitals have appeared by (LO–10, p. 97)
   a. 3 weeks post conception.
   b. 6 weeks post conception.
   c. 12 weeks post conception.
   d. 20 weeks post conception.

35. Which of the following does not adversely affect the health of a infant? (LO–11, pp. 100–106)
   a. the mother's nutrition during pregnancy
   b. caffeine exposure during pregnancy
   c. emotional upset of the mother during pregnancy
   d. calcium pills taken by the mother during pregnancy

36. A short-gestation infant is to a high-risk infant as _____ is to _____ . (LO–13, pp. 111–13)
   a. 39 weeks/6 pounds
   b. 35 weeks/4 pounds
   c. 6 pounds/32 weeks
   d. 4 pounds/37 weeks

37. For humans, the normal length of the gestation period is (LO–13, pp. 111–13)
   a. 30 to 33 weeks.
   b. 33 to 37 weeks.
   c. 35 to 39 weeks.
   d. 37 to 40 weeks.

38. Which of the following statements is true about recent studies of preterm infants? (LO–14, pp. 114–15)
   a. There are as many serious consequences now for preterm infants as there were 15 years ago.
   b. Social class differences do not affect the outcome for the infant.
   c. Outcomes are worse for an infant born with an identified problem than for others.
   d. Preterm infants generally have difficulty later in school.

39. The Brazelton Neonatal Behavioral Assessment Scale measures which of the following? (LO–15, p. 114)
   a. reflexes
   b. body color
   c. heart rate
   d. muscle tone

40. According to the extreme form of the bonding hypothesis, what time period is the critical period for bonding between mother and child? (LO–16, p. 115)
   a. the week before birth
   b. the initial days of the neonate's life
   c. the first six months
   d. all of the first year

Answers to Self-Test B

21. d	26. c	31. c	36. b
22. d	27. a	32. d	37. d
23. b	28. c	33. a	38. c
24. b	29. a	34. c	39. a
25. a	30. b	35. d	40. b

Questions to Stimulate Thought

1. According to Charles Darwin, evolution meant adaptation to the environment. What adapts? How is this related to genetic diversity and natural selection?
2. What is the genotype and the phenotype? How is each measured (can they be?), and what is their relationship to each other?
3. How is selective breeding like evolution?
4. How do heredity and environment interact? Give an example.
5. How is a zygote created?
6. What occurs during the germinal period? What might be the result if something went wrong with development during this period?

7. What occurs during the embryonic period? What divides the embryonic period from the germinal period? What might be the result if something went wrong with development during this period?

8. What occurs during the fetal period? What divides this period from the embryonic period? What ends this period of prenatal development? What might be the result if something went wrong with development during this period?

9. What effects can environmental factors have on the development of the fetus? Describe some. Define teratogen and give some examples.

10. How do babies get out of the uterus? Are there strategies to assist either the mother or the baby?

11. Compare and contrast two current methods of assessing the developmental state of the neonate.

12. The concept of premature birth has been replaced in modern practice. With what concepts has it been replaced and why?

13. What is bonding, and why might it be important?

Research Project

This research project demonstrates the concept of heritability in development. You will look at a variable for two different families (yours and the family of a student paired with you) and will get measures for parents, children, grandparents, uncles, aunts, and cousins. This is, therefore, a kinship study.

The measure you will take is height. Use Data Sheet 1 that follows to record the height for all of the aforementioned family members over 18 years of age. Record the same data for the family of your classmate. Then answer the questions that follow.

Data Sheet 1

Person/Sex	Family 1 Height	Family 2 Height
Self	_____	_____
Mother	_____	_____
Father	_____	_____
Grandmother 1	_____	_____
Grandmother 2	_____	_____
Grandfather 1	_____	_____
Grandfather 2	_____	_____
Sibling	_____	_____
Sibling	_____	_____
Aunt	_____	_____
Aunt	_____	_____
Uncle	_____	_____
Uncle	_____	_____
Cousin	_____	_____
Cousin	_____	_____
Other	_____	_____
Other	_____	_____

For each family, separate the data for the males from the females. What is the average height for the females in Family 1? In Family 2? What is the average height for the males in Family 1? In Family 2? What are the heights of the tallest and the shortest females in Family 1? In Family 2? What are the heights of the tallest and the shortest males in Family 1? In Family 2? (These "tallest" and "shortest" figures measure the range of heights.) Record your information in Data Sheet 2

Data	Family 1	Family 2
Average Female Height	_____	_____
Average Male Height	_____	_____
Tallest Female Height	_____	_____
Tallest Male Height	_____	_____
Shortest Female Height	_____	_____
Shortest Male Height	_____	_____

Questions

1. Which family in your sample is, on the average, taller, when you control for sex?
2. Of the taller family, how many females are taller than the females in the shorter family? How many of the males are taller than the males in the shorter family?
3. From your data, does it appear that height is an inherited trait?
4. What is the advantage of examining a variable like height, rather than a variable such as temperament or intelligence?

4 Physical and Perceptual Motor Development of Infants

Learning Objectives

After studying this chapter, you should be able to:

1. Describe three methods for studying perception in the nonverbal infant. (p. 124)
2. Describe the characteristics and appearance of the newborn. (p. 125)
3. Describe the reflexes present at birth, particularly the Moro and sucking reflexes, crying, and smiling, and explain their significance. (pp. 125–27)
4. Describe Brown's classification of infant states (of consciousness), including the sleeping-waking cycle. (pp. 128–29)
5. Describe the Brazelton Neonatal Behavioral Assessment Scale and explain its use. (pp. 130–31)
6. Explain the issues surrounding infant feeding. (p. 131)
7. Describe growth during the infant's first year, including cephalocaudal and proximodistal growth patterns, changes in gross and fine motor skills, and the role of rhythmic behavior. (pp. 133–39)
8. Describe growth during the infant's second year, including the deceleration in overall growth, the improvement in both gross and fine motor skills, and the role of rhythmic behavior. (pp. 135–39)
9. Define sensation and perception. (p. 141)
10. Explain the constructivist and ecological views of perceptual development and define the concept of the perceptual invariant. (pp. 142–43)
11. Describe the neonate's visual acuity and the use of the visual preference task to study it. (pp. 144–45)
12. Describe visual perception in the neonate, including that of color, objects and faces, and depth. (pp. 145–47)
13. Explain the distinction between egocentric and objective frames of reference, and describe the development of the perception of spatial relations. (pp. 148–49)
14. Describe the neonate's auditory perception and the intermodal coordination of visual and auditory information. (pp. 149–50)
15. Describe the state of the neonate's other senses (smell, taste, touch, and pain) and how they change in early development. (pp. 152–53)
16. Explain the concept and importance of intermodal perception and how it relates to the constructivist and ecological frameworks. (p. 153)

Summary

The neonate is born with reflexes and skills, such as breathing, sucking, swallowing, and elimination, that are needed to sustain life functions. Perceptual abilities, such as seeing, hearing, and smelling, and other reflexes, such as the Moro reflex, are also present. From birth, the newborn can communicate with its world—primarily through crying.

Muscular control develops during the infant's first year of life. Development follows a cephalocaudal pattern (proceeding from the head down) and a proximodistal pattern (proceeding from the center of the body toward the extremities). Rhythmic motor behaviors, such as kicking, waving, and banging, are common. These rapid, repetitious movements may represent an important transition between uncoordinated activity and complex, coordinated, voluntary control. For example, kicking movements have been observed to peak just before the onset of locomotion and to decline dramatically afterward. During infants' second year of life, growth decelerates. Infants eat less, and gross motor skills are refined. Gross motor skills are important for both emotional and physical development of infants because they provide infants with a sense of mastery of their world. Fine motor skills, such as using thumb and finger, holding a spoon, and scribbling with a pencil, also develop during infants' first two years.

Sensation and perception are the processes we use to gather and interpret information about the world. The two currently dominant theoretical frameworks for understanding perceptual development are the constructivist viewpoint espoused by Jean Piaget and the ecological framework proposed by Eleanor and James Gibson. Constructivists believe that perception is a kind of representation of the world that is based upon sensory input plus information retrieved from memory. They also believe that changes in perception during development result from changes in knowledge. The ecological viewpoint assumes that perceptual systems have evolved over time to directly pick up information about the world. The Gibsons assume that there are invariants in the world, to which the perceptual systems respond, that directly specify properties of the world. They also believe that perception works by attending to the appropriate information. Thus, according to ecological theorists, perceptual development involves changes in attention to relevant information, increased efficiency in the pickup of information, and increased sensitivity to the invariants in the world.

A variety of techniques have been developed for studying infant perception and sensation. Natural reactions are examined by presenting the infant with a stimulus and observing the infant's response. The preference technique involves the simultaneous presentation of two stimuli and observing if the infant prefers to attend to one rather than to the other. The infant's ability to discriminate between two stimuli can also be tested in this way. The habituation technique involves the repeated presentation of a stimulus until the infant stops attending to it. A different stimulus is then presented. If the infant attends to the new stimulus, he or she has dishabituated and has demonstrated the ability to discriminate between the two stimuli. The nonnutritive sucking technique uses the infant's tendency to suck even without receiving food to examine interest in visual or auditory stimuli.

Visual perception is one of the most explored areas of infant perception. Fantz has reported that infants, even neonates, show a visual preference for a display of stripes instead of a solid gray patch. Visual acuity in the neonate is about 20/600 but by six months has become 20/100. Visual acuity in one-month-old infants does not vary as a function of viewing distance. Recent investigations have suggested that infants are not entirely color-blind but may be partially color-blind. Depth perception has been demonstrated by Gibson and Walk, using a visual cliff and a natural reaction in six-month-old infants. Infants two to four months old can visually discriminate between the shallow and deep side of the visual cliff but do not necessarily perceive depth. Yonas and his colleagues used reaching behavior as a measure and found that 5½-month-old infants perceive depth. Spelke has demonstrated that four-month-old infants perceive partially occluded objects as unitary wholes, rather than as disconnected parts.

The perception of spatial relations changes from an egocentric frame of reference (using the body to determine spatial relations) in infancy to an objective frame of reference (involving the use of landmarks to determine spatial relations) sometime during the second year of life. Acredolo has found that, by 16 months of age, infants are able to respond objectively to locate things around them and that even younger infants can respond objectively in a familiar environment.

Research on hearing suggests that the ability to hear might exist before birth. Newborns can hear, but the sound must be louder than for an adult. Intermodal perception, the ability to perceive events in different perceptual modalities as a single unified event, has been demonstrated for auditory/visual coordination in four-month-old infants. Using a visual preference technique, Spelke found that even four-month-olds had a visual preference for a movie with sound over a movie without sound.

Research by Lipsett and his colleagues has shown that infants under 68 hours of age are sensitive to unpleasant odors and can discriminate between two different unpleasant odors. Infants two to seven days old can recognize the smell of their mother's milk on a breast pad as compared with a breast pad with no milk.

Sensitivity to taste may be present before birth since increased swallowing has been observed when saccharin is added to the amniotic fluid of a near-term fetus. Steiner has demonstrated differences in the facial expressions of newborns as a function of whether they are sucking a sweet or sour substance. Newborns are clearly responsive to touch since many reflexes are easily elicited by mild tactile stimulation. Studies of circumcision indicate that neonates can sense pain and that they can cope with it.

Research findings on intermodal perception in very young infants are more supportive of the Gibsons' ecological theory of perception than of Piaget's constructivist view.

Guided Review

You may want to look at the answers to the "Guided Review" statements as you read, or you may want to use the exercise as a form of self-test by covering up the answers below the statements with a sheet of paper and not consulting them until you have attempted to fill in the blanks of each statement.

1. The movements that govern newborns are called _____ . They are _____ and beyond their control.

   reflexes, automatic

2. A reflex that is a vestige of our evolutionary past is called the _____ reflex. It is like an emergency _____ reflex.

   Moro, grasping

3. Reflexes are often tested to assess the development of the neonate's _____ _____ .

   nervous system

4. The food-getting reflex of neonates is _____ . Infants engage in considerable nonnutritive sucking until about _____ year of age.

   sucking, one

5. Crying is the neonate's first _____ behavior. It first appears as a _____ response to discomfort.

   emotional or affective, reflexive

6. Adults can often distinguish the newborn's cries associated with _____ from those associated with _____ .

   pain or arousal, hunger

7. Watson argued that the parent (should or should not) _____ always respond to the crying neonate. He thought that the attention would act as a _____ and increase the incidence of crying.

   should not, reinforcer

8. Ainsworth and others with an _____ background argue a position that is _____ to Watson's. They believe that attention of the caregiver contributes to a _____ _____ between the infant and the caregiver.

   ethological, opposite, secure attachment

9. Brown described three states of sleep. _____ _____ exists when the infant lies motionless with eyes closed and does not respond to stimuli. During _____ _____ , there is little movement, but respirations may be irregular. During _____ _____ , there may be movement, eyelids may flutter, breathing is regular or _____ , and there may be _____ .

   Deep sleep, regular sleep, disturbed sleep, irregular, vocalizations

10. Brown also described four states of wakefulness. A _____ state is displayed by an infant with partially open and glassy eyes, who displays little movement but more _____ than in disturbed sleep. The infant who is awake with open and bright eyes, engages in a variety of movements, frets, has a reddish skin color, and breathes _____ when upset is displaying the state of _____ _____ . The state of _____ and _____ is more characteristic of older children. This state is similar to the state of alert activity except that _____ are integrated around a specific activity. The _____ _____ infant is awake but unreactive because attention is centered on some activity, such as _____ or _____ .

drowsy, vocalizations, irregularly, alert activity, alert, focused, movements, inflexibly focused, sucking, crying

11. Sleep occupies _____ to _____ hours of the neonate's day. By _____ month of age, infants begin to sleep longer at night, and by _____ months of age, their sleep patterns are more adultlike.

16, 17, one, four

12. About _____ percent of the neonate's sleep is _____ sleep. This form of sleep is correlated with _____ in adults and occupies about _____ percent of the adult sleep period. By _____ months of age, the infant's proportion of REM sleep falls to _____ percent.

50, REM, dreams, 20, three, 40

13. Discussions of infant feeding center on whether to _____ or _____ feed and on whether the infant should be fed on a _____ or on _____ .

breast, bottle, schedule, demand

14. It is generally believed that _____ feeding is healthier. However, the proportion of mothers who nurse their babies is only about _____ percent.

breast, 50

15. Watson argued for feeding by a _____ . He thought that it would teach _____ . Recently, there has been a tendency toward _____ feeding.

schedule, control, demand

16. The _____ pattern refers to growth from the top down. The _____ pattern describes a pattern of growth that starts at the center of the body and moves toward the extremities.

cephalocaudal, proximodistal

17. In the infant, the ability to hold the chest up while prone and to reach for seen objects develops by _____ or _____ months of age. Sitting with help usually appears by _____ months and rolling over by _____ months.

three, four, five, six

18. The infant's _____ can support some weight at birth and the stepping reflex is evident, but it is not until _____ or _____ months of age that walking with help is likely. Standing alone and perhaps pulling up to a standing position appears at about _____ months and walking by about _____ or _____ months.

legs, 8, 9, 11, 13, 14

19. The skills described in items 17 and 18 are _____ motor skills.
    gross

20. Because the motor pathways to the brain mature sooner for areas in the center of the body than for areas at the _____ , the development of the motor skills of the trunk and _____ precedes that of the _____ and _____ . The coordination of sensation with motor response is governed by the _____ areas. They develop _____ than the sensory and motor areas.
    extremities, arms, hands, fingers, association, later

21. Very brief tracking appears in the infant during the _____ month of life and improves over the next _____ or _____ months. Grasping and holding objects appears at about _____ or _____ months of age. A subtle use of the thumb in grasping develops by the _____ month. The skills described in this item are _____ motor skills.
    first, two, three, four, five, 12th, fine

22. During the second year, the infant's rate of growth _____ . The infant adds inches in height but few pounds, and the child's body becomes _____ and more _____ . By several months into the second year, the child becomes able to _____ and to _____ in a chair unassisted. The child can climb stairs by _____ months, walk downstairs with help by _____ months, and run efficiently without falling very often by _____ months.
    decelerates, leaner, muscular, run, sit, 18, 20, 24

23. During the second year, the child's intentions outdistance _____ . He or she wants to perform skills but cannot. The child typically asks for and acknowledges _____ .
    capabilities, help

24. During the first year of life, rapid, repetitious movement of the limbs, torso, and head, called _____ motor behavior, appears. Infants seem to find these acts _____ .
    rhythmic, pleasurable

25. Rhythmic stereotypies may represent a transition between _____ motor activity and _____ , _____ , _____ motor control. For example, kicking movements appear to peak just before the onset of _____ .
    uncoordinated, complex, coordinated, voluntary, locomotion

26. The number of brain _____ does not increase after birth, but the number of brain _____ does. In the prefrontal region of the brain, the concentration of _____ peaks at _____ months, decreases until about _____ to _____ months, and then increases at _____ to _____ years of age.
    cells, connections, dopamine, 5, 18, 24, two, three

27. The general processes that people use to gather and interpret information about the world are _____ and _____ . Sensation occurs when information contacts sensory _____ . Perception is the _____ of what is sensed.
    sensation, perception, receptors, interpretation

28. Piaget's theoretical framework is the _____ viewpoint. The _____ framework is taken by Eleanor and James Gibson.
    constructivist, ecological or direct perception

29. The constructivist argues that perceived reality is a _____ of the world based on the sensory input from your _____ plus information retrieved from _____ .
   representation or construction, eyes, memory

30. In the ecological view, _____ _____ represent information in the world to which the mind can respond directly. Because these invariants directly specify environmental properties, the child need not _____ internal representations to perceive them. Some perceptual invariants may even be perceived by _____ .
   perceptual invariants, build or construct, neonates

31. One of the challenges of studying perception in infants and young children is that the subjects do not yet possess adequate _____ to describe their world. However, one can assess an infant's perception by presenting two or more stimuli and measuring the infant's _____ for one or the other.
   language, preference

32. A review of the literature on visual acuity suggests that the acuity of the newborn is about _____ but improves to _____ by six months of age.
   20/600, 20/100

33. Recent studies of color vision in neonates indicate the possibility of partial _____-_____ .
   color-blindness

34. Objects in the visual world are perceived by adults as complete and whole even if the objects are _____ _____ . After viewing a rod with a block placed in front of it in phase 1 of an experiment, four-month-old infants looked longer at a rod with a _____ in it during the testing phase than they did a _____ rod.
   partly occluded, gap, complete

35. Fantz has shown that _____-month-old infants prefer looking at a _____ face rather than a _____ face.
   two, normal, rearranged

36. The _____ approach stresses that even higher-order information is directly available to the sensory receptors and need not be constructed by the mind. If so, one might expect higher-order information to be perceived by _____ .
   ecological, neonates

37. The purpose of the apparatus called the _____ _____ , designed by Gibson and Walk, was to simulate the appearance of a dangerous chasm without the danger of one. Infants in the age range of _____ to _____ months are less likely to crawl on the deep side than on the shallow side of the visual cliff.
   visual cliff, 6, 14

38. Infants as young as _____ months can use apparent _____ as a cue for depth. Younger infants seem capable of seeing _____ independent of _____ when viewing moving objects.
   5½, size, size, distance

39. Knowledge about the location of an object in the world must be based upon a _____ of _____ . Walking down the hall and turning to one's right is using an _____ frame of reference. Basing knowledge of an object's location on other objects in the environment is using an _____ frame of reference.
frame, reference, egocentric, objective

40. Piaget argued that infants in the first year of life are limited to an _____ orientation. Research by Acredolo indicates that infants as young as _____ months old can use an _____ frame of reference. One factor that increases the likelihood of using an objective frame of reference is _____ with the environment in which the individual is operating.
egocentric, 16, objective, familiarity

41. Some studies have indicated that a _____ can hear sounds. Immediately after birth, neonates _____ hear, although their sensory thresholds are somewhat _____ than those of adults. By the age of _____ months, infants can hear very _____ frequency sounds as well as adults.
fetus, can, higher, 24, high

42. Spelke believes that even _____ perceive visual and auditory information about the same event as a unitary episode. Her work suggests that infants as young as _____ months old have _____ perception. In her study, infants looked _____ at a film with a coordinated sound track than one for which the sound track did not match.
infants, four, intermodal, longer

43. Neonates apparently have a sense of _____ because they respond to asafetida in the air. Very young infants can apparently _____ the smell of a mother's breast, but not necessarily their own mother's.
smell, recognize

44. When the sucking of newborn babies is rewarded with a sweetened solution, the amount of sucking _____ . The rate of sucking is _____ for more-sweetened solutions. One study found that a sweet taste resulted in a _____ from a neonate, while a sour taste resulted in a _____ of the _____ .
increases, slower, smile, pursing, lips

45. A touch to the cheek of an infant results in a _____ - _____ response.
head-turning

46. Male infants react as if circumcision produces _____ . Research indicates, however, that infants cope _____ with this procedure.
pain, well

47. That perceptual modalities are coordinated is a fact. To the _____ , such as Piaget, experience teaches this coordination. According to Piaget, _____ interactions with the world make intermodal perception possible. The _____ perspective of the Gibsons stresses that some intermodal perceptual abilities are _____ .
constructivists, sensorimotor, ecological, innate

Key Terms Matching Exercise

Match the Key Term on the left with the correct definition on the right.

_____ 1. natural reaction (LO–1, p. 124)
_____ 2. preference technique (LO–1, p. 124)
_____ 3. habituation technique (LO–1, p. 124)
_____ 4. Moro reflex (LO–3, p. 125)
_____ 5. nonnutritive sucking (LO–3, p. 127)
_____ 6. reflexive smile (LO–3, p. 127)

a. Research technique that involves observing whether an infant chooses one stimulus over another; can be used to study infant perception

b. An organism's automatic response to a stimulus

c. Sucking behavior by the child that is unrelated to the child's feeding

d. When a stimulus is presented repeatedly until the infant no longer shows interest in it; a different stimulus is then presented to see if the infant now shows interest in the new object; a technique for studying infant perception

e. Smile in a neonate that does not occur in response to external stimuli

f. Startle response of the neonate that involves arching the back, throwing the head back, flinging out the arms and legs, and then rapidly closing them to the center of the body; triggered by bright light, loud noise, or the sudden loss of support

---

_____ 7. social smiling (LO–3, p. 127)
_____ 8. REM sleep (LO–4, p. 129)
_____ 9. scheduled feeding (LO–6, p. 131)
_____ 10. demand feeding (LO–6, p. 131)
_____ 11. cephalocaudal pattern (LO–7, p. 133)
_____ 12. proximodistal pattern (LO–7, p. 133)

a. Pattern of growth starting at the center of the body and moving toward the extremities

b. Pattern of growth occurring first at the top (or head) and gradually working its way down from top to bottom

c. Sleep state characterized by rapid eye movements and during which dreams are often reported

d. Smiling in an infant that occurs in response to a face

e. Feeding according to a predetermined cycle; designed to help children become orderly and controlled

f. When the timing and amount of a feeding are determined by the infant

_____ 13. gross motor skills (LO–7, p. 134)
_____ 14. fine motor skills (LO–7, p. 134)
_____ 15. sensory cortex (LO–7, p. 134)
_____ 16. motor cortex (LO–7, p. 134)
_____ 17. association areas of the cortex (LO–7, p. 134)
_____ 18. rhythmic motor behavior (LO–8, p. 137)

a. Motor behaviors involving small muscle groups, such as scribbling with a pencil
b. Motor behaviors involving large muscle groups, such as walking and climbing
c. Area of the brain where action originates
d. Rapid, repetitious movements of limbs, torso, and head, such as kicking and waving, that may be a transition between uncoordinated and coordinated motor behavior
e. Part of the brain where input from the sense organs is directly interpreted
f. Areas of the brain that coordinate the communication between sensation and action

_____ 19. rhythmic stereotypies (LO–8, p. 138)
_____ 20. sensation (LO–9, p. 141)
_____ 21. perception (LO–9, p. 141)
_____ 22. constructivist approach (LO–10, p. 142)
_____ 23. representation (LO–10, p. 142)

a. Detection of the environment through stimulation of receptors in the sense organs
b. Model of the world built up in the mind and based on sensory input plus information retrieved from memory
c. Belief that what one experiences is a construction, model, or picture based on sensory input plus information retrieved from memory—a kind of representation of the world one builds up in one's mind
d. Rhythmic behaviors performed without much variation, possibly representing an important transition between uncoordinated activity and complex, coordinated, voluntary motor control
e. The interpretation of what is sensed

_____ 24. direct perception or ecological view (LO–10, p. 143)
_____ 25. perceptual invariant (LO–10, p. 143)
_____ 26. visual acuity (LO–11, p. 144)
_____ 27. visual accommodation (LO–11, p. 144)
_____ 28. intermodal perception (LO–14, p. 149)

a. Ability to maintain high visual acuity over a range of viewing distances (by changing the shape of the lens)
b. View that the perceptual systems have evolved to directly respond to and pick up information in the environment
c. Ability to see details
d. Ability to perceive events coming to two different perceptual systems in a related, unified manner
e. Property of the world that remains constant over conditions of change and that directly provides information about some aspect of the world

1. b	5. c	9. e	13. b	17. f	21. e	25. e
2. a	6. e	10. f	14. a	18. d	22. c	26. c
3. d	7. d	11. b	15. e	19. d	23. b	27. a
4. f	8. c	12. a	16. c	20. a	24. b	28. d

Self-Test A

Choose the best alternative.

1. A psychologist moves an object toward an infant's face and observes that the infant retracts her head and puts her hands between her face and the object. The technique the psychologist has used is (LO–1, p. 124)
   a. preference.
   b. habituation.
   c. conditioned head-turning.
   d. natural reaction.

2. Which of the following techniques does the visual cliff use? (LO–1, pp. 124, 146–47)
   a. natural reaction
   b. preference
   c. habituation
   d. conditioned head-turning

3. Neonates spend most of their time (LO–2, p. 128)
   a. eating.
   b. crying.
   c. sleeping.
   d. exploring.

4. The first effective communicative behavior of the newborn infant is (LO–3, p. 127)
   a. smiling.
   b. cooing.
   c. babbling.
   d. crying.

5. Brown termed the state in infants characterized by open but glassy eyes, little movement, and some vocalizations as (LO–4, p. 128)
   a. drowsy.
   b. regular sleep.
   c. disturbed sleep.
   d. alert activity.

6. The Brazelton Neonatal Behavioral Assessment Scale is currently being scored according to which of the following four scales? (LO–5, p. 130)
   a. cuddliness, state, interaction, motoric
   b. state, interaction, motoric, physiological
   c. cuddliness, physiological, motoric, state
   d. state, interaction, cuddliness, physiological

7. A strong proponent of scheduled feeding was (LO–6, p. 131)
   a. Watson.
   b. Spock.
   c. Piaget.
   d. Gibson.

8. Infants gain control of their shoulders before they gain control of their legs. This illustrates the principle of (LO–7, p. 133)
   a. proximodistal development.
   b. cephalocaudal development.
   c. rhythmic behavior.
   d. differentiation.

9. The infant becomes able to sit with support at (LO–7, p. 134)
   a. three months of age.
   b. four months of age.
   c. five months of age.
   d. six months of age.

10. When does the child become able to run and to climb? (LO–8, p. 136)
   a. first year
   b. second year
   c. third year
   d. fourth year

11. What are the names of the processes used to gather and interpret information about the world? (LO–9, p. 141)
   a. sensation and perception
   b. vision and touch
   c. sight and hearing
   d. sensation and memory

12. Who of the following is most strongly associated with the constructivist views on the development of perception? (LO–10, p. 142)
   a. James and Eleanor Gibson
   b. Jean Piaget
   c. John Watson
   d. Arnold Gesell

13. The constructivist view of perception claims that perception is based on (LO–10, p. 142)
   a. invariants.
   b. direct information about the world.
   c. sensory input from your eyes plus information from memory.
   d. sensory input alone.

14. Visual acuity is _____ or higher in infants by six months of age. (LO–11, p. 145)
   a. 20/600
   b. 20/200
   c. 20/100
   d. 20/20

15. Spelke has demonstrated that infants of what age perceive objects as unified wholes after viewing two parts of an object that move in synchrony? (LO–12, p. 146)
   a. newborns
   b. four-month-olds
   c. six-month-olds
   d. eight-month-olds

16. An object is hidden on a child's right. The child is turned around to face in the opposite direction. The child then searches for the object on his right. He is (LO–13, p. 148)
   a. using an objective frame of reference.
   b. using an egocentric frame of reference.
   c. using a landmark.
   d. using information from large-scale space.

17. Research indicates that hearing may first occur (LO–14, p. 149)
   a. by the end of the first trimester of pregnancy.
   b. by late in the third trimester of pregnancy.
   c. at birth.
   d. by two months after birth.

18. Intermodal perception refers to the ability to (LO–14, p. 149)
   a. separate perceptions in one modality from perceptions in another.
   b. perceive events in two modalities as separate.
   c. perceive events in two modalities as unified.
   d. distinguish what is seen from what is felt.

19. Research has demonstrated that the sense of smell is working by what age? (LO–15, p. 152)
   a. three months
   b. three weeks
   c. three days
   d. less than 24 hours

20. Research on intermodal perception in young infants supports which theoretical account of perception? (LO–16, p. 153)
   a. ecological
   b. constructivist
   c. It supports both theoretical accounts of perception.
   d. It refutes both theoretical accounts of perception.

Answers to Self-Test A

1. d	5. a	9. c	13. c	17. b
2. a	6. b	10. b	14. c	18. c
3. c	7. a	11. a	15. b	19. d
4. d	8. b	12. b	16. b	20. a

Self-Test B

Choose the best alternative.

21. A psychologist interested in infant visual perception repeatedly presents a picture of a house to an infant until the infant ceases to attend to the picture. The psychologist then presents a picture of a different house to the infant. The psychologist is using which research technique? (LO–1, p. 124)
   a. natural reaction
   b. preference
   c. habituation
   d. conditioned head-turning

22. The research by Spelke and her colleagues examining visual perception of objects in four-month-old infants used which of the following techniques? (LO–1, pp. 124, 146)
   a. natural reaction
   b. preference
   c. habituation
   d. conditioned head-turning

23. The behavior of the newborn is (LO–2, p. 125)
    a. reflexive.
    b. controlled.
    c. intentional.
    d. indeterminant.

24. An experimenter puts a pacifier into a baby's mouth. When the baby sucks on the pacifier at a certain rate, a picture comes into focus. The experimenter is using which of the following research techniques? (LO–3, p. 127)
    a. habituation
    b. preference
    c. natural reaction
    d. nonnutritive sucking

25. Timmy is lying motionless, with his eyes closed, shows regular breathing and no vocalizations, and does not respond to outside stimulation. According to Brown's classification, Timmy is in which state? (LO–4, p. 128)
    a. alert activity
    b. disturbed sleep
    c. regular sleep
    d. deep sleep

26. If an infant is considered resistant to being held most of the time, she would be rated low on which category of the Brazelton Neonatal Behavioral Assessment Scale? (LO–5, p. 130)
    a. general muscle tone
    b. activity
    c. cuddliness
    d. defensive movements

27. The goal of scheduled feeding was to produce children who were (LO–6, p. 131)
    a. autonomous.
    b. orderly and controlled.
    c. independent.
    d. goal-directed.

28. Infants gain control of their trunk before they gain control of their fingers. This illustrates the principle of (LO–7, p. 133)
    a. proximodistal development.
    b. cephalocaudal development.
    c. rhythmic behavior.
    d. differentiation.

29. Which position does Esther Thelen take regarding the role of rhythmic behavior in development? (LO–7, pp. 137–38)
    a. It is a sign of developmental delay.
    b. It is a stage of sensorimotor development called circular reactions.
    c. It represents an attempt to establish relations with an "aloof" mother.
    d. It represents an important transition from uncoordinated to coordinated activity.

30. According to Caplan and Caplan, a preference for using one hand over the other first appears around the age of (LO–8, p. 137)
    a. 6–12 months.
    b. 12–24 months.
    c. 24–36 months.
    d. 5 years.

31. When light is focused on the retina, what is the immediate effect? (LO–9, p. 141)
    a. sensation
    b. perception
    c. vision
    d. vision and perception

32. Who is strongly associated with the ecological view of perception? (LO–10, p. 143)
    a. James and Eleanor Gibson
    b. Piaget and Inhelder
    c. information processing theorists
    d. John Locke and the empiricists

33. If an infant looks longer at one of two concurrent displays, the infant is showing (LO–11, p. 144)
    a. generalization.
    b. discrimination.
    c. habituation.
    d. fatigue.

34. Research on the visual cliff with infants has found that (LO–12, pp. 146–47)
    a. 6-month-old infants do not avoid the deep side, while 14-month-old infants do.
    b. 6-month-old infants as well as 14-month-old infants avoid the deep side.
    c. neither 6-month-old nor 14-month-old infants avoid the deep side.
    d. 6-month-old infants avoid the deep side, but 14-month-old infants no longer do.

35. Research by Yonas and his colleagues has demonstrated that infants 5½ months of age (LO–12, p. 147)
    a. reach toward the farther of two objects they view.
    b. reach toward the smaller of two objects they view.
    c. show no preference for reaching toward either a larger or smaller object they view.
    d. reach toward the larger of two objects they view if these objects are viewed through one eye.

36. An object is hidden on a child's right. The child is turned around to face in the opposite direction. The child then searches for the object on her left. She is (LO–13, pp. 148–49)
    a. using an objective frame of reference.
    b. using an egocentric frame of reference.
    c. using a simultaneous comparison.
    d. guessing.

37. Immediately after birth, infants (LO–14, p. 149)
    a. cannot hear.
    b. can hear, although their sensory thresholds are somewhat lower than those of adults.
    c. are capable of hearing only very high frequency sounds.
    d. can hear, although their sensory thresholds are somewhat higher than those of adults.

38. Spelke's work on intermodal perception has examined relations between which perceptual modalities? (LO–14, p. 150)
    a. vision and touch
    b. vision and hearing
    c. touch and hearing
    d. taste and smell

39. Sensitivity to taste has been observed (LO–15, p. 152)
    a. three months after birth.
    b. two months after birth.
    c. one month after birth.
    d. prior to birth.

40. Research on intermodal perception in young infants has demonstrated that (LO–16, p. 153)
   a. the main perceptual abilities are uncoordinated at birth and only slowly emerge through biological maturation.
   b. intermodal perception is possible only after many months of sensorimotor interactions with the environment.
   c. intermodal perception is present in early infancy.
   d. intermodal perception is present by the end of the second trimester of pregnancy.

Answers to Self-Test B

21. c	25. d	29. d	33. b	37. d
22. c	26. c	30. b	34. b	38. b
23. a	27. b	31. a	35. d	39. d
24. d	28. a	32. a	36. a	40. c

Questions to Stimulate Thought

1. What are sensation and perception, and why are they interesting problems for study? What practical problems might their study solve?
2. Compare and contrast two major current theoretical perspectives of perceptual development. What is the relationship of each to empiricism and nativism?
3. How might you reconcile the data presented on infant visual acuity and the results of the studies of depth, size, object, and face perception and imitation?
4. How is intermodal perception viewed by the constructivist and by the ecological theorist?
5. What is the state of the senses other than vision and audition at birth?
6. What is a reflex? Is it voluntary?
7. How are the various states of infant consciousness related to sleeping and waking?
8. What are the neonate's capabilities?
9. Describe the development of the infant's motor capabilities during the first year. What are the general patterns in this development?
10. How does motor development change during the second year?
11. What is the importance (if any) of the appearance of rhythmic behavior? Explain.

Research Project

This project involves observing the gross motor activity of infants. Pair up with another student in the class and go to a local playground or shopping mall. Observe two infants, one about 8 months old and the other about 20 months old. For each infant, describe five gross motor behaviors that the infant performs while you are observing. These behaviors can include reaching, sitting, walking, rocking, kicking, running, climbing, throwing, etc. Describe the same five behaviors, if possible, for each infant, noting differences in the way the infants perform the behaviors. Use the data sheet that follows for recording your observations. Then answer the questions.

Data Sheet

Infant 1: Sex _____   **Age** _____

Behavior 1 (_____ **):**

Behavior 2 (_____):

Behavior 3 (_____):

Behavior 4 (_____):

Behavior 5 (_____):

Infant 2: Sex _____   Age _____
Behavior 1 (_____):

Behavior 2 (_____):

Behavior 3 (_____):

Behavior 4 (_____):

Behavior 5 (_____):

Questions

1. What were the five behaviors you observed for each infant? Were they different?
2. In general, how can these behaviors be characterized or described for the 8-month-old? For the 20-month-old?
3. For the behaviors you observed that were the same for each infant, how would you characterize the differences in the performance of the behaviors by the two infants? That is, how did the infants differ in the way they did the behaviors?
4. From your observations of the two infants and the five behaviors at each age, what do you see as the course of development of gross motor behavior between 8 and 20 months? How do your specific findings compare with the general descriptions reported in the text?

5 Learning, Cognition, and Language in Infancy

Learning Objectives

After studying this chapter, you should be able to:

1. Describe learning, and list and explain the contributions of Pavlov, Skinner, and Bandura to theories of learning development. (pp. 161–68)
2. Describe classical conditioning and explain the conditioned stimulus, unconditioned stimulus, conditioned response, and unconditioned response. (pp. 161–62)
3. Describe the procedures for extinction and explain the meaning of spontaneous recovery. (p. 163)
4. Explain classical conditioning according to the stimulus substitution and information theories. (pp. 163–64)
5. Explain how children's fears might develop through classical conditioning and be eliminated through counterconditioning. (p. 164)
6. Describe the procedures of operant conditioning, including reinforcement, shaping, extinction, and spontaneous recovery. (pp. 165–66)
7. Describe three views of imitation. (pp. 166–67)
8. List and explain the general characteristics of sensorimotor thought and define the term *scheme*. (p. 168)
9. Name the six substages of the sensorimotor period and describe the infant's capacity in each. (pp. 170–71)
10. Give the Piagetian view of the sensorimotor development of object permanence and describe four non-Piagetian considerations. (pp. 172–73)
11. Describe the orienting response and relate it to habituation and dishabituation. (p. 174)
12. Describe the development of scanning in infancy. (pp. 174–75)
13. Describe the method of conjugate reinforcement for investigating infant memory and the concepts of conscious memory and infantile amnesia. (pp. 176–78)
14. Compare and contrast intelligence tests with infant developmental scales.(pp. 179–81)
15. Describe the assessment of infant intelligence with the Gesell test, the Bayley scales, the Cattell test, and the test developed by Uzgiris and Hunt. (pp. 179–81)
16. Describe the extent of continuity in the development of intelligence. (p. 181)
17. Describe the characteristics and functions of human language. (pp. 183–84)
18. List and define the five rule systems of language. (pp. 184–85)
19. Describe the behavioral (learning) view of language acquisition. (pp. 185–87)
20. Describe the nativist view of language acquisition. (pp. 187–91)
21. Define language universals, lateralization of language function, and critical or sensitive periods, and explain the relevance of the absence of humanlike language in other species. (pp. 187–91)
22. Describe the cognitive view of language acquisition. (pp. 191–92)
23. Define motherese, prompting, echoing, expanding, recasting, and labeling, and give one reason why each is important. (pp. 193–95)
24. Describe the child's preverbal accomplishments, such as babbling, pragmatic skills, and symbolic abilities, and give the relevance of each. (pp. 195–97)
25. Describe one-word utterances, the holophrase hypothesis, Eve Clark's theory of meaning, and underextensions and overextensions of words. (pp. 197–200)
26. Describe two-word utterances and telegraphic speech. (p. 200)

Summary

Learning can be defined as a relatively permanent change in behavior or thought that is caused by experience and that cannot be explained by reflexes, instincts, maturation, fatigue, injury, disease, or drugs. Pavlov's view of learning involved the association of biological and learned stimuli. Skinner argued for two kinds of learning—one as Pavlov described and a second based on the spontaneous actions of an organism that result in consequences in the environment that serve either to strengthen or weaken the behavior. A third kind of learning was proposed by Bandura, who argued that learning can occur through observation and imitation. Current research suggests that infants as young as 36 hours old may be able to imitate facial expressions of adults.

The technique developed by Pavlov is called classical conditioning. Classical conditioning is a procedure by which a neutral stimulus comes to elicit a response by being paired with a stimulus that regularly evokes the response. Classical conditioning may be explained by stimulus substitution. Proponents of this theory argue that the contiguity between the conditioned stimulus and the unconditioned stimulus creates a bond between them and that, eventually, the conditioned stimulus substitutes for the unconditioned stimulus. Classical conditioning may also be explained by information theory, which stresses that the conditioned stimulus acquires information value that provides the organism with information about the event that is to follow. Classical conditioning seems implicated in the learning of fears, some of which are maladaptive and irrational (phobias). Counterconditioning can be used to reduce these fears.

Piaget's theory of cognitive development is divided into four stages: sensorimotor, preoperational, concrete operational, and formal operational. The sensorimotor stage lasts from birth to about two years. During this stage, thought is not symbolic and is characterized by sensory and perceptual processes and action. By the end of this stage, the ability to use simple symbols develops. This view is in part supported by the appearance of deferred imitation at about 18 to 24 months of age.

Piaget described six substages of the sensorimotor period. In the first, knowledge is gained through simple reflexes, the only actions of which the infant is capable. In the second substage, the child becomes capable of primary circular reactions, which are the infant's attempts to repeat an action that initially occurred by chance. The third substage is characterized by secondary circular reactions, which are actions the infant repeats because they caused an interesting event to occur in the environment. The fourth substage involves the coordination of secondary circular reactions and also the appearance of intentionality. The infant can use one action to be able to perform another. The fifth substage is characterized by tertiary circular reactions. The infant systematically explores the effects of a variety of actions on an object. Novelty and curiosity appear. The final substage is the internalization of schemes. The child becomes able to use primitive symbols, and mental representation appears.

The development of object permanence is one of the most important achievements of the sensorimotor stage. The child develops the ability to understand that objects and events continue to exist even though the child is not in direct contact with them.

Attention involves focusing perception to produce increased awareness of a stimulus. Newborns can detect a contour and fixate on it. Both orientation and size of the stimulus affect fixation. Older infants scan both internal and external parts of a pattern, while younger infants fixate primarily on external parts.

Using a conjugate reinforcement technique, researchers have demonstrated memory for as long as three days in infants as young as two months old. With a reactivation technique, the recall interval can be extended up to four or five weeks. A distinction is made between conscious memory and the type of memory infants show in the conjugate reinforcement setting. Conscious memory involves feelings of having experienced something before. Conscious memory may not exist until 18 months to two years of age. Infantile amnesia exists for events that occur prior to three years of age and may indicate that memory in the strict sense does not occur until then.

Infant intelligence tests are usually called developmental scales and are oriented toward motor development, in contrast to the heavy verbal orientation of intelligence tests for older children and adults. Perhaps as a consequence of this, infant intelligence tests have been better at assessing the effects of malnutrition, drugs, and maternal deprivation than at predicting later intelligence. However, recent research on two aspects of attention in infancy—decrement of attention and recovery of attention—suggests more continuity with intelligence in childhood.

Language has several characteristics, including infinite generativity and displacement, and is a complex set of rules. The five most prominent rule systems are: (1) phonology, the sound system of a language; (2) morphology, rules regarding the smallest units of language that carry meaning (morphemes); (3) syntax, rules governing how words are combined into sequences; (4) semantics, the meaning of words and sentences; and (5) pragmatics, rules about the social context of language.

The first of three different theories used to explain language development is the behavioral view, which sees language as verbal behavior. This learning theory explains language acquisition through shaping, reinforcement, and imitation. With regard to shaping and reinforcement, however, Brown and Hanlon found that mothers reinforce the truth value rather than the grammatical correctness of statements. Imitation also cannot totally explain language learning. All children master language, despite large individual differences among children in imitation. A further argument against the behavioral position is that it is difficult to explain infinite generativity based on learning principles alone. Children appear to generalize complex rules in mastering language.

The second theory of language development is the nativist theory, which assumes a biological component to language development. One argument for the nativist position is that there are language universals—properties that appear in all languages. There also appears to be brain lateralization of language function. The left hemisphere of the brain controls language processing for the majority of people. Broca's and Wernicke's areas are involved in speech production and speech comprehension, respectively. A third argument for the nativist position is that there is evidence of a critical or sensitive period in language development. Puberty appears to close the critical period for fully acquiring the phonological rules of different languages. The lateralization of language in the brain may be subject to a critical period also. Prior to puberty, a child whose left hemisphere is damaged might be able to shift language to the right side of the brain. A fourth argument for the nativist position is that language appears to be a species-specific behavior. Communication systems in nonhuman species are not like language.

The third theory of language development is the cognitive theory, which claims that the innate equipment humans have is not specifically linguistic and that language develops from general cognitive abilities. According to cognitivists, the child's growing intelligence and desire to express meanings—together with language input—"drive" the acquisition of language. The observation that a child's early utterances indicate knowledge of semantic rather than linguistic categories supports this claim. Also, evidence indicates that children can identify semantically deviant sentences as wrong before they can identify syntactically deviant sentences as wrong. Another argument for the cognitive theory of language development is the fact that human language appeared too recently for a large amount of purely linguistic machinery to have evolved in the brain.

A number of environmental factors may contribute to the acquisition of language. These include motherese, prompting, echoing, expanding, and recasting. Research has not demonstrated that expansion aids language acquisition, but the other techniques appear to. Another experience that may facilitate language development is the labeling game that children play with their parents.

Language development occurs in a number of different stages. In the preverbal stage, infants develop babbling, which may be necessary for the development of articulatory skills. Preverbal infants also develop pragmatic skills for communicating. These include eye contact, pointing in conjunction with vocalizing, and differences in behavior that allow the infant to either request or assert. In the one-word stage, infants use single words that can belong to different semantic categories. The holophrase hypothesis proposes that the single word stands for a complete sentence with limitations on production. Eve Clark, however, distinguishes between words and concepts. According to Clark, children may have more concepts than they yet have words for. This leads to the underextension and overextension of words during the one-word stage. The two-word stage allows different meanings to be captured. A semantic analysis of the two-word stage gives a promising view of the richness of children's language ability. During the two-word stage, some children seem to use word order that would mark the appearance of syntax while other children do not. Also, during the two-word stage, language has been described as telegraphic because articles, auxiliary verbs, and other connectives are left out.

Guided Review

You may want to look at the answers to the "Guided Review" statements as you read, or you may want to use the exercise as a form of self-test by covering up the answers below the statements with a sheet of paper and not consulting them until you have attempted to fill in the blanks of each statement.

1. A relatively permanent change in the mind or behavior that involves experience and is not due to reflexes, maturation, instincts, or the influence of fatigue, injury, disease, or drugs is called _____ . Learning involves a _____ in mind or behavior. This change is _____ _____ and is the result of _____ .

   learning, change, relatively permanent, experience

2. Pavlov was the first to describe the process of association that we now call _____ _____ as a kind of learning.

   classical conditioning

3. In a classical conditioning procedure, the stimulus that can elicit a response before any learning occurs is called the _____ stimulus. The _____ stimulus begins the procedure as a neutral stimulus, not eliciting any particular response. The response elicited by the unconditioned stimulus is called the _____ response. In Pavlov's research, the tuning fork started to elicit salivation in the dog. This salivation was the _____ response.

unconditioned, conditioned, unconditioned, conditioned

4. The process of presenting the conditioned stimulus without the unconditioned stimulus is called _____ . It results in the _____ of the _____ response. After extinction and a subsequent rest, the conditioned response can reappear. This is the phenomenon called _____ _____ . Elimination of the response recovered in spontaneous recovery is accomplished through _____ .

extinction, reduction or suppression, conditioned, spontaneous recovery, extinction

5. Pavlov argued for a _____ _____ explanation for classical conditioning. He believed that _____ helps to create a bond between the _____ _____ and the _____ _____ . Eventually, the _____ _____ substitutes for the _____ _____ . However, those who assert that the child uses a conditioned stimulus as a sign or expectancy that an unconditioned stimulus will follow ascribe to _____ theory.

stimulus substitution, contiguity, conditioned stimulus, unconditioned stimulus, conditioned stimulus, unconditioned stimulus, information

6. Irrational fears are called _____ . _____ and _____ demonstrated that these fears could be learned by _____ _____ . They taught _____ to fear _____ by creating a _____ _____ while the child played with the _____ . Later, the child displayed fear of similar objects, a phenomenon called _____ _____ .

phobias, Watson, Rayner, classical conditioning, Albert, rats, loud noise, rat, stimulus generalization

7. In a separate experiment, _____ used _____ to _____ fears classically conditioned in a child named _____ .

Watson, counterconditioning, weaken, Peter

8. Papousek has demonstrated _____ _____ in _____ . However, he found that the learning process can take _____ to _____ trials over a _____ - week period.

classical conditioning, infants, 150, 200, three

9. Voluntary responses involve _____ behavior, while classical conditioning involves _____ behavior.

operant, reflexive

10. In a study of infant conditioning, Rheingold showed that _____ could be increased by simple _____ of _____ . The investigators measured frequency of vocalizations during an initial _____ period. In the _____ trials that followed, all vocalizations were reinforced. Finally, there was an _____ phase that was similar to the baseline phase. One reinforcer for vocalizing was a _____ .

vocalizations; contingencies; reinforcement; baseline; conditioning; extinction; smile, soothing sound, or caress

11. Learning by watching is called _____ . It is also called _____ or _____ learning. A modeled response does not require _____ .

imitation, modeling, observational, reinforcement

12. According to Piaget, the infant must be _____ months old before _____ is possible. He called earlier demonstrations _____ - _____ because the infant only performed actions mastered early in life and _____ by the infant. Recent demonstrations have apparently demonstrated _____ in _____ .

nine, imitation, pseudo-imitation, seen, imitation, neonates

13. The newborn is in Piaget's _____ stage. During the sensorimotor period, the infant develops the ability to organize and coordinate his or her _____ and _____ .

sensorimotor, sensations, actions

14. The _____ is the basic unit for an organized pattern of sensorimotor functioning that _____ during the sensorimotor period.

scheme or schema, develops

15. The first substage of the sensorimotor period is simple _____ . During this substage, the infant develops the ability to produce simple _____ in the absence of a triggering stimulus.

reflexes, reflexes

16. A scheme based upon a reflex divorced from its eliciting stimulus is called a _____ . A primary circular reaction is a _____ based upon an infant's attempt to reproduce an interesting or pleasurable event that first happened accidentally. Habits and circular reactions are _____ during this substage in that the infant repeats them in the same way each time.

habit, scheme, stereotyped

17. The infant becomes _____-oriented during the substage of secondary circular reactions. According to Piaget, primitive _____ is possible during this substage, and schemes are not _____ directed.

object, imitation, goal

18. The coordinated combination of schemes is a development of the substage of coordination of _____ circular reactions. During this substage, the quality of _____ develops, which involves the separation of _____ and _____ in accomplishing simple feats.

secondary, intentionality, means, goals

19. During the substage of tertiary circular reactions, the infant _____ new possibilities with objects. All such exploration is _____ .

explores, physical

20. During the final substage of the sensorimotor stage, the infant _____ the actions of the previous substage. According to Piaget, a _____ is an internalized sensory image or word that represents an event.

internalizes, symbol

21. The understanding that objects and events do not cease to exist when out of perceptual contact is called _____ _____ . One aspect of the concept of object permanence is the understanding of self-world _____ .

object permanence, differentiation

22. If an infant shows no reaction when an interesting toy is hidden, the assumption is that he (has/has not) _____ developed object permanence. The sensorimotor substage during which strong, active search for a hidden toy appears is Substage _____ .
has not, 4

23. Other theorists and some researchers have argued that the development of object permanence is more _____ than Piaget described. Some claim that his description of object permanence ignores psychological _____ "variables" and that the _____ - _____ _____ is not as consistent as he described.
gradual, performance, A-B error

24. _____ involves focusing perception to produce increased awareness of a stimulus. The _____ response involves turning toward the source of sensory stimulation. It also involves _____ changes, such as _____ of the pupils of the eyes and an increased _____ _____ in the brain.
Attention, orienting, physiological, dilation, blood flow

25. The orienting response is made to _____ stimuli. As stimulation is _____ or _____ , the orienting response decreases. This decrease is called _____ .
new, continued, repeated, habituation

26. A new stimulus presented after habituation causes _____ if the individual detects a _____ between the new stimulus and the old one.
dishabituation, difference

27. Newborn infants are able to fixate on _____ . Young infants tend to scan more of the contour and boundary features of a stimulus. This called the _____ effect. When exposed to their mother's face, one-month-old infants concentrated on the external details, such as the hairline and chin, while two-month-old infants spent more time looking at the _____ .
contours, externality, eyes

28. _____ pertains to retaining information over time. A research technique that combines aspects of operant conditioning with a memory test is called the _____ _____ technique. Use of it has demonstrated memory in infants as young as _____ _____ old. A _____ technique involving _____ 24 hours before the test can extend the apparent retention.
Memory, conjugate reinforcement, three months, reactivation, reexposure

29. _____ memory of a stimulus involves feeling that you have seen the stimulus before. Neonates (do/do not) _____ have conscious memory. Conscious memory seems to appear after _____ months of age. According to Piaget, conscious memory is _____ _____ _____ _____ .
Conscious, do not, six, memory in the strict sense

30. Adults' lack of memory for events that occurred before about three years of age is referred to as _____ _____ .
infantile amnesia

31. To assess development in infancy, measures called _____ _____ have been devised. They investigate the _____ _____ among infants.
developmental scales, individual differences

32. One of the early contributors to the developmental testing of infants was _____ _____ .
The scores from his scale involve four categories of behavior: _____ , _____ ,
_____ , and _____ - _____ . They can be combined to yield an overall
score called the _____ _____ .
Arnold Gesell, motor, language, adaptive, personal-social, developmental quotient

33. The developmental scales most widely used today were developed by _____ _____ .
They include a _____ scale, a _____ scale, and an _____
_____ _____ .
Nancy Bayley, Mental, Motor, Infant Behavior Profile

34. For normal children, the correlation between scores on infant developmental scales and later measures of
intelligence is _____ . One way to get continuity with measures of intelligence is to use more precise
measures of _____ _____ in infancy. In particular, measures like
habituation, called _____ of _____ , and one like dishabituation,
called _____ of _____ , can be used to better predict standard
intelligence performance than the usual developmental scales.
low, information processing, decrement, attention, recovery, attention

35. _____ are symbols that, by convention, stand for things other than themselves. The finite set of rules
used by the speaker, listener, and writer to generate an infinite number of meaningful sentences is called
_____ _____ . The power of language to communicate knowledge
across both time and space is called _____ .
Words, infinite generativity, displacement

36. The basic speech sounds are called _____ , and the study of these sounds is called
_____ .
phonemes, phonology

37. The smallest unit of meaning in a language is the _____ . Morphemes such as *ed* have meaning in
that they _____ what other morphemes mean. Morphology is the study of the rules that govern the
combining and sequencing of _____ .
morpheme, change, morphemes

38. _____ refers to the rules for combining words into acceptable phrases and sentences. The formal
description of a language's syntactic rules is called _____ .
Syntax, grammar

39. Chomsky and many other contemporary linguists refer to the actual order of the words in a sentence as the
_____ structure. The syntactic relationships among the words in a sentence are referred to
as the _____ structure. If a sentence has two different deep structures, its meaning is _____ .
surface, deep, ambiguous

40. Semantic rules are those that pertain to the _____ of words and sentences. The sentence "The car
looked at the mechanic" does not make _____ sense.
meaning, semantic

41. The rules of pragmatics deal with the use of language in _____ . Of particular importance
is the _____ _____ in which the language is used.
conversation, social context

42. Supporters of the _____ view of language acquisition argue that language is learned. A major proponent of this view has been _____ _____ _____ . The three principles from learning theories that behaviorists have invoked to explain the acquisition of language are _____ and _____ , _____ , and the _____ _____ of rules.

behavioral, B. F. Skinner, shaping (and) reinforcement, imitation, creative generalization

43. Roger Brown and his associates have found that mothers respond to their children's _____ - _____ utterances in a positive, reinforcing way. They respond positively to the _____ value of the statement, not the _____ .

ill-formed, truth, syntax

44. Rote repetition of parents' speech is the simplest form of _____ . Some recent work suggests that imitation might have a _____ function or that it might provide _____ to analyze and understand an utterance.

imitation, consolidation, time

45. The number of novel utterances that the child in theory might produce is _____ . This pertains to the claim that language has _____ _____ . This is a problem for the behavioral explanation of language acquisition.

infinite, infinite generativity

46. Human infants might be born with an _____ mechanism than helps them to acquire language.

innate

47. The nativist theory of language acquisition emphasizes the _____ aspects of language function.

universal

48. In most human brains, language is controlled by structures in the _____ hemisphere. Speech production appears to be controlled by _____ area, while language comprehension appears to be controlled by _____ area.

left, Broca's, Wernicke's

49. The sad case of Genie illustrates the concept of a _____ or _____ period for language acquisition. The event that appears to end the critical period for language is _____ . A person who immigrates after puberty is not likely to ever eliminate his or her accent. That is not true of those who immigrate at a younger age. This, too, may be evidence for a _____ _____ in language development.

critical, sensitive, puberty, critical period

50. _____ _____ have not been found to have language functions comparable to humans. Terrace argues that the chimpanzee imitates and responds to subtle cues from the trainer and does not expand upon the trainer's statements. Thus, the chimpanzee lacks the capacity for _____ _____ .

Lower animals, infinite generativity

51. A growing group of language researchers argue that language derives more from general _____ abilities than from specific linguistic ones. The focus of these thinkers is on the _____ and _____ levels of language, rather than on the phonological, morphological, or syntactic levels.

cognitive, semantic, pragmatic

52. According to Slobin, _____ is acquired before syntax in all languages. Recent evidence has shown that children can detect sentences that are _____ deviant before they can detect syntactically deviant sentences.

meaning, semantically

53. Finally, according to some estimates, language itself has existed for, at most, 100,000 years. From an evolutionary perspective, _____ functions are much older than language functions.

cognitive

54. If your sentences are short, with exaggerated intonation contours, and you pause for a long time between utterances, stress important words, and repeat yourself frequently, you are speaking _____ . This dialect is used with _____ language users.

motherese, immature

55. _____ involves rephrasing a sentence if it appears that the child has not understood it. Repeating what the child has said to you is called _____ . Restating a child's utterance in another, more sophisticated, form is called _____ . In addition to mothers, motherese also has been observed in _____ and in _____-year-olds.

Prompting, echoing, expanding, fathers, four

56. In her research, Fernald found that _____ percent of mothers' vocalizations to their babies involved expanded pitch contours and/or whispering. Morgan found that exaggerated intonation contours tend to occur at

_____ _____ _____ .

77, syntactic phrase boundaries

57. In one research study, mothers' tendencies to _____ the vocalizations of their one-year-old babies were positively correlated with communicative competence of these babies. _____ has been found to have some positive effects on children's use of linguistic structures.

imitate, Recasting

58. The process of labeling via the _____ _____ _____ may account for a large part of a child's early vocabulary. Also, the technique of elaborating on an interest that a child initially indicates, called _____ _____ _____ _____ _____ , is useful in tailoring language exposure to the child's _____ level.

great word game, following in order to lead, maturational

59. An early preverbal linguistic behavior that first appears between three and six months of age is _____ . The infant's earliest communications skills are directed at _____ _____ . A shifting of eye contact between an adult and a toy is a _____ . One prerequisite for the mastery of language is the use and comprehension of _____ .

babbling, attracting attention, request, symbols

60. The possibility that the single-word utterance of the one-word stage really represents a complete sentence that the baby has in mind is called the _____ hypothesis. However, it is also possible that the one-word utterance represents a thought corresponding to just _____ _____ . According to Clark, during the one-word stage, the process of acquiring _____ is advanced beyond the process of acquiring language so that there are many concepts for which no language exists.

holophrase, one word, concepts

61. _____ is the use of a word to include a whole set of objects that are not related to or are inappropriate for the word's meaning. If a child sees a house from the window of her house and says, "house," and yet, when walking past a house on the street, the child does not name it so, the child is _____ the meaning of the word *house*.

Overextension, underextending

62. The two-word utterance usually makes its appearance between _____ and _____ months of age. The speech use at this time has been referred to as _____ speech because articles, auxiliary verbs, and other connectives are usually left out. It is not clear whether children in the two-word stage have any understanding of the rules of _____ .

18, 24, telegraphic, syntax

Key Terms Matching Exercise

Match the Key Term on the left with the correct definition on the right.

____ 1. learning (LO–1, p. 161)
____ 2. classical conditioning (LO–2, p. 162)
____ 3. unconditioned stimulus (UCS) (LO–2, p. 162)
____ 4. conditioned stimulus (CS) (LO–2, p. 162)
____ 5. unconditioned response (UCR) (LO–2, p. 162)
____ 6. conditioned response (CR) (LO–2, p. 162)

a. Neutral stimulus that acquires the ability to elicit a response by being associated with an unconditioned stimulus

b. Response that is unlearned and elicited by the unconditioned stimulus

c. Relatively permanent change in the mind or behavior that occurs through experience and cannot be accounted for by reflexes, instincts, maturation, fatigue, injury, disease, or drugs

d. Procedure by which a neutral stimulus comes to elicit a response by being paired with a stimulus that regularly evokes the response

e. Response that is learned through pairing the unconditioned stimulus with the conditioned stimulus

f. Stimulus that can elicit a response in an organism prior to learning

_____ 7. S-S learning (LO–2, p. 162)

_____ 8. extinction (LO–3, p. 163)

_____ 9. spontaneous recovery (LO–3, p. 163)

_____ 10. stimulus substitution theory (LO–4, p. 163)

_____ 11. information theory (LO–4, p. 164)

_____ 12. phobia (LO–5, p. 164)

a. After extinction and a rest period, there is a return of the conditioned response, although in a diminished fashion

b. Explanation of classical conditioning that argues that the central nervous system is constructed in such a way that the contiguity between the conditioned stimulus and unconditioned stimulus creates a bond that eventually allows the conditioned stimulus to substitute for the unconditioned stimulus

c. Procedure in operant conditioning when the reinforcer that followed a behavior is no longer presented; in classical conditioning, occurs when the conditioned stimulus is no longer paired with the unconditioned stimulus; also a decrease in the conditioned response due to nonreinforcement or absence of the UCS

d. Another term for classical conditioning, emphasizing the significance of the association between stimuli

e. Irrational fears that may be acquired via classical conditioning

f. Explanation of classical conditioning that stresses the informational value of the conditioned stimulus; that is, the organism sees the conditioned stimulus as a sign of the unconditioned stimulus that follows

_____ 13. counterconditioning (LO–5, p. 164)

_____ 14. baseline (LO–6, p. 165)

_____ 15. conditioning trial (LO–6, p. 165)

_____ 16. imitation (LO–7, p. 166)

_____ 17. scheme, schema (LO–7, p. 168)

_____ 18. habit (LO–9, p. 170)

a. Learning that requires the coordination of motor activity with a mental picture of an act

b. Scheme based on a simple reflex that is completely divorced from its eliciting stimulus

c. Basic unit for an organized pattern of sensorimotor functioning

d. In a conditioning procedure, the initial phase in which the target behavior is observed and measured prior to any attempt to change the behavior

e. Procedure for weakening a conditioned response (phobia); the conditioned stimulus is associated with a new response that is incompatible with the old (for example, smiling, relaxing)

f. Each individual instance that the conditioning process is used

_____ 19. primary circular reaction (LO–9, p. 170)
_____ 20. secondary circular reaction (LO–9, p. 170)
_____ 21. coordination of secondary circular reactions (LO–9, p. 170)
_____ 22. intentionality (LO–9, p. 171)
_____ 23. tertiary circular reactions (LO–9, p. 171)
_____ 24. internalization of schemes (LO–9, p. 171)

a. Separation of means and goals in accomplishing simple feats
b. Schemes in which the infant purposefully investigates new possibilities with objects by changing what is done to them and exploring the results
c. Scheme based upon the infant's attempt to reproduce an interesting event that followed the infant's chance action on an object
d. Scheme based on the infant's attempt to reproduce an interesting event concerning the infant's body that initially occurred by chance
e. When the infant's mental functioning shifts from a purely sensorimotor plane to the ability to use primitive symbols
f. When the infant readily combines and recombines previously learned schemes in an organized way

_____ 25. symbol (LO–9, p. 171)
_____ 26. object permanence (LO–10, p. 172)
_____ 27. A-B error (LO–10, p. 173)
_____ 28. orienting response (LO–11, p. 174)
_____ 29. dishabituation (LO–11, p. 174)
_____ 30. saccadic movements (LO–12, p. 174)

a. The knowledge that objects and events continue to exist even when one is not in direct perceptual contact with them
b. Internalized sensory image or word that represents an event
c. Renewed interest shown to a different stimulus presented after habituation has occurred to an original stimulus
d. Changes in eye fixation while looking at a complex pattern
e. Physiological changes that accompany increased attention to a stimulus, such as an increase in muscle tone and perspiration or a change in heart rate
f. Search error by infants, in which they search for an object where it has been found before, rather than in a new location

____ 31. externality effect (LO–12, p. 175)

____ 32. memory (LO–13, p. 175)

____ 33. conjugate reinforcement technique (LO–13, p. 176)

____ 34. infantile amnesia (LO–13, p. 178)

____ 35. developmental scales (LO–14, p. 179)

____ 36. developmental quotient (DQ) (LO–14, p. 179)

a. Technique used to assess memory in infants; an infant is presented with a stimulus that his or her action causes to move, which is reinforcing to the infant; after some time, the stimulus is reintroduced and the behavior of the infant is measured

b. Intelligence tests created for infants

c. The finding that, as children and adults, we have little or no memory for events experienced before three years of age

d. Overall developmental score for the infant, based on his or her performance on Gesell's scale

e. The observation that, up until one month of age, infants tend to fixate on the external parts of a pattern and exclude the internal parts

f. Feature of cognition that involves retaining information over time

____ 37. Bayley Scales (LO–15, p. 179)

____ 38. Mental scale (LO–15, p. 179)

____ 39. decrement of attention (LO–15, p. 181)

____ 40. recovery of attention (LO–15, p. 181)

____ 41. infinite generativity (LO–17, p. 183)

____ 42. displacement (LO–17, p. 183)

a. Ability to combine a finite number of individual words into an infinite number of sentences

b. One of the scales from the Bayley Scales; includes such things as manipulation of objects and examiner interaction

c. Novelty preference; indexed by the relative amount of looking given to novel rather than familiar stimuli

d. Power of language to communicate knowledge across time and space

e. Amount or rate of decay in looking at a repeated or constant stimulus

f. The currently most widely used developmental scale; composed of a Mental scale, a Motor scale, and an Infant Behavior Profile

____ 43. phonemes (LO–18, p. 184)

____ 44. phonology (LO–18, p. 184)

____ 45. morpheme (LO–18, p. 184)

____ 46. morphology (LO–18, p. 184)

____ 47. syntax (LO–18, p. 184)

____ 48. grammar (LO–18, p. 184)

a. Study of rules that govern the sequencing of phonemes in a language

b. Smallest unit of language that carries meaning

c. Speech sound that marks the minimal difference between it and another sound used in a language

d. Rules of a language involved in combining words into acceptable phrases and sentences (order)

e. Formal description of syntactic rules

f. Study of the rules involved in the combining and sequencing of morphemes

_____ 49. surface structure (LO–18, p. 184)
_____ 50. deep structure (LO–18, p. 184)
_____ 51. semantics (LO–18, p. 185)
_____ 52. pragmatics (LO–18, p. 185)
_____ 53. language universals (LO–21, p. 187)
_____ 54. lateralization of language (LO–21, p. 187)

a. Syntactic relations among words in a sentence
b. Actual order of words in a spoken sentence
c. Rules that pertain to the social context of language and how people use language in conversation
d. The finding that language processing in most people is controlled by the left hemisphere of the brain
e. Set of language rules that pertain to the meaning of words and sentences
f. Properties of language that are true for all languages

_____ 55. Broca's area (LO–21, p. 187)
_____ 56. Wernicke's area (LO–21, p. 187)
_____ 57. motherese (LO–23, p. 193)
_____ 58. prompting (LO–23, p. 193)
_____ 59. echoing (LO–23, p. 193)

a. Section of the temporal lobe that is heavily involved in speech comprehension
b. Rephrasing a sentence if it appears not to have been understood
c. Repeating what is said by an immature language speaker
d. Section of the frontal lobe responsible for speech production
e. Characteristic way in which adults talk to young language learners; involves simple, short sentences, exaggerated intonation contours, long pauses between sentences, and great stress on the important words

_____ 60. expanding (LO–23, p. 193)
_____ 61. register (LO–23, p. 194)
_____ 62. baby talk register (LO–23, p. 194)
_____ 63. recasting (LO–23, p. 195)
_____ 64. labeling (LO–23, p. 195)

a. Providing a name for a specified object
b. A restatement in a more sophisticated form of what a language learner has already said
c. Rephrasing the same or similar meaning in a different way
d. Register characterized by six features, including a higher than normal frequency, occasional whispering, and a longer than normal duration in speaking separable verbs
e. Way of speaking to individuals of a particular category

_____ 65. babbling (LO–24, p. 196)
_____ 66. holophrase (LO–25, p. 197)
_____ 67. overextending (LO–25, p. 199)
_____ 68. underextending (LO–25, p. 199)
_____ 69. telegraphic speech (LO–26, p. 200)

a. Tendency of children to misuse words by not applying one word's meaning to other appropriate contexts for the word
b. Tendency of children to misuse words by applying one word's meaning to include a whole set of objects that are not related to or are inappropriate for the word's meaning
c. Use of mainly nouns and verbs in children's sentences and the omission of articles, auxiliary verbs, and other connectives
d. Vocalization that appears between three and six months of age; the baby produces many different sounds that may be instrumental in developing articulatory skills
e. Single word that implies a whole sentence in the young child's mind.

Answers to Key Terms Matching Exercise

1. c	11. f	21. f	31. e	41. a	51. e	61. e
2. d	12. e	22. a	32. f	42. d	52. c	62. d
3. f	13. e	23. b	33. a	43. c	53. f	63. c
4. a	14. d	24. e	34. c	44. a	54. d	64. a
5. b	15. f	25. b	35. b	45. b	55. d	65. d
6. e	16. a	26. a	36. d	46. f	56. a	66. e
7. d	17. c	27. f	37. f	47. d	57. e	67. b
8. c	18. b	28. e	38. b	48. e	58. b	68. a
9. a	19. d	29. c	39. e	49. b	59. c	69. c
10. b	20. c	30. d	40. c	50. a	60. b	

Self-Test A

Choose the best alternative.

1. All of the following are examples of learning except which? (LO–1, p. 161)
   a. A child becomes able to read.
   b. A child grows stronger and becomes able to lift a chair.
   c. A child begins to ride a two-wheeled bicycle.
   d. A child begins to turn the television on in the morning to watch Superman.

2. The importance of consequences of behavior for learning are most strongly stressed in which type of learning? (LO–1, p. 165)
   a. classical conditioning
   b. operant conditioning
   c. observational learning
   d. cognitive behavior modification

3. A child is about to cross a street when her mother pulls her back and screams because there is a car coming. The child is now afraid to cross streets. This is an example of (LO–2, p. 164)
   a. classical conditioning.
   b. operant conditioning.
   c. observational learning.
   d. cognitive behavior modification.

4. A child is about to cross a street when her mother pulls her back and screams because there is a car coming. The child is now afraid to cross streets. The fear of crossing streets is a (an) (LO–5, p. 164)
   a. unconditioned stimulus.
   b. conditioned stimulus.
   c. unconditioned response.
   d. conditioned response.

5. The explanation that classical conditioning is based on the organism using the conditioned stimulus as a sign that an unconditioned stimulus will follow is a component of (LO–4, p. 164)
   a. information theory.
   b. stimulus substitution theory.
   c. cognitive behavior modification.
   d. higher-order conditioning.

6. A criticism of classical conditioning as the only kind of learning is that (LO–5, p. 165)
   a. it fails to capture the active nature of the child in influencing the environment.
   b. it is not biologically based.
   c. it relies too heavily on imitation, and imitation is not the only way in which children learn.
   d. it cannot explain the way fears develop.

7. According to Piaget, the ability to think about concrete events without directly acting them out or perceiving them is characteristic of which substage of the sensorimotor period? (LO-9, p. 171)
   a. Substage 3
   b. Substage 4
   c. Substage 5
   d. Substage 6

8. An infant hits the palm of one hand with a finger of the other and triggers his palmar grasp. He attempts to repeat this sequence. Which of the following most closely describes this behavior? (LO–9, p. 170)
   a. reflexes
   b. primary circular reactions
   c. secondary circular reactions
   d. tertiary circular reactions

9. An infant kicks her feet and notices that a doll hanging over her crib swings. She then kicks her feet again to make the doll swing. This is an example of (LO–9, p. 170)
   a. reflexes.
   b. primary circular reactions.
   c. secondary circular reactions.
   d. tertiary circular reactions.

10. An infant sees his mother go out the door. He briefly looks at the spot where she disappeared, as if expecting her to reappear. He soon stops looking for her and plays with his toes. This infant is most likely in which of Piaget's sensorimotor substages? (LO–10, p. 172)
    a. Substage 1
    b. Substage 2
    c. Substage 3
    d. Substage 4

11. All of the following are criticisms of Piaget's view of object permanence except which? (LO–10, p. 173)
    a. His sequence of behaviors cannot be replicated.
    b. There are more behavioral accomplishments than he described.
    c. He ignored performance variables that influence behavior.
    d. Performance may depend on learning how to search, not on where the object is.

12. All of the following are parts of the orienting response except which? (LO–11, p. 174)
    a. increased muscle tone
    b. dilation of the pupils in the eyes
    c. change in heart rate
    d. constriction of blood vessels in the head

13. What is the age range for the observation of the externality effect? (LO–12, p. 175)
    a. birth to two weeks
    b. birth to one month
    c. birth to two months
    d. birth to six months

14. An infant is resting on a pressure transducer so that, when she presses her head back with anything over a certain force, a doll in front of her moves. She learns to press her head back hard enough to make the doll move. One week later, the doll is reintroduced, and the infant's head-pressing is measured. This procedure is an example of (LO–13, p. 176)
    a. habituation.
    b. natural response.
    c. the conjugate reinforcement technique.
    d. nonnutritive sucking.

15. Dr. Smith claims that the reason a child can use the correct form of making a negative statement is that use was reinforced. Dr. Smith most likely takes which view of language development? (LO–19, p. 186)
    a. nativist view
    b. critical period hypothesis
    c. behavioral view
    d. cognitive view

16. A child says to his father, "More milk, Daddy." The father says back to his son, "Shall I get you some more milk?" This is an example of (LO–23, p. 195)
    a. prompting.
    b. echoing.
    c. expanding.
    d. recasting.

17. The nativist view of language acquisition argues that (LO-20, p. 187)
    a. language is innate.
    b. language is acquired through reinforcement.
    c. language is acquired based upon sensorimotor knowledge.
    d. the acquisition of language is complex and relies on built-in structures, as well as on principles of learning and cognition.

18. Jan suffered a blow to the head and now has difficulty understanding what people mean when they speak to her. Jan's problem would support which of the following views? (LO–20, p. 187)
    a. Language is learned through reinforcement.
    b. Language has a biological base.
    c. Language comes from general cognitive principles.
    d. There are universal properties to language.

19. The finding that children are unable to use such terms as "more" or "all-gone" until they acquire object permanence would support which view of language acquisition? (LO–22, pp. 191–92)
   a. nativist view
   b. critical period hypothesis
   c. behaviorist view
   d. cognitive view

20. What is thought to cause the onset of babbling? (LO–24, p. 196)
   a. maturation
   b. imitation
   c. reinforcement
   d. secondary circular reactions

Answers to Self-Test A

1. b	5. a	9. c	13. b	17. a
2. b	6. a	10. b	14. c	18. b
3. a	7. d	11. a	15. c	19. d
4. d	8. b	12. d	16. d	20. a

Self-Test B

Choose the best alternative.

21. A psychologist is interested in teaching an infant to press a panel. The first thing that the psychologist does is count the number of times that the infant presses the panel in the minute before learning occurs. This is referred to as (LO–6, p. 165)
   a. the baseline period.
   b. the conditioning phase.
   c. the intervention phase.
   d. the extinction period.

22. In teaching an infant to press a panel, a psychologist makes a light go on every time the infant presses the panel. Now, in a 10-minute period, the psychologist keeps the light from going on when the infant presses the panel. This is referred to as (LO–3, p. 163)
   a. the baseline period.
   b. the conditioning phase.
   c. the response phase.
   d. the extinction period.

23. Learning that is based on associations of conditioned and unconditioned stimuli is called (LO–2, p. 162)
   a. classical conditioning.
   b. operant conditioning.
   c. observational learning.
   d. insight learning.

24. A psychologist says, "slowly, slowly," while at the same time presenting a relaxing scene that slows down the man's heart rate. After repeated pairings, the man's heart rate slows down to the words "slowly, slowly." This is an example of (LO–2, p. 162)
   a. operant conditioning.
   b. classical conditioning.
   c. observational learning.
   d. insight learning.

25. An explanation for classical conditioning claims that the contiguity between the conditioned and unconditioned stimulus creates a bond between them and that, eventually, the conditioned stimulus can work in place of the unconditioned stimulus. This explanation is based on (LO–4, p. 163)
    a. information theory.
    b. cognitive behavior modification.
    c. stimulus substitution theory.
    d. higher-order conditioning.

26. Classical conditioning is most useful for describing the process by which children acquire (LO–5, p. 164)
    a. language.
    b. motor skills.
    c. depth perception.
    d. fears.

27. The appearance of true imitation of novel acts, such as sticking out the tongue, which cannot be seen on one's own body, marks which substage of sensorimotor development? (LO–7, p. 167)
    a. Substage 3
    b. Substage 4
    c. Substage 5
    d. Substage 6

28. An infant hits his father's hand away to get a ball that he sees but that his father's hand blocks him from getting. Of which behavior is this an example? (LO–9, p. 171)
    a. simple reflexes
    b. primary circular reactions
    c. secondary circular reactions
    d. coordination of secondary circular reactions

29. An infant pulls on a string with varying amounts of force to observe the effects of the force on an object attached to the end of the string. This behavior is an example of (LO–9, p. 171)
    a. tertiary circular reactions.
    b. coordination of secondary circular reactions.
    c. secondary circular reactions.
    d. primary circular reactions.

30. An infant recovers an object under a cup on her right. The object is now hidden on her left, under a cloth. She lifts up the cup on her right again to search for the object. This child is in which of Piaget's substages of sensorimotor development? (LO–10, p. 173)
    a. Substage 3
    b. Substage 4
    c. Substage 5
    d. Substage 6

31. Who has described more than six landmarks in the development of object permanence in a criticism of Piaget's work? (LO–10, p. 173)
    a. Uzgiris and Hunt
    b. Harris
    c. Corrigan
    d. Gratch

32. An infant sees a picture and shows an increase in muscle tone and perspiration. This is an example of (LO–11, p. 174)
    a. the orienting response.
    b. saccadic eye movements.
    c. the externality effect.
    d. selective attention.

33. When presented with the picture of a triangle, the infant fixates only on the corners or lines of the triangle. This is an example of (LO–12, p. 175)
    a. saccadic movements.
    b. the orienting response.
    c. the externality effect.
    d. organizational processing.

34. Research using the conjugate reinforcement technique has demonstrated retention for as long as three days for infants as young as (LO–13, p. 176)
    a. one week.
    b. two months.
    c. three months.
    d. six months.

35. While a mother and child are being observed, the child makes the following utterances: "Him gave me candy," and "The 'Cosby Show' is on TV on Monday." The mother's response to the first statement is, "Yes, he did, didn't he?" Her response to the second statement is, "No, it is on Thursdays." These observations argue against which behavioral process as an explanation for syntactic development? (LO–19, p. 186)
    a. imitation
    b. shaping
    c. reinforcement
    d. classical conditioning

36. Angie says, "milk dog." Her father doesn't understand what she means and says, "milk dog." This illustrates (LO–23, p. 193)
    a. elaborating.
    b. echoing.
    c. expanding.
    d. recasting.

37. Which of the following arguments or data supports the biological basis of language development? (LO–20, p. 187)
    a. Parents reinforce the truth of statements rather that correct grammar.
    b. Children create and generalize rules.
    c. Language is infinitely productive.
    d. Children acquire language rapidly under nonideal learning conditions.

38. Universal characteristics that exist for all languages are evidence for which theory of language acquisition? (LO–20, p. 187)
    a. behaviorist view
    b. nativist view
    c. cognitive view
    d. Both a and b are correct.

39. Genie was a child whose family isolated her from language. Discovered at 13½ years of age, she has since learned vocabulary and been able to produce up to three-word utterances. However, her language skills lag far behind her cognitive skills. This is evidence in favor of which of the following? (LO–21, p. 189)
    a. linguistic universals
    b. lateralization of language function
    c. a critical period for language development
    d. infinite generativity

40. The finding that children develop semantic abilities before they develop syntactic abilities supports which theory of language acquisition? (LO–22, p. 192)
   a. behaviorist view
   b. nativist view
   c. cognitive view
   d. Both a and b are correct.

Answers to Self-Test B

21. a	25. c	29. a	33. c	37. d
22. d	26. d	30. b	34. b	38. b
23. a	27. b	31. a	35. c	39. c
24. b	28. d	32. a	36. b	40. c

Questions to Stimulate Thought

1. Are classical conditioning and instrumental conditioning two kinds of learning, or only two different sets of procedures for what is essentially the same process?
2. Both learning and development involve changes. Are they the same?
3. How do you know what infants pay attention to?
4. Do infants really have a memory?
5. If developmental scales do not predict later performance, what good are they?
6. Is language learned?
7. Is language innate?

Research Project

In this exercise, you examine prompting, echoing, and expansion, using naturalistic observation. Refer to the definitions of these terms in your text if necessary. Go to a local shopping mall and observe a mother with an infant 18 to 24 months old for 15 minutes. Record three instances of speech by the mother to the infant and classify those instances as prompting, echoing, or expanding. Note on the data sheet the mother's statements and also the infant's response to each of the mother's three different statements and then answer the questions that follow.

Data Sheet

Speech	Response of Infant	Age _____	Sex _____
Sentence 1			
Sentence 2			
Sentence 3			

Questions

1. What types of techniques were used by the mother with the infant you observed?
2. How did the infant respond to the statements made by the mother?
3. From your observations, do you think that prompting, echoing, and expanding are effective techniques in aiding infants to learn language? Why or why not? What variables might have affected the quality of data you collected? Might your conclusions have been different if you had observed a different mother-infant pair? How?

6 Social and Personality Foundations and Development in Infancy

Learning Objectives

After studying this chapter, you should be able to:

1. Describe two possible ways in which biological factors could influence social and personality development in infancy. (pp. 207–8)
2. Describe Bronfenbrenner's ecological model for the impact of sociocultural factors on social and personality development in infancy. (pp. 208–9)
3. List the changes that accompany the onset of parenthood. (p. 211)
4. Describe the concept of reciprocal socialization. (pp. 211–12)
5. Explain how the family is a system of interacting individuals. (pp. 212–13)
6. Explain how the construction of relationships reflects continuity and coherence. (p. 214)
7. Define the concept of attachment from the ethological, psychoanalytic, social learning, and cognitive developmental points of view. (pp. 214–18)
8. Describe the development of attachment. (pp. 218–19)
9. Explain Ainsworth's concepts of secure and insecure attachment. (pp. 219–21)
10. Explain the relationship between the formation of attachment and the construction of relationships. (pp. 221–24)
11. Describe the effect of differences in temperament on the formation of attachment. (pp. 224–25)
12. Describe the development of attachment to the father and his role in the social and personality development of the infant. (pp. 226–29)
13. Describe the effects of both sibling and peer relationships on social and personality formation in infancy. (pp. 231–32)
14. Define several types of day care and describe its role and importance in the social and personality formation of the infant. (pp. 232–34)
15. Describe the functions of emotion in infancy and discuss the preverbal infant's communication and recognition of emotions. (pp. 235–36)
16. Explain Erikson's concept of trust. (p. 237)
17. Explain both Mahler's and Erikson's theories regarding the development of the self during infancy. (pp. 237–40)
18. Describe Rheingold's findings on the development of independence. (p. 240)
19. Explain Kopp's four phases in the development of self-control. (p. 241)
20. Describe seven ways in which early experience could be linked to the development of later disorders. (pp. 243–45)
21. Define child abuse and describe possible facilitating conditions. (pp. 245–46)
22. Define infantile autism. (pp. 246–47)

Summary

Inhibition is one aspect of personality that may be influenced by biological factors. Ethologists also focus on biological factors, such as sensitive periods, in social and personality development. Sociocultural influences, such as the social settings in which the child lives and the general cultural climate, also influence development.

Families are important agents of socialization for the child. Behaviorists' approach to socialization has been that it is a one-way process, with adults molding the child. The current view is that socialization is reciprocal: Parents socialize children and, in turn, are socialized by them. Studies of early socialization have looked at micro behaviors, such as eye gazing, and also at more molar exchanges to determine the match of affective tone between mother and infant. When the infant is very young, the mother carries the load in facilitating the interaction. Later, the mother and child both initiate or "drive" the relationship.

The contemporary view of socialization emphasizes the transactions between a changing child and a changing social environment. There is continuity in the parent-child relationship over time, and relationships are carried forward to influence new relationships. Children who are rejected by their mothers elicit angry responses from their teachers, while children who have mothers who cuddle them elicit similar behavior from their teachers. Negative social interaction between husband and wife is linked to negative affect shown by the father toward the infant. This suggests that families are systems that should be explored in explaining the child's social behavior.

Attachment is an affectional tie that one individual has for another that persists over time and space. Freud believed that oral gratification provided the mechanism for attachment and that, as a result, the infant became attached to the one who fed him or her. Social learning theory has explained attachment as resulting from primary and secondary reinforcement, with both feeding and contact comfort existing as primary reinforcers. Cognitive theorists interpret attachment as a motivational system based on the need to express competence in interpersonal exchanges. In this view, the development of object permanence is necessary for the development of attachment. The ethological perspective proposed by Bowlby argues that the infant and mother instinctively trigger each other's behavior to form an attachment bond and that executor responses and signaling responses both play a role in the development of the attachment system.

Attachment develops from undifferentiated responding to mother and stranger, to fear of strangers, and finally, to using the mother as a base for exploration. Ainsworth describes secure attachment as when infants use mothers as a secure base for exploration, respond positively to being picked up, and move away freely to play when put down. Insecure attachment is evidenced by ambivalent attachment behavior, heightened separation anxiety, and avoidance of proximity with the caregiver. Situational differences can affect measures of attachment. For example, if an infant is seated on the mother's lap, he or she shows less distress toward a stranger. Attachment relationships carry forward into other relationships. Attachment also may be related to temperament. Attachment between father and infant occurs at the same time as attachment between mother and infant. Fathers can be just as sensitive to infants as mothers. However, mothers operate more in a caregiving role than do fathers, while fathers are identified more with a play role.

Infants are, to some extent, socialized by siblings and peers, as well as by parents. During the second year, younger siblings initiate more sibling conflict than during the first year. Infants as young as six months of age interact socially by smiling, touching, and vocalizing. By around 14 months of age, infants use toys to facilitate peer interactions. By 18 months of age, a display of affect may accompany a positive peer interaction. Both positive and negative interactions are more common in the second year than the first.

Another social environment in which some infants spend much time is day care. Infants may begin day care at one or two years of age or earlier. For some infants, day care is a positive experience; for others, it is a negative experience. In day-care centers that are university based and/or staffed, the programs for infants and young children are good and the infants are not different in attachment behavior from infants reared at home by their mothers. For some infants, there may be positive benefits in social development from day-care experience. Good quality day care does not have any negative effects on the social or cognitive development of the infant.

Emotions begin to develop during infancy. Crying and smiling are both important in attachment. Emotion is thought to have adaptive and survival-promoting functions. It also serves communicative and regulative functions. Even one-month-old infants display a wide range of emotional expressions, including joy, interest, anger, surprise, and fear. Infants seem able to distinguish between emotions by four months of age, preferring to look at a face expressing joy than one expressing anger. Emotion language appears at about 18 to 20 months of age.

Several facets of personality develop during infancy. According to Erikson, trust or mistrust, a basic personality orientation to the world, is the outcome of infancy. Infants also develop a sense of self and the beginnings of independence. A mirror technique, observing infants' response to their reflections in a mirror, is often used as a measure of self-recognition. Mahler describes the process of separation-individuation—when the child acquires individual characteristics—as a critical development of the first three years. A sense of trust and a sense of self are both needed for separation-individuation to develop. Rheingold has observed that independence develops during the first two years, as measured by the distance that infants of varying ages are willing to move from their mothers to explore their environment.

Self-control also begins to develop during infancy. It begins with the ability to control arousal states in the first few months and continues with the ability to engage in voluntary sensorimotor acts. Self-control requires the emergence of representational thinking and recall memory and an ability to regulate behavior on the basis of demands from caregivers, even in the absence of the caregivers. It thus does not appear until 18 to 24 months of age.

Some problems and disturbances appear during infancy. Some, such as certain forms of mental retardation, are influenced by biological factors. Environmental factors, such as experiences that change family relationships, may also contribute to disturbances. Child abuse is an example of a contemporary environmental problem in our culture, in part because of the culture of violence in America. In contrast, infantile autism seems to have a strong biological base. It is characterized by an inability of the young child to relate to other people and is often accompanied by speech problems.

Guided Review

You may want to look at the answers to the "Guided Review" statements as you read, or you may want to use the exercise as a form of self-test by covering up the answers below the statements with a sheet of paper and not consulting them until you have attempted to fill in the blanks of each statement.

1. Kagan believes that _____ has a genetic basis. The inhibited infant is _____ and _____ , while the disinhibited infant is more likely to be _____ .
    inhibition, shy, introverted, extraverted

2. The _____ may modify this biological tendency, but the inhibited child is not likely to ever be _____ .
    environment, extraverted

3. According to the ethological view, a _____ period could explain the role of early mother-infant interaction.
    sensitive

4. According to _____ , the actual social setting in which the child lives is the _____ . Such contexts as the _____ , _____ , _____ , and _____ are important in this respect. The infant helps to _____ this environment; that is, the infant is not viewed as a _____ recipient of such experiences.
    Bronfenbrenner, microsystem, family, school, peers, neighborhood, construct, passive

5. According to Bronfenbrenner, the _____ refers to the relations between microsystems or between contexts. The contexts that influence the child's development without the child having any direct role make up the _____ .
    mesosystem, exosystem

6. According to Bronfenbrenner, the macrosystem is composed of the _____ and _____ of the culture.
    attitudes, ideologies

7. A new infant is likely to result in a couple having less free _____ and less extra _____ . When both parents work, there are concerns about the effects of _____ _____ .
    time, money, day care

8. Mothers may develop " _____ _____ ," a kind of depression that may last _____ _____ into the infant's life. The father's _____ is key to adaptation by the _____ in the infant's first year of life.
    "postpartum blues," nine months, involvement, mother

9. The traditional view is that the child is formed by the parents' socialization techniques. Hartup has referred to these perspectives as _____ _____ theories. However, we now view the socialization process as a _____ one. One of the most studied examples of reciprocal socialization in infancy involves mutual _____ . Currently, studies of reciprocal interchanges are likely to be done at a _____ level rather than at the level of specific behaviors.
    social mold, reciprocal, gazing, molar

10. When the infant is young, most of the responsibility for facilitating interaction falls on the _____ . This is likely to persist for at least _____ year. The interaction becomes more equal in the _____ year.

mother, one, second

11. The _____ can be thought of as a system defined in terms of generation, gender, and role. Pederson, Anderson, and Cain found that positive interaction between the husband and wife (was/was not) _____ related to their positive interaction with their infant but that negative interaction (was/was not) _____ . The new role of the woman in our society may require the _____ to do more of the traditionally female duties.

family, was not, was, father

12. According to Sroufe and Fleeson, there is _____ in relationships over time, and previous relationships _____ later ones. Sroufe and Fleeson's observations of children indicate that children who have a history of _____ attachment tend to be more socially competent in preschool settings, children who have experienced maternal _____ tend to misbehave until punished, and children who generally are treated as cute and charming usually come from a family with a history of _____ maternal behavior.

continuity, influence, secure, rejection, seductive

13. _____ refers to a relationship between two individuals in which each person feels strongly about the other and does a number of things to ensure the continuation of the relationship.

Attachment

14. The basis of Bowlby's ethological theory of attachment is that the infant and the mother have _____ that trigger each other's behavior to form an attachment bond. _____ responses refer to the infant's smiling, crying, and calling that are attempts to elicit behaviors from the mother. _____ responses include clinging, following, sucking, and physical approach. They bring the infant and mother in close contact, and the infant is the main actor. These responses can also be made by the _____ .

instincts, Signalling, Executor, mother or father

15. According to Bowlby, during the first phase in the development of attachment, the infant does not _____ . Anyone can elicit _____ . During the second phase, the infant focuses on the _____ _____ . During the third phase, the _____ of attachment _____ , and in the final phase, the elements become _____ into a _____ system of attachment.

discriminate, smiles, primary caregiver, intensity, increases, integrated, mutual

16. According to Freud, the infant becomes attached to a person who provides _____ satisfaction. The infant is most likely to attach to the _____ because of the _____ experience. Erikson added the concept of _____ on the part of the infant.

oral, mother, feeding, trust

17. Those who believe that the caregiver-infant attachment bond is a learned phenomenon call upon the process of _____ to explain its formation. Food is the _____ reinforcer, and since the caregiver is associated with food, he or she becomes a _____ reinforcer for the infant.

reinforcement, primary, secondary

18. In a classic study by _____ and _____ , infant monkeys were raised by surrogate mothers. They were _____ either by a soft, cloth mother or a hard, wire mother. Regardless of where the monkeys nursed, they spent more time with the _____ surrogate.

Harlow, Zimmerman, fed, cloth

19. According to cognitive developmental theory, a prerequisite to the formation of a stable attachment is the cognitive skill of _____ _____ . Object permanence relative to persons seems to appear _____ than object permanence for inanimate objects.
object permanence, sooner

20. The longitudinal study of Schaffer and Emerson found that attachment became focused on the _____ at about six months. The fear of strangers appeared at about _____ months. Ainsworth observed that Ugandan infants began to show the most intense attachment to the mother at about _____ months.
mother, eight, seven

21. According to Ainsworth, an infant who uses the caregiver as a "safe" base from which to explore is said to have a(n) _____ attachment, while an infant who is ambivalent, tends to avoid proximity with the caregiver, and shows heightened separation anxiety is said to have a(n) _____ attachment. Some insecurely attached infants do not go near or approach the mother at reunion. This is called insecurely attached _____ . Other insecurely attached infants kick the mother as she picks them up. This is called insecurely attached _____ .
secure, insecure, avoidant, resistant

22. Clarke-Stewart argues that _____ of the mother is an important determinant of infant behavior and that _____ contact may also be important.
nearness, eye

23. Waters, Wippman, and Sroufe found that children who were securely attached at 18 months of age _____ more with their mothers in a test six months later than did avoidant or resistant infants. A different group of infants, who had been designated as securely or insecurely attached at 15 months of age, were assessed for social competence at the age of 3½. The previously securely attached children received _____ scores in competence than did the previously insecurely attached children. Van Pancake has recently found that children with a history of anxious-avoidant attachment have less positive relationships with their _____ than their securely attached counterparts. However, work done by Lewis seems to indicate a _____ difference in this effect.
shared, higher, peers, sex

24. In one investigation, mothers who had problems with their one-year-old infants reported a _____ relationship with their own parents. Uddenberg reported a link between a mother's relationship with her own mother and the incidence of _____ difficulties in the _____ period, feelings of _____ as a parent, and _____ feelings toward the _____ . Main, Kaplan, and Cassidy found that the child's _____ of the parent following separation was related to parental reports of rejection in their own childhoods.
poor, psychiatric, postpartum, inadequacy, negative, infant, avoidance

25. A recent argument has been made that the differences in attachment (that is, between secure and insecure attachment) may be due primarily to differences in _____ among infants. A recent study by Weber, Levitt, and Clark found that mothers of _____ babies were more likely to have a temperament involving intensity of reaction than the mothers of _____ and _____ babies. This suggests a role for the temperament of the _____ .
temperament, avoidant, secure, ambivalent, mother

26. During the Colonial period, the father's role was that of a teacher of _____ . With the Industrial Revolution came the father's role as the _____ . By the end of World War II, the father was expected to provide a _____ - _____ model. Since the 1970s, fathers are evaluated with regard to the extent that they are involved with their children in an _____ and _____ way.

morals, breadwinner, sex-role, active, nurturant

27. Lamb has defined involvement with the child in terms of _____ , _____ , and _____ . In families in which the mother is a homemaker, the father spends about _____ to _____ percent as much time as the mother interacting with the child. This rises to about _____ percent when the mother works. The biggest discrepancy in parental roles is that the typical father takes no ultimate _____ for the child's welfare and care.

interaction, accessibility, responsibility, 20, 25, 33, responsibility

28. At about the same time that infants form attachments to their mothers, they bond to their _____ . Infants seem to prefer fathers for _____ and mothers for _____ .

fathers, play, comfort

29. In a study of nontraditional Swedish couples in which the _____ took parental leave to care for their infants, the fathers were _____ likely to discipline, vocalize to, hold, soothe, and kiss than the mothers.

fathers, less

30. Recent work suggests that, between the ages of _____ and _____ , _____ siblings initiate more conflict that previously.

one, two, younger

31. _____ , _____ , and _____ are the means of peer interaction in the first year. In one study, an infant who was well liked tended to approach peers in a positive way, with a _____ . In the same study, an infant who was avoided frequently by peers often initiated encounters with other infants by _____ their _____ .

Smiling, touching, vocalizing, smile, grabbing, toys

32. _____ are very important in peer interaction in the second year. However, toys may initially _____ interaction. It takes time for the toddler to coordinate play with a _____ and a _____ .

Toys, decrease, toy, peer

33. While positive peer _____ increase during the second year, so also do _____ ones. In particular, there are more _____ over _____ .

interactions, negative, fights, toys

34. In one recent study, positive _____ during peer interaction in the toddler period predicted _____ in the preschool period.

affect, popularity

35. In 1984, the number of women in the labor force with children under the age of six (with spouse present in the home) was _____ million. Currently, about _____ million children are in formal, licensed day care, and another _____ million attend nursery school. The number of children in _____ day care can only be estimated.

6.2, 2, 5, unlicensed or informal

36. If the attachment behavior of children in high-quality, university-staffed day-care centers is compared with that of home-reared children, the differences are _____ . However, one study found some differences if the day care was begun during the _____ year of life.
    minimal, first

37. Most views of emotion claim that it has _____ and _____-_____ functions, serves as a form of _____ , and has _____ functions. For example, _____ serves as a linkage between certain events and possible danger. The infant who _____ likely is telling others that he or she is feeling pleasant, while the infant who cries may be communicating that something is _____ . Infants can use emotional displays to regulate the _____ between themselves and others.
    adaptive, survival-promoting, communication, regulative, fear, smiles, unpleasant, distance

38. Interviews with mothers revealed that the mothers believe that their one-month-old infants display _____ , _____ , _____ , _____ , _____ , and _____ . In work by Malatesta and Haviland, and Izard et al., judges were able to reliably code several emotions in _____ -month-old infants and _____ -to _____ -month-old infants, respectively.
    joy, interest, anger, surprise, fear, sadness, three, one, nine

39. The first emotional displays are a _____ , _____ , _____ , and a reflexive _____ . The next display to emerge is probably the _____ smile in response to a _____ . Between _____ and _____ months of age, _____ , _____ , and _____ emerge. The infant begins to show _____ at about _____ months of age.
    startle, distress, disgust, smile, social, face, three, four, surprise, anger, sadness, fear, six

40. In one study, infants spent more time looking at a facial expression of _____ than a _____ one or an _____ one. Apparently, _____ of emotional displays precedes _____ of emotional displays.
    joy, neutral, angry, production, recognition

41. During the second year, the toddler's ability to _____ increases. Emotional language emerges at about _____ to _____ months.
    communicate, 18, 20

42. If an infant feels that the world is predictable and that he can depend upon his mother, he will develop a feeling of _____ . This is actually an _____ that develops as a result of care that is _____ and _____ .
    trust, expectancy, consistent, warm

43. The sense of _____ that develops from inconsistent care produces _____ _____ of new experiences.
    mistrust, fearful apprehension

44. Erikson's views are very compatible with _____ views on attachment.
    Ainsworth's

45. Children recognize their reflection in a mirror by about _____ months of age. Among the animals, only humans and the _____ _____ have this ability. It seems to be tied to the ability to form a _____ _____ of one's face. This accomplishment is taken as an indication of the development of a sense of _____ .
    18, great apes, mental image, self

46. Mahler believes that toddlers develop independence by a process of _____ -
_____ . First, they break the _____ relationship with the mother.
That is _____ . Then they acquire individual characteristics. That is _____ ,
the development of an _____ , _____ .
separation-individuation, symbiotic, separation, individuation, independent, autonomous self

47. Harter thinks that Mahler has put too much emphasis on the _____ and that many of her
observations have not been _____ .
mother, documented

48. According to Erikson, a necessary precursor to the development of independence is the development of a sense of
early _____ . Major changes in competencies can result in the dependent child beginning to
experience an _____ _____ . If the child does not develop a sense of
_____ - _____ and _____ _____ , he or she may develop lasting
_____ and _____ .
trust, autonomous will, self-control, free will, shame, doubt

49. Rheingold found that infants' reaction to strange environments really resulted from being _____ and
_____ _____ . The separation itself was not the problem because the same infants would
_____ their mothers to _____ .
placed, left alone, leave, explore

50. Kopp has described _____ stages in the development of self-control. From birth until about _____
months of age, arousal states are modulated and reflex patterns become more organized. This is
_____ modulation. From _____ to about _____ months of age, the infant
develops the ability to use and modify the _____ act. This is _____
modulation. During the next months, the infant shows awareness of social or task demands. This is
_____ . True self-control is characterized by the appearance of _____
thinking and _____ _____ .
four, 3, neurophysiological, 3, 12, voluntary, sensorimotor, control, representational, recall memory

51. Genetic, prenatal, and environmental factors _____ to influence the outcome of the infant.
interact

52. According to Sroufe, _____ regulation, harmonious _____ , and the
formation of an _____ relationship are central developmental tasks for the infant.
biological, relationships, attachment

53. When a caregiver harms his or her charge, it is called _____ . Parke has developed a
model of child abuse based on an understanding of the _____ _____ .
American society is _____ . This is a _____ influence. The child may be
_____ or _____ , the parents may be experiencing severe _____ ,
or there may be a parental history of _____ . These are _____ influences. There may no
family or friends nearby nor any crisis centers. This is a _____ influence.
child abuse, social environment, violent, cultural, unattractive, unwanted, stress, abuse, familial, community

54. A prominent characteristic of infantile autism is the apparent inability of an autistic child to _____ to
other people. An autistic child not only has a deficit in _____ but will actually protest
close _____ . A speech problem characteristic of autism is called _____ ,
in which the child simply _____ what is said. A third characteristic of autism is hyperreactivity
to a _____ in routine.
relate, attachment, contact, echolalia, repeats, change

Key Terms Matching Exercise

Match the Key Term on the left with the correct definition on the right.

—— 1. mesosystem (LO–2, p. 208)
—— 2. microsystem (LO–2, p. 208)
—— 3. exosystem (LO–2, p. 208)
—— 4. macrosystem (LO–2, p. 209)
—— 5. social mold theories (LO–4, p. 211)

a. Behavioral theories that view socialization as a one-way process, considering the child to be the product of the parents' training techniques

b. Refers to relations between microsystems, or connections between contexts

c. Contexts that influence the child's development even though the child does not have an active role in those contexts

d. Refers to the attitudes and ideologies of the culture

e. Actual social setting in which the child lives

—— 6. reciprocal socialization (LO–4, p. 211)
—— 7. molar exchanges (LO–4, p. 211)
—— 8. second-order effects (LO–5, p. 213)
—— 9. attachment (LO–7, p. 215)
—— 10. executor responses (LO–7, p. 216)

a. Global clusters of responses rather than specific behaviors in reciprocal interchanges

b. Indirect effects, such as the way a relationship between spouses mediates the way a parent acts toward the child

c. View that children and parents socialize each other, rather than parents just socializing children

d. Behaviors (for example, clinging, following, and physical approach) that bring infant and mother into close contact, with the infant the main actor

e. Relationship between two individuals, in which each person feels strongly about the other and does things to ensure the continuation of the relationship

—— 11. signalling responses (LO–7, p. 216)
—— 12. contact comfort (LO–7, p. 216)
—— 13. secure attachment (LO–9, p. 219)
—— 14. insecure attachment (LO–9, p. 219)
—— 15. separation-individuation (LO–17, p. 238)

a. Relationship in which the infant uses the mother as a base from which to explore the environment; infants respond positively to being picked up and, when put down, move away freely to play

b. Process characterized by the child's emergence from the symbiotic relationship with the mother and the acquisition of individual characteristics in the first three years of life

c. Relationship in which an infant shows ambivalent attachment behavior and heightened separation anxiety in strange situations and tends to avoid proximity with the caregiver

d. Behaviors (for example, smiling, crying, and calling) that the infant engages in to elicit reciprocal behaviors from the mother

e. Tactile stimulation with a soft stimulus

____ 16. neurophysiological modulation (LO–19, p. 241)

____ 17. sensorimotor modulation (LO–19, p. 241)

____ 18. control (LO–19, p. 241)

____ 19. self-control (LO–19, p. 241)

____ 20. autism (LO–22, p. 246)

____ 21. echolalia (LO–22, p. 246)

a. Refers to the infant's ability to engage in a voluntary act and change the act in response to events that might arise

b. Inability of an infant or child to relate to other people; often accompanied by speech problems and lack of flexibility in adapting to new routines and changes in daily life

c. Speech pattern in which the child repeats what is heard rather than responding

d. Behavior of the infant that is based on representational thinking, reflecting knowledge of social rules as well as the demand characteristics of situations, even in the absence of caretakers

e. Form of control in which arousal states are modulated and reflex patterns become more organized in terms of functional behavior

f. Emerging ability of infants to show awareness of demands defined by caregivers and to initiate, maintain, modulate, or cease physical acts, communication, and emotional signals accordingly.

Answers to Key Terms Matching Exercise

1. b	5. a	9. e	13. a	17. a
2. e	6. c	10. d	14. c	18. f
3. c	7. a	11. d	15. b	19. d
4. d	8. b	12. e	16. e	20. b
				21. c

Self-Test A

Choose the best alternative.

1. Kagan argues that which of the following has a genetic basis? (LO–1, p. 207)
    a. temperament
    b. attachment
    c. inhibition
    d. intelligence

2. According to Bronfenbrenner, if a mother is yelled at by her boss and comes home and yells at her son, the aspect of the world that is influencing the mother is the son's (LO–2, pp. 208–9)
    a. microsystem.
    b. exosystem.
    c. macrosystem.
    d. mesosystem.

3. The period of depression that may appear after the birth of a baby (LO–3, p. 210)
    a. is called postpartum blues.
    b. can have disastrous consequences for bonding.
    c. predicts child abuse.
    d. is found more in fathers than in mothers.

4. The view that children socialize parents as well as being socialized by them (LO–4, p. 211)
   a. is referred to as social mold theory.
   b. supports social mold theory.
   c. is used as evidence to refute reciprocal socialization.
   d. is referred to as reciprocal socialization.

5. Research by Pederson found that (LO–5, p. 213)
   a. conflict between spouses is related to negative affect from the mother to the infant.
   b. conflict between spouses is related to negative affect from the father to the infant.
   c. affection between spouses is related to positive affect from the mother to the infant.
   d. affection between spouses is related to positive affect from the father to the infant.

6. Sroufe and Fleeson observed that a preschool teacher is more likely to become angry with a child who (LO–6, p. 214)
   a. is seductive to adults.
   b. has a dependent relationship with her mother.
   c. is clingy and whiney.
   d. has been rejected by her mother.

7. Executor responses and signalling responses are components of which theory of attachment? (LO–7, p. 216)
   a. ethological
   b. psychoanalytic
   c. behavioral
   d. cognitive

8. According to data from Schaffer and Emerson, fear of strangers occurs at about (LO–8, p. 218)
   a. 6 months of age.
   b. 7 months of age.
   c. 8 months of age.
   d. 10 months of age.

9. According to Ainsworth, an infant who moves away freely from the mother to explore the environment, but looks at the mother occasionally, would be classified as (LO–9, p. 219)
   a. securely attached.
   b. insecure-avoidant.
   c. insecure-resistant.
   d. unattached.

10. According to research by Michael Lewis and colleagues, infants whose attachment relationships were classified as ambivalent and who at age six appeared withdrawn would most likely be classified in which of the following categories? (LO-10, p. 223)
    a. depressed girls
    b. depressed boys
    c. schizoid boys
    d. schizoid girls

11. According to research by Weber, Levitt, and Clark, a mother with a temperament that involves intensity of reaction is more likely to have an infant who is _____ than mothers who are not. (LO–11, p. 225)
    a. securely attached
    b. ambivalent
    c. avoidant
    d. Both b and c are correct.

12. By the end of World War II, which role of fathers had become important? (LO–12, p. 226)
    a. breadwinner
    b. moral teacher
    c. caregiver
    d. sex-role model

13. At what age do toys become used as a medium for playing with peers? (LO–13, p. 232)
    a. 6 months
    b. 12 months
    c. 14 months
    d. two years

14. According to research, infants in university based or staffed day-care programs (LO–14, p. 234)
    a. are more cognitively advanced than home-reared infants.
    b. are more socially advanced than home-reared infants.
    c. are less attached to their mothers than home-reared infants.
    d. show few differences in cognitive or social development from home-reared infants.

15. Research on displays of emotions in infants has found that (LO–15, p. 236)
    a. infants one month of age display a wide range of emotions.
    b. infants six months of age show only three or four emotional expressions.
    c. infants' expression of emotion begins at about eight months of age.
    d. infants less than three months of age only express displeasure.

16. According to Erikson, the developmental task of infancy is (LO–16, p. 237)
    a. developing self-control.
    b. developing trust.
    c. separation-individuation.
    d. becoming attached to the mother.

17. The process of emerging from the symbiotic relationship with the mother and acquiring individual characteristics is called (LO–17, p. 238)
    a. developing self-control.
    b. developing trust.
    c. separation-individuation.
    d. attachment.

18. To study the development of independence in infants, Rheingold measured (LO–18, p. 240)
    a. the distance the infants would move from their mothers.
    b. the amount of clinging that infants engaged in after separation.
    c. the amount of distress observed during separation.
    d. the amount of distress infants showed to the approach of a stranger.

19. An infant reaches for a rattle on her high-chair tray, picks it up, and throws it on the floor, watching the results when it hits. According to Kopp, this infant is in which stage of the development of self-control? (LO–19, p. 241)
    a. neurophysiological modulation
    b. sensorimotor modulation
    c. control
    d. self-control

20. A childhood disorder that is characterized by echolalia and an inability to relate to other people is (LO–20, p. 246)
    a. child abuse.
    b. mental retardation.
    c. introversion.
    d. infantile autism.

Answers to Self-Test A

1. c	5. b	9. a	13. c	17. c
2. b	6. d	10. b	14. d	18. a
3. a	7. a	11. c	15. a	19. b
4. d	8. c	12. d	16. b	20. d

Self-Test B

Choose the best alternative.

21. Which of the following is not seen as having a strong biological component in social development? (LO–1, pp. 207–8)
    a. extraversion
    b. introversion
    c. being insecurely attached
    d. sensitive periods in attachment

22. A researcher who wants to study social interactions between children observes Timmy at home playing with his friend Jim. Which of Bronfenbrenner's systems is most directly involved? (LO-2, p. 208)
    a. microsystem
    b. mesosystem
    c. exosystem
    d. macrosystem

23. For preschool children, parents assume the role of (LO–3, p. 210)
    a. feeders.
    b. comforters.
    c. holders.
    d. limit-setters.

24. The theories that focus exclusively on the way in which the child is shaped by the environment are called (LO–4, p. 211)
    a. social mold theories.
    b. cognitive theories.
    c. biological theories.
    d. reciprocal theories.

25. Research by Cowan and Cowan has observed that, after the birth of the first baby, roles of the husband and wife (LO–5, p. 213)
    a. become less traditional.
    b. become more traditional.
    c. stay consistent with how they were prior to the birth of the child.
    d. can change in a variety of ways, with no consistent pattern from family to family.

26. Research by Waters, Wippman, and Sroufe has found that more socially competent preschoolers have a history of (LO–6, p. 214)
    a. secure attachment.
    b. maternal rejection.
    c. good health.
    d. seductive maternal behavior.

27. The view that attachment occurs through oral gratification is a component of which theory? (LO–7, p. 216)
    a. ethological
    b. psychoanalytic
    c. behavioral
    d. cognitive

28. Research by Schaffer and Emerson reported which of the following findings on the development of infant attachment? (LO-8, p. 218)
    a. Attachment appears at three months of age.
    b. Fear of strangers occurs at six months of age.
    c. Attachment is initially only to the mother.
    d. Attachment is as intense to other specific caregivers as to the mother.

29. Sammy approaches his mother after a brief separation but pushes her away and hits her when she picks him up. Which of Ainsworth's categories describes his behavior? (LO–9, p. 220)
    a. securely attached
    b. insecurely attached—avoidant
    c. insecurely attached—resistant
    d. insecurely attached—denial

30. Research by Waters, Wippman, and Sroufe found what behaviors in preschool children who were insecurely attached as infants? (LO–10, p. 222)
    a. overt aggression
    b. peer leader
    c. clinging to teacher
    d. withdrawal

31. In research by Weber, Levitt, and Clark, what was related to an infant's behavior toward a stranger? (LO–11, p. 225)
    a. attention span
    b. persistence
    c. adaptability
    d. distractibility

32. Research by Lamb on the role of the father in contemporary families found what difference between families in which the mother works and families in which the mother does not work? (LO–12, pp. 226–27)
    a. Fathers interact more if the mother works.
    b. Fathers interact less if the mother works.
    c. Fathers assume less responsibility if the mother works.
    d. Fathers assume more responsibility if the mother works.

33. What behavior appears in the younger of two siblings during the second year that was not present during the first year? (LO–13, p. 231)
    a. more physical aggression
    b. more nurturing behavior
    c. more moral references
    d. more negotiations

34. According to the text, the majority of infants of working mothers are (LO–14, p. 233)
    a. cared for in family day-care homes.
    b. in licensed day-care centers.
    c. cared for by relatives.
    d. cared for at home by unrelated baby-sitters.

35. Infants have been shown to be able to distinguish between different facial expressions of emotion by as young as (LO–15, p. 236)
    a. two months of age.
    b. four months of age.
    c. six months of age.
    d. eight months of age.

36. Judy is consistently fed when hungry and is kept warm and dry by her mother. She expects the world to be a good place. Whose theory does this illustrate? (LO–16, p. 237)
    a. Ainsworth
    b. Mahler
    c. Rheingold
    d. Erikson

37. Which of the following techniques is used to test for the sense of self? (LO–17, pp. 237–38)
    a. separating the infant from the mother
    b. having a stranger approach the mother
    c. observing the infant move away from the mother
    d. observing the infant react to his or her reflection in a mirror

38. According to Mahler, what behavior on the part of the mother makes the separation-individuation process difficult for an infant? (LO–17, pp. 238–39)
    a. overprotection
    b. emotional unavailability
    c. emotional support
    d. Both a and c are correct.

39. Kopp calls the ability to control arousal states (LO–19, p. 241)
    a. neurophysiological modulation.
    b. sensorimotor modulation.
    c. control.
    d. self-control.

40. Which of the following is not usually considered a factor in child abuse? (LO–21, pp. 245–46)
    a. violence in the culture
    b. history of child abuse in the parent's family
    c. psychosis
    d. stressful family situations

Answers to Self-Test B

21. c	25. b	29. c	33. a	37. d
22. b	26. a	30. d	34. c	38. b
23. d	27. b	31. c	35. b	39. a
24. a	28. d	32. a	36. d	40. c

Questions to Stimulate Thought

1. Do parents' reasons for having a child matter? That is, do the reasons have an impact on subsequent parenting and child development?
2. Define attachment. What difference does temperament make?
3. How are later child relationships related to the initial attachment bond?
4. Compare and contrast sibling and peer influences.
5. Is home rearing by the natural mother better for the child?
6. Are infants born with emotions?
7. What is the relationship between trust and independence?

Research Project

In this exercise, you look at attachment behavior using naturalistic observation. Go to a local shopping mall and observe a mother with a 12- to 18-month-old infant for 15 minutes. Describe the behaviors that you see on the data sheet that follows and then answer the questions.

Data Sheet

Behaviors	Child	Age _____	Sex _____
Talking			
Laughing			
Tickling			
Clinging			
Crying			
Escaping			
Retrieving			
Mutual Gaze			
Hitting			
Smiling			
Yelling			
Generally Positive Interaction			
Generally Negative Interaction			

Questions

1. What kinds of behaviors did your mother-infant pair engage in? Did the infant use the mother as a base for exploration? Was the infant allowed to explore?
2. Would you characterize the infant as secure or insecure? Were interactions generally positive or generally negative? Did the relationship seem warm and affectionate or hostile? Why?

7 Physical and Cognitive Development in Early Childhood

Learning Objectives

After studying this chapter, you should be able to:

1. Describe the patterns of growth in height and weight in early childhood, including their variations. (pp. 258–59)
2. Explain the evaluation of motor and perceptual development in early childhood. (pp. 259–61)
3. Describe early childhood nutrition and explain the role it plays in the child's health. (pp. 261–63)
4. Explain the relation between health and the development of an understanding about health on the child's development. (p. 264)
5. Define the operation and explain the nature of preoperational thought. (pp. 269–70)
6. Describe the symbolic function substage of the preoperational period. (pp. 270–75)
7. Explain the egocentrism of the preoperational period. (pp. 270–74)
8. Define animism. (pp. 274–75)
9. Describe the substage of intuitive thought. (pp. 275–76)
10. Explain the criticisms of Piaget's account of early childhood cognitive development based on learning and task characteristics. (pp. 276–77)
11. Describe the development of attention during the early childhood period. (pp. 277–79)
12. Compare and contrast long and short-term memory and describe how short-term memory increases during the early childhood period. (pp. 279–80)
13. Explain the role of the analysis of task dimensions in understanding the changes in reasoning and problem solving during the early childhood period. (pp. 280–81)
14. Define the mean length of utterance (MLU) and describe its development during the early childhood period. (pp. 281–83)
15. Describe the phonological characteristics of language during the early childhood period. (p. 284)
16. Explain the changes in morphology, including the plural, possessive, third-person singular, and the overgeneralization of rules, during the early childhood period. (p. 284)
17. Describe the increasing complexity of the syntax used during early childhood and the mastery of *wh-* questions. (pp. 284–85)
18. Describe the changes in semantics during early childhood. (p. 286)
19. Describe the improvements in displacement, knowledge of articles, and modifications in speech style for the listener during early childhood. (pp. 286–87)
20. Define the child-centered approach to education and its relevance to the early childhood period. (pp. 289–90)
21. Describe the roles of the preschool and compensatory education in early childhood. (pp. 290–93)

Summary

Growth slows down during early childhood. The average child grows 2½ inches in height and gains between five and seven pounds a year during this period. Ethnic origin and nutrition seem to be important contributors to the growth variability. Children with growth problems can often be treated with hormones directed at the pituitary gland. The deprivation of affection may also cause alterations in the release of hormones by the pituitary gland, leading to deprivation dwarfism.

Motor development is assessed in infants through 2½ years of age by the Bayley Motor Scale, which emphasizes postural control, locomotion, and prehensile activity. The Denver Developmental Screening Test is used for children from birth through six years of age. It evaluates such behaviors as the ability to sit, walk, broad-jump, pedal a tricycle, catch a bounced ball, and hop on one foot. It also evaluates fine motor behaviors, such as the child's ability to stack cubes, reach for objects, and draw a person. A more detailed test of gross motor skills is the DeOreo Fundamental Motor Skills Inventory, which evaluates such things as jumping, skipping, balancing, and running speed.

Adequate nutrition is necessary for growth, and the average preschool child should receive 1,400 to 1,800 calories a day, with a diet that includes protein, carbohydrates, fats, vitamins, and minerals. Without adequate nutrition, there can be growth retardation. A concern in our culture today is the excessive amount of fat in the diet. Animal studies demonstrate the importance of protein in the diet of the pregnant mother and in the diet of the subsequent offspring. Both body weight and brain cell count are affected by the amount of protein in the diet.

The health care needs of children can be understood by considering health in relation to motor, cognitive, and social development. Advanced mobility increases young children's risk of accidents and exposure to hazards in the environment. Children's understanding of the causes of illness has been related to Piaget's stages of cognitive development. The preoperational thinker believes that magic or mere association causes illness. The concrete operational thinker believes that temporal or spatial proximity exists between illness and its source. Parents must be sensitive to the use of language to identify emotional and physical feeling states and must make sure that the phrases "feel good" and "feel bad" are not confused with good and bad behavior. Parents can model good health behavior, such as wearing seat belts or not smoking, to their children. Children, even young ones, can profit from a regular exercise program.

The preoperational period is the second stage in Piaget's theory of cognitive development. During this time, stable concepts are formed, mental reasoning emerges, magical belief systems are constructed, and egocentrism is perceptually based. The early part of this period is the symbolic function substage. During this substage, the child has the ability to develop mental representations of objects and events. Drawing, language, and symbolic play appear. The second substage is called the intuitive thought substage. During this period, children begin to reason about matters and have opinions but cannot explain how they know what they know. The child at this age cannot correctly classify objects into groups that belong together, nor can the child correctly reason about an object belonging simultaneously to two different classes. Thinking is egocentric during the preoperational period, in that the child is unable to distinguish between his or her own perspective and the perspective of another. Animism also characterizes thought at this period. Children incorrectly attribute human qualities to inanimate objects.

Several studies have challenged Piaget's view of the child between two and seven years of age. For example, research by Gelman has shown that, with small numbers of objects, even three-year-old children can demonstrate conservation of number.

Information processing speed is slower in younger children than in older children. Age differences in cognition often involve controlled processes and knowledge. Capacity is difficult to measure. Attention increases with age. Vurpillot found that six and nine-year-old children systematically scan a set of pictures being compared, but four-year-old children do not. Short-term memory retains information for about 20 to 30 seconds. With rehearsal, short-term memory can retain information longer. Memory span increases from two digits in two to three-year-old children, to about five digits in seven-year-old children. Speed and efficiency of processing may be related to the increase in digit span.

The mean length of utterance (MLU) is one measurement devised to measure progress in language development. Phonology is still developing after MLU has reached three. Consonant clusters and difficult phonemes such as *r* appear late. In the development of morphology, Brown has found that plurals appear before passives, which appear before the third-person singular form. This is interesting because all of these require adding *s* to the word. Evidence for morphological rules comes from the errors children make by generalizing the rule to irregular forms, such as "foots" for "feet." There also is evidence of overgeneralization of syntactic rules. An example of this is applying rules for forming *wh-* questions to "how come" questions. Semantic knowledge is also expanding as children advance beyond the two-word stage. Vocabulary grows rapidly. Some classes of words, such as spatial adjectives and possessive verbs, are not fully understood until well into the childhood years. Understanding of pragmatics is also growing between the ages of two and six. Preschool children develop a command of displacement and begin to be sensitive to the conversational needs of others. The ability to change speech style according to the listener first appears around age four.

Project Head Start was a program in compensatory education targeted at children from low-income families. It offered preschool experiences with the hope that these early experiences might counteract the disadvantages these children normally experienced and allow them to profit from regular schooling later. Project Follow Through assessed the effectiveness of different kinds of educational programs at helping children from low-income families progress. Children in academically oriented approaches performed better on achievement tests and were more persistent on tasks. Children in affective education approaches were absent from school less and were more independent. Thus, different approaches had different outcomes in the kinds of behavior they fostered. Long-term follow-up studies show positive effects of Head Start in the number of people who go to college and who are employed full time, comparing individuals who participated in Head Start with initially similar others who did not receive that experience.

Guided Review

You may want to look at the answers to the "Guided Review" statements as you read, or you may want to use the exercise as a form of self-test by covering up the answers below the statements with a sheet of paper and not consulting them until you have attempted to fill in the blanks of each statement.

1. In Montessori schools, children are encouraged to work _____ , to _____ tasks in a prescribed manner once they have been begun, and to put materials away in _____ places. The teacher serves as a _____ of a process of _____ .
    independently, complete, assigned, facilitator, discovery

2. The Montessori approach includes tasks designed to promote _____ and _____ development. However, critics believe that _____ development is neglected and that _____ _____ is restricted.
    sensory, perceptual, social, imaginative play

3. The _____ of growth that began in the second year continues during early childhood. The average child grows _____ inches in height and gains _____ to _____ pounds a year. Both boys and girls become _____ during this time. The relative size of the _____ decreases.
    slowing, 2½, five, seven, leaner, head

4. In early childhood, the _____ _____ slows down and becomes more _____ . However, the _____ system is still more susceptible to _____ than it will be in middle and late childhood.
    heart rate, regular, skeletal, injury

5. The most important factors with regard to individual differences in height are _____ _____ and _____ . _____ , _____ -class, and _____ children are taller than _____ , _____ -class, and _____ - _____ ones. Maternal _____ during pregnancy costs the offspring about _____ inch in height by age five. In the United States, _____ children tend to be taller than _____ children.
    ethnic origin, nutrition, Urban, middle, firstborn, rural, lower, later-born, smoking, ½, black, white

6. One hormone that helps to control growth is secreted by the _____ gland located at the base of the brain. Deprivation dwarfism is a type of growth _____ that may result from a deprivation of _____ . This results in alterations in the release of hormones by the pituitary gland.
    pituitary, retardation, affection

7. The _____ _____ Scale can be used to evaluate the motor development of children up to the age of 2½ years. The Denver Developmental Screening Test can be used for children through the age of _____ . The Denver Developmental Screening Test is a simple way to identify _____ development because it evaluates language and social skills as well as both gross and fine motor skills. A more recent test that provides a more detailed assessment of gross motor skills is the _____ _____ _____ _____ Inventory.
    Bayley Motor, six, delayed, DeOreo Fundamental Motor Skills

8. Knowledge of large-scale spaces is known as _____ . In a study of three- to five-year-old children, evidence was found that children as young as three showed _____ ability to learn large-scale layouts. However, older children made _____ _____ .

mapping, some, fewer errors

9. The constituent of good nutrition that is essential for growth and development and that is conspicuously absent in the diets of peoples in the Third World is _____ . Animal studies have shown that the development of the _____ is directly related to the level of this nutrient in the diet. A study of South African black children found that adequate nutrition during the second through the seventh years resulted in _____ _____ than a control group with unchanged nutrition.

protein, brain, higher IQs

10. American children eat too much _____ . In part, this results from a taste for _____ _____ . It is very likely that this sort of diet is bad for the _____ .

fat, fast food, heart

11. According to Maddux, two issues that must be addressed concerning children and health are _____ _____ to prevent future health problems and the _____ _____ of each developmental period.

early intervention, unique problems

12. A particular problem of the preschool period is the increased risk of _____ that comes with the child's increased _____ .

accident, mobility

13. Children should be restrained in _____ _____ to ensure their safety while riding in an automobile. Children one to four years of age are particularly susceptible to accidental _____ , those five to nine years of age have higher rates of _____ accidents, and older children and adolescents have higher rates of accidents on _____ _____ .

car seats, poisoning, pedestrian, recreational equipment

14. The link between _____ and _____ —that is, the child's understanding of health—has been described in Piagetian terms. In the _____ stage, _____ thought dominates. The cause of illness is explained in _____ terms. In the _____ stage, _____ _____ thought is dominant. The child believes that there is temporal or spatial _____ between illness and its source. During this stage, the child begins to take responsibility for personal health by _____ germs.

health, cognition, phenomenistic, preoperational, magiclike, contagion, concrete operational, proximity, avoiding

15. According to one group, health education for preschool children should stress three goals: (1) _____ feelings and being able to _____ them to adults, (2) identifying sources of _____ , and (3) _____ the sources of assistance.

identifying, express, help, using

16. One problem that needs consideration are children's level of _____ skill. They may not have the _____ to describe the feeling. They may not be able to distinguish between _____ distress and _____ illness.

linguistic, word, emotional, physical

17. Parents have the responsibility for _____ the child health-related behavior while they _____ their child's _____ . The self-management of _____ does not occur before the age of _____ .

teaching, monitor, health, diabetes, 12

18. The _____ that results from hospitalization can interfere with _____ during _____ and the development of _____ and _____ in the toddler and early childhood years.
    separation, attachment, infancy, independence, exploration

19. Many children are in _____ physical condition when they begin _____ . Between 1975 and 1985, 6- to 17-year-old children showed _____ improvement in physical fitness.
    poor, school, no

20. The preoperational period lasts from _____ to _____ years of age. The child develops _____ concepts, mental _____ , and _____ _____ systems. _____ declines.
    two, seven, stable, reasoning, magical belief, Egocentrism

21. The first phase of the preoperational period is the _____ _____ substage. The child has the ability of mental _____ . Symbolic thought is expressed by children's _____ and their use of _____ .
    symbolic function, representation, drawings, language

22. Scribbles become pictures about the age of _____ . By age _____ , the child usually has represented a _____ .
    three, four, person

23. The inability to distinguish between one's own perspective and the perspective of another is called _____ . The _____ _____ task was devised by Piaget and Inhelder to study egocentrism in children. When asked what a doll seated across the table sees, preoperational children often describe _____ _____ _____ .
    egocentrism, three mountains, their own view

24. _____-taking ability increases with age and is not strongly influenced by general _____ . The correlation between perspective taking in different dimensions is _____ .
    Perspective, intelligence, low

25. The view that inanimate objects are alive or that plants and similar forms have human qualities is called _____ . Recent evidence suggests that what appears to be animism might actually be _____ _____ or lack of _____ .
    animism, game playing, knowledge

26. During the substage called _____ _____ , children are sure of their knowledge without being aware of how they know. When asked to put an assortment of objects into groups of similar items, the intuitive child cannot because he or she has not yet developed the skill of _____ . The _____ -year-old child can't _____ - _____ ; the _____ -year-old probably can.
    intuitive thought, classification, six, cross-classify, nine

27. About the age of _____ , the child begins to _____ _____ . Many of the questions involve asking " _____ ?" This phenomenon demonstrates the child's _____ .
    three, ask questions, why, curiosity

28. Some have suggested that the lack of higher-level thought in preschoolers may result from _____ variables or inadequate _____ opportunities. Gelman has shown that _____ training can improve performance on the _____ problem. She has also demonstrated improvement in the _____ concept with _____ training.

    task, learning, attentional, conservation, number, reinforcement

29. A two-year-old may have an attention span of _____ minutes, a three-year-old _____ minutes. In the classroom, the child's attention span is _____ .

    two, ten, longer

30. Preschool children are captured by the _____ features of a display rather than the ones relevant to a current task. After the age of six or seven, attention seems to come under _____ control so that older children attend to stimuli that are _____ to a particular task.

    salient, cognitive, relevant

31. Short-term memory appears to retain information for up to _____ seconds. The retention duration of short-term memory can be increased by various _____ strategies. The relatively permanent part of memory is called _____ - _____ memory. Both the storage and retrieval processes for long-term memory are more _____ than those for short-term memory.

    30, rehearsal, long-term, effortful

32. A test in which you hear a short list of stimuli read and are then asked to repeat the digits is called a _____ - _____ task. The memory-span task can be used to assess _____ - _____ memory. The memory span increases sharply between _____ and _____ years of age. This seems best explained by increases in _____ of _____ . For young adults, there is evidence that it might be related to _____ ability.

    memory-span, short-term, two, seven, speed, processing, intellectual

33. _____ _____ reasoning requires a child to compare the number of objects in a _____ with the number of objects in the larger set. According to Piaget, this is a _____ _____ ability.

    Class inclusion, subset, concrete operational

34. The _____ _____ psychologist analyzes the task into component steps. In the class inclusion problem, these steps might be to _____ the key elements of the problem and to formulate a _____ . The plan might be: _____ the subset, _____ the larger set, and make a _____ . There are then _____ ways in which the child can fail to solve the problem.

    information processing, encode, plan, count, count, comparison, many

35. The information processing approach yields a list of important _____ to teach children. This is in sharp contrast to the _____ approach.

    skills, Piagetian

36. The method developed by Roger Brown to chart the child's progress from the two-word stage involves measuring the _____ _____ _____ _____ . You record a speech sample, count the number of _____ in each utterance, and calculate the mean.

    mean length of utterance, morphemes

37. During the preschool years, pronouncing _____ _____ may be a problem. Some phonological rules for pronouncing word endings may not be mastered until _____ years of age.

    consonant clusters, eight

38. The correct use of plurals, possessives, and *ed* for the past tense is evidence that children beyond the two-word stage know some _____ rules. Brown found that children learn the rule for _____ first, then the rule for _____ , and finally the rule for creating the _____ - _____ _____ .

morphological, plurals, possessives, third-person singular

39. Jean Berko's study of preschool and first-grade children demonstrated knowledge of morphological rules using _____ words. Her work provided an explanation for _____ of rules to irregular forms.

fictional, overgeneralization

40. The understanding and use of a *wh-* question requires not only the placing of a _____ word at the beginning of the sentence but also the _____ of the auxiliary verb. "How come is that man crying?" is an example of overgeneralization of the _____ rule.

***wh-*, inversion, inversion**

41. Akiyami's findings that American preschool children have more difficulty understanding _____ - _____ statements than _____ - _____ statements and that Japanese-speaking children show just the opposite problem suggest that how children learn _____ rules depends upon the language being learned.

true-negative, false-negative, syntactic

42. The speaking vocabulary of a six-year-old child has been estimated to be between _____ and _____ words. This means a new-word rate of _____ to _____ words per day between the ages of one and six. One way to learn words this fast is by _____ _____ ; that is, deriving clues to the meaning of a word by the way the word is used in a sentence.

8,000, 14,000, five, eight, fast mapping

43. One class of words not well understood until well into the childhood years are the _____ words, such as *more, less, above,* and *longer.* Two types of relational words that are difficult for preschoolers to understand are _____ _____ and _____ _____ .

relational, spatial adjectives, possessive verbs

44. The ability to talk about things not physically present is _____ . It appears about the age of _____ . About the age of _____ , evidence of sensitivity to the _____ of others in conversation is displayed by preschoolers' correct use of _____ and their use of different _____ of speech with a _____ - _____ - _____ child and a _____ .

displacement, three, four, needs, articles, styles, two-year-old, peer

45. Five-year-old children are deficient in the ability to make polite _____ , even though they can _____ them.

requests, understand

46. The most popular form of education before the first grade has been described as _____ - _____ because the emphasis is on providing the child with an _____ experience in learning. Children who have attended preschool demonstrate greater developmental _____ than children who have not attended such programs.

child-centered, individualized, maturity

47. The first attempt at compensatory education in the United States was _____ _____
_____ . The purpose of this program was to _____ the early environment of children from low-income families.

Project Head Start, enrich

48. The attempt to determine whether some types of enrichment programs worked better than others was called
_____ _____ _____ . The Oregon model of Project Follow Through produced better academic _____ and task _____ , but the students in the Far West Laboratory model were _____ less and were more _____ . The highly _____ University of Kansas model produced task _____ but less _____ .

Project Follow Through, performance, persistence, absent, independent, structured, persistence, independence

49. Lazar, Darlington, and their collaborators have found _____ long-term effects of _____ preschool education with _____ - _____ children.

positive, competent, low-income

50. One long-term follow-up study of Head Start students has found that _____ have shown a greater effect than _____ , who seem no better off.

males, females

Key Terms Matching Exercise

Match the Key Term on the left with the correct definition on the right.

____ 1. Montessori approach (LO–21, p. 256)
____ 2. deprivation dwarfism (LO–1, p. 259)
____ 3. phenomenistic stage (LO–4, p. 264)
____ 4. contagion stage (LO–4, p. 264)
____ 5. operations (LO–5, p. 269)
____ 6. symbolic function substage (LO–6, p. 270)

a. Internalized set of actions that allow the child to do mentally what before was done physically
b. Stage during which the preoperational child may explain the relation between sources of illness and the body in magiclike terms or believes that the relation is due to mere association
c. Growth retardation due to lack of affection
d. Stage during which the concrete operational child believes that there is at least temporal or spatial proximity between illness and its source
e. Approach to education in which children are encouraged to work independently, to complete tasks in a prescribed manner once started, and to put materials away in assigned places; teacher serves as facilitator
f. First part of preoperational period, during which the child begins to use mental representations to represent object not actually present

_____ 7. egocentrism (LO–7, p. 270)
_____ 8. three mountains task (LO–7, p. 270)
_____ 9. animism (LO–8, p. 274)
_____ 10. intuitive thought (LO–9, p. 275)
_____ 11. short-term memory (LO–12, p. 279)
_____ 12. long-term memory (LO–12, p. 279)

a. Task involving a display set up on a table; the child is seated on one chair at the table and a doll on one of three others; then the child is asked what the doll is seeing in each of several positions

b. Memory storage for considerable periods of time

c. Inability to distinguish between one's own perspective and the perspective of someone else

d. Belief that nonliving objects have lifelike qualities and are capable of action

e. Memory storage in which stimuli are stored and retrieved for up to 30 seconds, if not rehearsed

f. Part of the preoperational stage; characterized by beginning to reason about various matters and frequently asking questions

_____ 13. memory span task (LO–12, p. 279)
_____ 14. class inclusion reasoning (LO–13, p. 280)
_____ 15. syllogism (LO–13, p. 282)
_____ 16. mean length of utterance (MLU) (LO–14, p. 281)
_____ 17. overgeneralization (LO–16, p. 284)
_____ 18. relational words (LO–18, p. 286)

a. Comparing the relative number of objects in a subset with the number of objects in the larger set

b. Words that specify associations among objects, events, or people

c. Measure of short-term memory in which a short list of digits is presented at a rapid pace and the individual is asked to repeat the digits back

d. In language, the application of normative rules to exceptions

e. Type of reasoning problem, consisting of two premises and a conclusion

f. Measure of language development that uses morphemes as the unit of analysis

_____ 19. child-centered education (LO–20, p. 289)
_____ 20. compensatory education (LO–21, p. 290)
_____ 21. Project Head Start (LO–21, p. 290)
_____ 22. Project Follow Through (LO–21, p. 290)
_____ 23. task persistence (LO–21, p. 291)
_____ 24. independence (LO–21, p. 291)

a. Educational technique emphasizing the individual child
b. Child engaging in self-instruction over a specified period of time
c. A child or group of children engaging in a task without an adult
d. Programs to provide children from low-income families with an enriched environment, to put them on an equal level with children who are not disadvantaged
e. Program to see which of several different educational programs were effective
f. Program designed to give children from low-income families an enriched early environment to help them acquire skills and experiences necessary for success in school

Answers to Key Terms Matching Exercise

1. e	5. a	9. d	13. c	17. d	21. f
2. c	6. f	10. f	14. a	18. b	22. e
3. b	7. c	11. e	15. e	19. a	23. b
4. d	8. a	12. b	16. f	20. d	24. c

Self-Test A

Choose the best alternative.

1. During the preschool years, the average child gains about _____ inches and _____ pounds a year. (LO-1, p. 258)
   a. 2½/five to seven
   b. 3/three to five
   c. 3½/five to seven
   d. 4/six to eight

2. Deprivation dwarfism refers to children who have stunted growth because (LO–1, p. 259)
   a. they do not receive adequate nutrition.
   b. they are exposed to excessive levels of cigarette smoke.
   c. they are allowed unlimited access to caffeine.
   d. they do not receive enough affection.

3. Which of the following measures motor skills in children only up until the age of 2½ years? (LO–2, p. 259)
   a. Bayley Motor Scale
   b. Gesell Developmental Schedules
   c. Denver Developmental Screening Test
   d. DeOreo Fundamental Motor Skills Inventory

4. The American Heart Association recommends that the daily limit for calories from fat should be approximately (LO–3, p. 262)
   a. 15 percent.
   b. 20 percent.
   c. 35 percent.
   d. 40 percent.

5. Justin believes that, if he is bad, he will get sick. According to Bibace and Walsh, Justin is in which stage of thinking about health? (LO–4, p. 264)
   a. contagion
   b. phenomenistic
   c. animistic
   d. egocentric

6. According to Piaget, an internalized set of actions that are organized and conform to certain rules of logic are (LO–5, p. 269)
   a. structures.
   b. schemes.
   c. operations.
   d. symbols.

7. A child is asked to classify a set of shapes into groups that go together. She first puts a square down, then a circle on top of it for a head. Next, she chooses two triangles for the legs and two rectangles for the arms. This child is most likely in which of Piaget's stages of cognitive development? (LO–5, p. 270)
   a. sensorimotor
   b. preoperational
   c. concrete operational
   d. formal operational

8. A child drawing a picture makes a circle that she says is an airplane. This child is most likely in which stage? (LO–6, p. 270)
   a. Substage 5
   b. Substage 6
   c. symbolic function substage
   d. intuitive substage

9. A child believes that, if his mother comes into his room at night, she will be able to see his dream. This form of egocentrism is characteristic of which of Piaget's stages of cognitive development? (LO–7, p. 270)
   a. sensorimotor
   b. preoperational
   c. concrete operational
   d. formal operational

10. A child says that the moon follows her when she goes for a walk because the moon likes her. This is an example of (LO–8, p. 274)
    a. egocentrism.
    b. a classification skill.
    c. logical reasoning.
    d. animistic reasoning.

11. Timmy is asked if he can be a boy and an Egyptian at the same time. He replies, "No!" Timmy is in which of Piaget's stages of cognitive development? (LO–9, p. 275)
    a. concrete operational stage
    b. formal operational stage
    c. symbolic function substage
    d. substage of intuitive thought

12. Gelman presented preschool children with two plates—one with two mice and one with three mice. Gelman found that (LO–10, p. 277)
    a. her results supported Piaget's descriptions.
    b. her children did better at earlier ages than Piaget's descriptions.
    c. her children did worse at earlier ages than Piaget's descriptions.
    d. her children did worse than Piaget's descriptions, but her research was seriously flawed.

13. Research on visual scanning in young children has documented systematic visual scanning in children as young as (LO–11, p. 278)
    a. three years of age.
    b. four years of age.
    c. five years of age.
    d. six years of age.

14. Short-term memory is often measured by (LO–12, p. 279)
    a. having a child recall what he or she ate yesterday.
    b. a memory span task.
    c. a recognition task.
    d. an intermodal presentation of information.

15. The units of analysis in calculating a child's mean length of utterance (MLU) are (LO–14, p. 281)
    a. morphemes.
    b. phonemes.
    c. whole words.
    d. syllables.

16. Which of the following phonological sounds is mastered last? (LO–15, p. 284)
    a. *t*
    b. *d*
    c. *r*
    d. *m*

17. After singing a song for his parents, Michael says, "I singed that song good." The use of the word *singed* is an example of (LO–16, p. 284)
    a. overextension.
    b. underextension.
    c. creative generalization of rules.
    d. the use of relational words.

18. As he sees his father walk out, a child says, "Where Daddy is going?" This error is an example of what kind of development? (LO–17, p. 284)
    a. phonological
    b. syntactic
    c. semantic
    d. pragmatic

19. Which of the following pairs is most difficult for four-year-old children to understand? (LO–18, p. 286)
    a. big/small
    b. tall/short
    c. high/low
    d. wide/narrow

20. At what age do children begin to use definite and indefinite articles? (LO–19, p. 287)
    a. five
    b. seven
    c. eight
    d. two

Answers to Self-Test A

1. a	5. b	9. b	13. d	17. c
2. d	6. c	10. d	14. b	18. b
3. a	7. b	11. d	15. a	19. d
4. c	8. c	12. b	16. c	20. a

Self-Test B

Choose the best alternative.

21. What instrument can be used to assess motor development in three to six-year-old children? (LO–2, p. 259)
    a. Apgar scale
    b. Bayley Motor Scale
    c. Denver Developmental Screening Test
    d. Brazelton Neonatal Behavioral Assessment Scale

22. A diet rich in _____ increases the number of cells in the brains of rats. (LO–3, pp. 262–63)
    a. protein
    b. fat
    c. vitamins
    d. carbohydrates

23. A child who believes that she can get ill if she visits a sick friend is in which of the following stages? (LO–4, p. 264)
    a. preoperational stage
    b. formal operational stage
    c. phenomenistic stage
    d. contagion stage

24. Which of the following characterizes preoperational thought? (LO–5, pp. 269–70)
    a. reversible thought
    b. coordination between action and perception
    c. decentration
    d. symbolic functioning

25. Susie uses words and pictures to stand for objects that are not present. According to Piaget, she is in the (LO–6, p. 270)
    a. concrete operational stage.
    b. symbolic function substage.
    c. substage of intuitive thought.
    d. sensorimotor stage.

26. Mark is describing a shape to a friend so that his friend can pick out an object of the same shape. Mark says, "It looks like my mommy's hat." This is an example of (LO–7, p. 270)
    a. egocentric thinking.
    b. animistic reasoning.
    c. logical reasoning.
    d. decentration.

27. Karen thinks that thunder roars because the clouds are angry. She is displaying (LO–8, p. 274)
    a. egocentric thinking.
    b. animistic reasoning.
    c. logical reasoning.
    d. decentration.

28. Jane believes that people made the lakes and the rivers, but she cannot tell why she believes that. Jane is most likely in which substage? (LO–9, p. 275)
    a. substage of tertiary circular reactions
    b. symbolic function substage
    c. substage of intuitive thought
    d. substage of internalization of schemes

29. The understanding that a glass of milk remains the same if it is poured from a tall, thin glass into a short, fat glass is (LO–10, p. 276)
    a. egocentrism.
    b. animism.
    c. conservation.
    d. classification.

30. Preschool children are apt to attend most to _____ stimulus features when performing a task. (LO–11, pp. 278–79)
    a. salient
    b. relevant
    c. critical
    d. Both b and c are correct.

31. The memory span in a seven-year-old is about (LO–12, p. 279)
    a. two digits.
    b. three digits.
    c. four digits.
    d. five digits.

32. Which of the following tasks has been analyzed into component steps by Trabasso? (LO–13, pp. 280–81)
    a. memory span task
    b. class inclusion task
    c. animism problem
    d. conservation of liquid

33. One of the most useful measures of language development is (LO–14, p. 281)
    a. semantic development.
    b. the use of pragmatics.
    c. the mean length of utterance.
    d. the onset of babbling.

34. After many years, Angie can finally pronounce the word *sunshine* correctly, instead of saying "shunshine." This illustrates what kind of development? (LO–15, p. 284)
    a. phonological
    b. morphological
    c. syntactic
    d. semantic

35. Learning to use *s* to form a plural structure is an example of what kind of development? (LO–16, p. 284)
    a. phonological
    b. morphological
    c. syntactic
    d. semantic

36. After racing down the street with his uncle, Peter says, "I runned very, very fast!" The use of the term *runned* is an example of what kind of development? (LO–16, p. 284)
    a. phonological
    b. morphological
    c. syntactic
    d. semantic

37. Donna answers the phone when her father calls. When she realizes that it is her father, she says, "You don't come home. Why you don't come home?" This speech sample is a good example of what kind of development? (LO–17, p. 284)
   a. syntactic
   b. phonological
   c. pragmatic
   d. semantic

38. The speaking vocabulary of a six-year-old is estimated to range from (LO–18, p. 286)
   a. 1,000 to 2,000 words.
   b. 7,000 to 12,000 words.
   c. 8,000 to 14,000 words.
   d. 10,000 to 20,000 words.

39. At around what age do children begin to show sensitivity to the communicative needs of others? (LO–19, p. 287)
   a. two
   b. four
   c. six
   d. nine

40. Which approach to compensatory education produced children who performed best on achievement tests? (LO–21, p. 291)
   a. parent education programs
   b. affective-centered programs
   c. Piagetian-based programs
   d. direct instruction programs

Answers to Self-Test B

21. c	25. b	29. c	33. c	37. a
22. a	26. a	30. a	34. a	38. c
23. d	27. b	31. d	35. b	39. b
24. d	28. c	32. b	36. b	40. d

Questions to Stimulate Thought

1. Is physical growth determined by genetic or environmental factors?
2. What are the implications of the nature of preoperational thought for teaching in the early elementary grades?
3. Can the drawbacks (relative to adult thinking) of preoperational thought be explained in information processing terms (that is, perception, attention, memory, and so on)?
4. Is language learned?
5. Is there a biological basis for language?
6. What might happen if a child had to acquire two different languages at the same time?
7. What are the assumptions of attempts at compensatory education?
8. Does (can) compensatory education work? Why or why not?

Research Project

This project is designed to give you exposure to the kinds of errors children make when they are acquiring language. Pair up with another student in the class. One of you will act as the experimenter while the other will act as the observer. You will test two different children—one who is two years of age, the other five years of age—on three different tasks evaluating their understanding and use of the passive construction. You will present an act-out task, an imitation task, and a production task. The sentences and task descriptions follow. Use the data sheet provided for recording your observations and then answer the questions that follow.

Sentences for All Tasks

a. The car hit the truck.
b. The dog was kicked by the cat.
c. The boy was bit by the dog.
d. The boy hit the cat.
e. The truck was hit by the car.
f. The cow stepped on the horse.
g. The cat kicked the dog.
h. The cat was hit by the boy.
i. The dog bit the boy.
j. The horse was stepped on by the cow.

Task Descriptions

1. **Act-out task:** Have the following objects available: a toy car and truck, a toy doll, and a toy horse, cow, dog, and cat. Read the sentences one at a time and have the child act out the sentences with the toys.
2. **Imitation task:** Read each of the sentences to each child and have the child repeat the sentences back to you.
3. **Production task:** Use the toys to perform the actions in each of the sentences for the child. Ask the child to tell you what happened, starting with the first noun in the sentence. For instance, for sentence e, roll the car along so that it hits the truck and then ask the child to tell you what happened, beginning with the truck.

Data Sheet

Task	Child 1 Sex _____ Age _____		Child 2 Sex _____ _____Age	
Act-Out Task				
Sentence a				
Sentence b				
Sentence c				
Sentence d				
Sentence e				

Sentence f

Sentence g

Sentence h

Sentence i

Sentence j

Imitation Task

Sentence a

Sentence b

Sentence c

Sentence d

Sentence e

Sentence f

Sentence g

Sentence h

Sentence i

Sentence j

Production Task

Sentence a

Sentence b

Sentence c

Sentence d

Sentence e

Sentence f

Sentence g

Sentence h

Sentence i

Sentence j

Questions

1. What did the two-year-old child do on the act-out task? the imitation task? the production task? Was performance on one task better than on the others? If so, which? What sorts of errors appeared in the act-out task? the imitation task? the production task? Were the errors similar in the various tasks?
2. What did the five-year-old child do on the act-out task? the imitation task? the production task? Was performance on one task better than on the others? If so, which? What sorts of errors appeared in the act-out task? the imitation task? the production task? Were the errors similar in the various tasks?
3. Compare the two children. What differences, if any, did you see in their performance on these three tasks? How would you account for the differences? What is the nature of language learning that seems to be occurring during this time?
4. What criticisms could be leveled at the procedures you used in this demonstration? For example, do you think that each task should have had different questions?

---

8 Social and Personality Development in Early Childhood

Learning Objectives

After studying this chapter, you should be able to:

1. Define the authoritarian, authoritative, permissive-indulgent, and permissive-indifferent parenting styles and explain their effects on the child's subsequent social behavior. (pp. 301–3)
2. Compare and contrast sibling and parent-child relationships. (pp. 303–4)
3. Explain the influence of birth order on development. (p. 305)
4. Describe the development of sibling interactions and the older sibling's role as teacher. (p. 305)
5. Describe the effect of a working mother on the child's social and personality development. (p. 306)
6. Describe the effects that divorce can have on the child's social and personality development. (pp. 307–9)

7. Describe the role that peers play in the development of social competence and perspective taking and the changes in peer relationships in early childhood. (pp. 310–12)

8. Describe how the worlds of parents and peers coordinate yet are distinct. (pp. 312–14)

9. Define and explain four functions of play. (p. 314)

10. Describe onlooker, parallel, associative, and cooperative play and rituals. (pp. 315–17)

11. Describe the cognitive factors associated with pretend play. (pp. 317–19)

12. Explain how play is assessed and play's relationship to cognition and language. (pp. 319–20)

13. List the advantages and disadvantages of television. (pp. 320–23)

14. Describe television's role as a social agent, including the social context in which it is watched. (pp. 323–24)

15. Explain the relationship between the formal features of television and attention to and memory of the content. (pp. 324–25)

16. List two characteristics of the "I" (knower, active observer) and the "me" (product of observing process, what is known), define self-concept and self-esteem and relate them to the "I" and "me," and provide one reason why this issue is important for understanding the development of personality. (pp. 327–29)

17. Define the concepts of sex role, sexual or gender identity, and androgyny, and explain androgyny's relationship to an understanding of sex-role development. (pp. 329–35)

18. Describe the role of hormones in sex-role development during the prenatal period. (pp. 329–30)

19. Describe the cognitive factors that might be involved in the formation of sex roles. (pp. 330–31)

20. Describe how parents influence children's sex-role development. (p. 331)

21. Explain how the environment, including parents, peers, and teachers, influences the formation of sex roles. (pp. 331–34)

22. Describe both the issues and the efficacy of changing sex-typed behavior. (pp. 334–35)

23. Define moral development. (p. 336)

24. Describe Piaget's theory of moral reasoning and define the moral realist and the moral autonomist. (pp. 336–38)

25. Distinguish the study of moral behavior from the study of moral reasoning and describe how social learning theory might explain them. (pp. 338–39)

26. Describe the sources and effects of guilt. (p. 339)

27. Define altruism and explain its relationship to empathy and the part that role-taking and perspective-taking skills play in each. (pp. 339–40)

Summary

Four types of parenting styles are associated with different aspects of the child's social behavior. Authoritarian parents are restrictive, punitive, and controlling. Their children tend to be anxious about social comparison, to fail to initiate activity, and to be ineffective in social interaction. Authoritative parents encourage the child to be independent, place limits and demands on the child, demonstrate a high degree of warmth toward the child, and engage in extensive verbal give-and-take. Their children tend to be socially competent, self-reliant, and socially responsible. Permissive-indulgent parents are highly involved in their children's lives but do not control or set limits on their behavior. Their children tend to show a disregard for rules and regulations. Permissive-indifferent parents are uninvolved in their children's lives and do not control them. Their children tend to exhibit lack of self-control.

Sibling relationships are generally more negative than parent-child relationships. Siblings may have a stronger socializing influence on a child than parents in such areas as dealing with peers, coping with difficult teachers, and discussing taboo subjects. Toddlers with a younger sibling place increased demands on the mother or engage in behavior that will attract the mother's attention. The older sibling may begin to act aggressively toward the younger sibling when the younger sibling is about one year old. During infancy and toddlerhood, more sibling rivalry appears between cross-sexed siblings than same-sexed siblings. This trend may reverse in elementary school. In general, firstborn children receive more attention from the mother than later-born children. A younger sibling tends to observe and imitate an older sibling, while an older sibling generally does not do this with a younger sibling.

Divorce is common in the American culture, and 40 to 50 percent of children born in the 1970s will spend some time in a single-parent home. Research suggests that separations and divorces have fewer negative effects on the child than living in a family with conflict. However, the time immediately after the divorce is still conflict-ridden for many families, and children receive less adequate parenting than before the divorce. The support systems available, the age of the child at the time of the divorce, and the sex of the child with respect to the sex of the custodial parent are all variables that can affect the outcome of the divorce on the child. Remarriage often occurs and can bring with it many different kinds of families, with attending complications and conflicts. Stepparent and stepchild relationships are often conflict-ridden. Many divorced women go back to work. Children with working mothers (divorced or otherwise) must help out, and many are unsupervised for large segments of time. This may provide an impetus for development or be a negative experience.

Peers are children of about the same age or behavioral level. Social contacts and aggression are characteristic of same-age peers. Peer groups allow the child to receive feedback about his or her abilities relative to others of the same age. The presence of peers can be used as a therapeutic technique to allow social learning in deficient individuals or socially deprived individuals. Cross-cultural research has observed aggressiveness, prosocial activity, and sociable behavior in peer relations in six different cultures. Children who have more frequent peer contacts generally score higher on perspective-taking tasks. Peer relationships are different from interactions with adults.

Play is an important activity that may serve several functions, including affiliation with peers, tension release, advances in cognitive development, and exploration. Play therapy has been used in therapeutic settings with young children to provide a medium through which the therapist can learn about the child's conflicts and methods of coping with them.

Parten described six categories of play: unoccupied play, solitary play, onlooker play, parallel play, associative play, and cooperative play. Younger children engage more in solitary and parallel play, and older children engage more in cooperative and associative play. Children also engage in pretend play, trying out many different adult roles. Pretend play is a function of the child's level of cognitive development. It does not appear until the end of the sensorimotor period, becomes more social during the preoperational period, and declines and is replaced by rule-governed play during the concrete operational period. Younger children use toys as part of the description of pretend play, while older children describe pretend play according to actions performed.

Children watch a great deal of television. Television has two primary functions: entertainment and communication. Television provides the child with information about a wider variety of views and knowledge than may be available from the child's immediate environment. It also exposes children to violence and aggression, which they may then imitate. Because it is a pictorial medium, it may interfere with the use of the printed media. But television can also teach children that it is better to behave in prosocial rather than antisocial ways. Children also learn from commercials, which are often about high-sugar food products. Certain features of television, such as animation, unusual voices, and sound effects, are associated with child-oriented content, and children both attend to such material more and remember its content better than material that does not include such features.

The development of the self, independence, and identity are interrelated. The self is particularly important in understanding development in the humanistic view. A distinction has been made between the "I" (the self as knower) and the "me" (the self as object). Research on memory has found that information that is self-generated is remembered better than other information. Also, information that is encoded in terms of the self is remembered better than information not so encoded. Initially, the view of the self focuses on external characteristics. At about age six or seven, children begin to describe themselves in terms of psychological traits.

Sex-role development is a multi-faceted issue, with biological, cognitive, and environmental influences. A number of biological arguments have been offered to explain differences in males and females. Erikson has argued that psychological differences between males and females come from anatomical differences between the two groups; that is, that anatomy is destiny. Thus, he believes that, because of genital structure, males are more intrusive and aggressive, while females are more inclusive and passive. A second biological argument is that hormonal levels, particularly of testosterone, are responsible for aggression and that, since males have more testosterone, they are more aggressive than females. Further evidence of the influence of hormones comes from a study of children of mothers who received androgen (a male sex hormone) during pregnancy. The daughters played more like boys than girls, and the sons engaged in more rough-and-tumble play than average. However, these children were being treated with cortisone, and the cortisone treatment may have affected their behavior rather than the prenatal exposure to androgen.

Cognitive factors are also important in sex-role development. According to Kohlberg, children are trying to make sense of their world and create categories that simplify information processing. Sex categories allow the child to generate expectations about another person on the basis of the person's sex and to also develop expectations about his or her own appropriate behavior. Sexist language, such as the use of the pronoun *he* when referring to everyone, may limit or constrain thinking in those situations. Developmental research has found that children do not have strong beliefs about sex-appropriate behavior until they develop gender constancy, the recognition that gender will not change. They become very rigid in what they consider appropriate behavior for boys and girls in the early concrete operational period and become more flexible several years later.

Toy preferences are demonstrated in young children prior to gender constancy and are possibly tied to environmental influences. Fathers, who play an important role in sex typing both boys and girls, are more likely to behave differently toward sons and daughters than mothers are. Parents often encourage boys and girls to engage in different kinds of play behaviors, even in infancy. Parents treat boys and girls differently, allowing boys more freedom and protecting girls more. Peers also play a role in socializing sex-typed behavior by criticizing those who play in cross-sex activities and reinforcing those who play in sex-appropriate activities. In elementary school, female teachers reinforce feminine behaviors in both boys and girls. Attempts have been made, based on both psychoanalytic and behavioral models, to change the behavior of gender-deviant or gender-rigid children, most often males. Behavior modification involving parents and teachers has had the best long-term results.

Morality concerns the rules and conventions about what people should do in their interactions with other people. Several different theories have emerged to explain how this develops in children. Piaget viewed moral development in two stages. The stage of moral realism is associated with younger children. In this stage, children evaluate good or bad based on the consequences of behavior, without regard for intention. The child sees rules as unchangeable and given from a higher authority and believes that punishment is mechanically connected to transgressions. In Piaget's second stage of moral development—moral autonomy—the child believes that the intention of the actor is the primary consideration in evaluating an action as good or bad. The child understands that rules are conventional and open to negotiation. In Piaget's view, it is in the peer group where social understanding comes about.

Moral behavior has primarily been studied by social learning theorists, who invoke the processes of reinforcement, punishment, and imitation to explain how children learn moral behavior. A key ingredient of moral development from the social learning perspective is the child's ability to resist temptation and to develop self-control. Cognitive rationales are more effective in getting a child to resist temptation than threats or punishments alone. A second behavior that has been examined is delay of gratification, which is closely related to resistance to temptation. Mischel believes that self-control, including the ability to delay gratification, is influenced by cognitive factors. The child can instruct himself or herself to be more patient. Cognitive social learning theory assumes that cognitive processes determine moral competence and that reinforcement and incentives determine moral performance.

Moral feelings are also an important aspect of moral development. Guilt can be instrumental in preventing the performance of a behavior or in making reparations after a transgression. Feelings of empathy for the distress of another appear early and may lead a young child to attempt to alleviate the other's distress. Altruistic behavior— behavior that involves attempts to be helpful to another—can appear as early as two years of age, although it increases with development. It may be motivated by the child's developing feelings of empathy. The appropriateness of the altruistic response is a function of the child's level of cognitive development and, in particular, may be related to the child's ability to take the perspective of another and realize what will comfort someone else.

Guided Review

You may want to look at the answers to the "Guided Review" statements as you read, or you may want to use the exercise as a form of self-test by covering up the answers below the statements with a sheet of paper and not consulting them until you have attempted to fill in the blanks of each statement.

1. _____ parents are restrictive, have a _____ orientation, and place _____ and _____ on the child. There is very little verbal _____-_____-_____.

   Authoritarian, punitive, limits, controls, give-and-take

2. Authoritarian parenting is associated with the following social behaviors of the child: anxiety about social _____ , _____ to initiate activity, and _____ social interactions.

   comparisons, failure, ineffective

3. The _____ parenting style encourages _____ within limits. There is extensive verbal _____ - _____ - _____ and a high degree of _____ and _____ .

   authoritative, independence, give-and-take, warmth, nurturance

4. Authoritative parenting produces children with _____ social skills, particularly _____ - _____ and social _____ .

   good, self-reliance, responsibility

5. According to Maccoby and Martin, authoritarian parents are _____ and _____ , as well as _____ , _____ , and _____ - _____ . This style is also called _____ _____ .

   demanding, controlling, rejecting, unresponsive, parent-centered, power assertive

6. According to Maccoby and Martin, authoritative parents are _____ and _____ . However, they are also _____ , _____ , and _____ - _____ . Maccoby and Martin call this style _____ - _____ .

   demanding, controlling, accepting, responsive, child-centered, authoritative-reciprocal

7. According to Maccoby and Martin, the permissive-indulgent parent is _____ , but _____ and _____ . Neglecting parents are undemanding but _____ . Maccoby and Martin call this _____ - _____ parenting.

   undemanding, accepting, responsive, rejecting, permissive-indifferent

8. Permissive-indulgent children grow up showing a disregard for _____ . Permissive-indifferent children grow up with a lack of _____ - _____ .

   rules, self-control

9. During the first year of a child's life, the interaction moves from an emphasis on _____ to include more play and visual-vocal exchanges. During children's second and third years, parents often handle discipline issues by _____ _____ . As the child grows older, parents increasingly use _____ to deal with the child. Maccoby believes that these changes are linked to the _____ of the child.

   caretaking, physical manipulation, reasoning, maturation

10. The relations of siblings with their parents are generally _____ than their relations with each other. One pervasive characteristic of sibling relationships is _____ .

    better, competition

11. Siblings can be a stronger socializing influence than parents. This is especially true in such areas as _____ interaction, coping with difficult _____ , and _____ subjects.

    peer, teachers, taboo

12. The appearance of a younger sibling _____ the amount of _____ that mothers give to the older sibling and may stimulate an increase in the older child's _____ behavior. Toward the end of the first year of the younger sibling's life, the older sibling may sometimes begin to act _____ toward the younger sibling.

    decreases, attention, disruptive, aggressively

13. One constant of sibling interaction is _____ between the siblings. It tends to _____ during the elementary school years.
    rivalry, increase

14. Birth order accounts for only a _____ proportion of the variance in the prediction of social competence. However, it appears that mothers do give more _____ to firstborn children. This may be explained by differences in _____ surrounding the arrival of the two children.
    small, attention, novelty

15. Older siblings are often effective _____ for their younger siblings. Older _____ are more competent than older _____ at teaching.
    models, sisters, brothers

16. About _____ percent of children born during the 1970s will spend some part of their childhood in a single-parent home. About _____ percent of all American families are so-called blended families. There has been a slight _____ in the tendency of fathers to engage in _____ - _____ duties.
    50, 11, increase, child-rearing

17. One longitudinal study found that full-time mothering resulted in adolescents who were more competent _____ but who were also more _____ , and _____ . An educated, nonworking mother may discourage _____ in her children and may inject more _____ into the parent-child relationship than the child can handle.
    intellectually, fearful, conforming, independence, mothering

18. Hoffman argues that the working mother is a more _____ model for socialization of today's child than that of a full-time mother. This is especially true for _____ .
    realistic, daughters

19. Children of divorced parents are treated _____ by teachers. In one study, they were rated more _____ on _____ , _____ , _____ , and ability to cope with _____ .
    differently, negatively, happiness, emotional adjustment, stress

20. _____ has more influence than family structure on the child's development. Divorce may not solve the conflict problem because, in the first year after a divorce, conflict usually _____ . Adjustment problems for children are particularly evident in the _____ year after a divorce.
    Conflict, increases, first

21. The _____ of the relationship between the ex-spouses predicts the nature of the child's _____ in divorced families.
    quality, adjustment

22. Divorce when children are _____ has a more negative effect on development than when the children are _____ . The mother needing to go to work and not being able to afford quality day care may interfere with _____ . _____ children may blame themselves for the divorce and have unrealistic hopes for their parents' _____ . According to Santrock and Warshak, children living with the _____ - _____ _____ are more socially competent than those with the opposite custody arrangement.
    infants, older, attachment, Preschool, reconciliation, same-sex parent

23. People of about the same age are _____ , although same _____ _____ might be a better definition.
peers, behavioral level

24. Mixed-age groups produce more _____ and _____ behavior than _____ groups. _____ _____ and _____ are more characteristic of same-age groups. According to Hartup, an important function of the peer group is to provide a source of _____ and _____ about the world outside the family.
dominant, altruistic, peer, Social contacts, aggression, information, comparison

25. Work with animals suggests that peers can provide _____ for arrested social development. Similar work with human infant isolates indicates that the technique _____ with humans. A case history compiled by _____ _____ on a group of six World War II orphans indicated that peer associations alone provided protection against _____ and _____ .
therapy, works, Anna Freud, delinquency, psychosis

26. One cross-cultural study indicated that in _____ different cultures, _____ , _____ , and _____ were rarely seen among peers but were observed in parent-child interactions. _____ , _____ activity, and _____ behavior were usually seen in peer interactions.
six, dependency, nurturance, intimacy, Aggressiveness, prosocial, sociable

27. The ability to take someone else's point of view is called _____ _____ . In Norway and Hungary, the children from farm regions were _____ at a visual perspective-taking task than children from villages and towns.
perspective taking, poorer

28. The frequency of _____ and _____ peer interactions increases throughout early childhood. However, the proportion of _____ exchanges _____ . In the classroom, the problem of aggressive behavior can be addressed using _____ _____ , although this approach works better with _____ , _____ children than with those who are _____ _____ .
positive, negative, aggressive, decreases, behavior modification, withdrawn, isolated, acting out

29. Play increases the probability that children will _____ with each other. According to Freud, the function of play is _____ reduction. According to Piaget, play allows the child to _____ his or her cognitive skills. According to Berlyne, play satisfies an _____ drive present in all people.
affiliate, tension, practice, exploratory

30. _____ _____ developed different categories of play, based on observations of children in free play at nursery school. When in _____ play, a child may stand in one spot, look around the room, or perform random movements with no goal. A kind of play in which a child plays alone and independently of those around him or her is called _____ play. _____ play describes a child who is essentially watching others play. In _____ play, a child plays alone but with toys similar to those being used by others. _____ play is characterized by social interaction and little or no organization. If group identity and organization are added, associative play becomes _____ play.
Mildred Parten, unoccupied, solitary, Onlooker, parallel, Associative, cooperative

31. Observations more recent than Parten's have found that children engage in _____ associative and cooperative play than in the 1930s. The bulk of Parten's observations, however, were _____ .

    less, replicated

32. A form of spontaneous play that involves controlled repetition is called a _____ . The rituals of three-year-olds are _____ , but those of five-year-olds are more _____ .

    ritual, longer, complex

33. Pretend play appears at about _____ months of age. During pretend play, the child may try out several different _____ . It is at about this time that children develop imaginary _____ . The incidence of pretend play peaks between _____ and _____ years of age.

    18, roles, playmates, five, six

34. Valid assessment of play will require an _____ definition of the phenomenon, a _____ setting in which to test, and a _____ interpretation of play content.

    operational, standardized, standardized

35. With development, children move from a _____ conception of pretend play to an _____ conception.

    material, ideational

36. For Piaget, pretend play signals the appearance of a special function, called the _____ function. This function overlays _____ on _____ patterns, _____ , or _____ .

    semiotic, meanings, sound, gestures, images

37. _____ and _____ are television's primary functions.

    Communication, entertainment

38. Elementary school children watch as much as _____ hours of television each day. Recently, two- to five-year-old children have been found to watch television about _____ hours per week. Systematic viewing apparently begins by _____ years of age.

    6, 28, 2½

39. The use of _____ media is correlated with television watching. Its use increases until the age of _____ and then decreases. The correlation between use of pictorial and printed media is _____ .

    pictorial, 12, low

40. Prime time television averages _____ violent acts per hour. As recently as the early 1970s, _____ _____ _____ contained as many as 25 acts of violence per hour.

    5, Saturday morning cartoons

41. Children who view violent cartoons exhibit _____ violent acts than children who view cartoons with the violence removed.

    more

42. The amount of television viewing by children is _____ correlated with the socioeconomic status and educational level of the parents.

    inversely

43. Children learn early that certain formal features of television indicate certain kinds of content. For example, animation indicates _____ - _____ content. The formal features help to promote both _____ to and _____ for messages presented.

    child-oriented, attention, memory

44. William James distinguished the "I" as _____ from the "me," the things _____ . _____ - _____ and _____ - _____ are viewed as the latter.
observer, known, Self-concept, self-esteem

45. The psychological tradition that places the strongest emphasis on the self and the self-concept is _____ . Humanistic psychologists believe that how the child perceives himself or herself—the child's _____ _____ - _____ —is the key to personality. These psychologists take the _____ approach to the study of children's development.
humanism, global self-concept, phenomenological

46. The self as knower is reflected in the finding that information that is _____ - _____ is better remembered than information that is passively encountered. _____ - _____ in the coding of information is a very efficient retrieval cue.
self-generated, Self-reference

47. Children as young as _____ years old have some idea that they have a _____ self to which others do not have access.
three, private

48. During early childhood, children describe themselves in terms of _____ features. The use of psychological traits in self-description does not appear until at least _____ years of age.
external, six

49. According to Freud, human behavior is related to _____ process. According to Erikson, psychological differences stem from _____ differences. Erikson's view is called the "_____ is _____" view.
reproductive, anatomical, anatomy, destiny

50. In a study by Ehrhardt, the female offspring of mothers who had been given androgen during the gestation period had more _____ characteristics than their unaffected sisters. The male offspring of mothers who had been given androgen during the gestation period displayed more _____ - _____ - _____ play than their unexposed brothers. However, this study has been criticized because the children required lifelong treatment with _____ , which has the side effect of producing a high activity level. It is also possible that the knowledge that the children were androgenized altered the _____ of the parents and peers and created a self-fulfilling prophecy.
masculine, rough-and-tumble, cortisone, expectations

51. According to Kohlberg, the categories of male and female become relatively stable by the age of _____ . After self-categorization, the child attempts to make his or her behavior _____ with the category.
six, consistent

52. One conclusion from the Hyde studies is that the use of *he* as the gender neutral form influences the formation of a _____ _____ in children. An alternative explanation of Hyde's data is that even the youngest children have had many years of hearing *he* and *they* used as equivalents. Therefore, sexist thought might be seen as a product of experience with sexist _____ .
gender schema, language

53. Fathers are more likely to treat sons and daughters _____ . Boys from father-absent homes display more _____ behaviors than those from father-present homes. This might be explained by the single mothers being _____ and _____ about their sons' independence.
differently, feminine, overprotective, apprehensive

54. Different types of play activities are _____ in boys and girls. Parents play more actively with and respond more positively to physical activity in _____ . With increasing age, _____ are less likely to be allowed by parents to be away from home without supervision.
encouraged, boys, girls

55. Children who engage in sex-inappropriate activity are usually _____ or _____ by their peers. Those who engage in sex-appropriate activities are _____ by their peers.
criticized, ignored, rewarded

56. In elementary school, the sexes tend to _____ themselves. There appears to be a social class difference in the extent to which the sexes are segregated during play, with working- or lower-class children exhibiting _____ sex segregation.
segregate, more

57. Of the two sexes, _____ are the recipients of more scolding and other forms of negative attention from _____ .
boys, teachers

58. Boys who play with mostly feminine sex-typed toys may be judged _____ _____ . Parents have been taught _____ _____ techniques, and attempts have been made to teach gender-deviant boys _____ skills. These interventions have led to normal sex-typed behavior for as long as _____ years.
gender deviant, behavior modification, athletic, three

59. Attempts to teach children in school about androgyny have been most successful when _____ are involved. However, the question of teaching children to violate socially approved behavior patterns raises an _____ question.
girls, ethical

60. During the 18-month to three-year-old age period, children show a great deal of interest in _____ - _____ _____ and also begin to _____ themselves and others according to gender. By the time they are three, children know the _____ _____ for toys, games, clothing, and so forth. During the three- to seven-year-old age period, children increasingly enjoy being with _____ - _____ peers and understand gender _____ . _____ consistently hold the more stereotypical views about gender.
sex-typed play, classify, sex stereotypes, same-sex, constancy, Boys

61. The rules and conventions about how people should behave in their interactions with other people are called _____ development. The three domains of moral reasoning involve how children _____ about rules for ethical conduct, how they _____ in the face of temptation, and their _____ after a moral decision.
moral, reason, behave, feelings

62. According to Piaget, the more primitive stage in the development of moral reasoning is the stage of _____ _____ . For the moral realist, the _____ of a behavior determine its morality. The _____ believes that the rules are handed down by an all-powerful _____ and that they are unchangeable. The moral realist also believes in _____ _____ if a rule is broken.
moral realism, consequences, realist, authority, immanent justice

63. The child functioning in Piaget's moral reasoning stage of _____ _____ has at least some formal operational characteristics. The moral autonomist considers the _____ of the actor. He or she also understands that rules are socially agreed upon _____ that are subject to change. The moral autonomist realizes that a transgression must be _____ to result in punishment.
moral autonomy, intentions, conventions, witnessed

64. Piaget believed that the increased social understanding that the child develops comes about through the mutual give-and-take of _____ _____ .
peer relationships

65. The study of moral reasoning identifies what children _____ is right and wrong. The study of moral _____ investigates what children actually do in a situation.
believe, behavior

66. The reinforcement of behavior consistent with laws and social customs is likely to result in that behavior being _____ . The effectiveness of reward and punishment depends upon the _____ of their application. The effectiveness of a model depends upon the _____ of the model.
repeated, consistency, characteristics

67. From the social learning perspective, an important component of the development of moral development is the child's ability to _____ _____ . The ability to resist temptation has been tied to _____ of _____ . _____ - _____ is involved both in the ability to resist temptation and the ability to delay gratification.
resist temptation, delay, gratification, Self-control

68. The effectiveness of punishment in developing children's ability to resist temptation is enhanced by a _____ _____ , such as explaining the consequences of an act.
cognitive rationale

69. The understanding of another's feelings is called _____ . This is the _____ side of moral development.
empathy, positive

70. According to psychoanalytic thought, guilt is _____ turned inward and comes from the part of the personality structure called the _____ . Psychoanalysts also believe that guilt-prone individuals avoid moral transgressions to avoid _____ .
hostility, superego, anxiety

71. Behaviors such as _____ are described as altruistic. Children as young as _____ years old may display altruistic behavior by, for example, showing empathy toward a hurt child. In older children, _____ behavior usually follows the show of empathy.
sharing, two, helping or altruistic

72. The understanding that other people have feelings and perceptions that are different from one's own refers to _____ - _____ and _____ - _____ skills. Children who have well-developed role-taking skills display more _____ behavior than children with less well-developed skills.
role-taking, perspective-taking, altruistic

Key Terms Matching Exercise

Match the Key Term on the left with the correct definition on the right.

—— 1. authoritarian parenting (LO–1, p. 301)
—— 2. authoritative parenting (LO–1, p. 301)
—— 3. permissive-indulgent parenting (LO–1, p. 302)
—— 4. permissive-indifferent parenting (LO–1, p. 302)
—— 5. siblings (LO–2, p. 303)
—— 6. peers (LO–7, p. 310)

a. Brothers and sisters
b. Parenting style in which the parents are very uninvolved in their children's lives and place no limits on their behavior
c. Parenting style in which the parents are highly involved in their children's lives but do not control or place limits on their children's behavior
d. Children about the same age; can also be children who interact at about the same behavioral level
e. Parenting style in which the parents are restrictive, punitive, and controlling, and engage in little verbal give-and-take with the child
f. Parenting style in which the parents encourage independence but still place limits, demands, and controls on the child; there is extensive verbal give-and-take, and the parents demonstrate much warmth toward the child

---

—— 7. perspective taking (LO–7, p. 311)
—— 8. play therapy (LO–9, p. 314)
—— 9. unoccupied play (LO–10, p. 315)
—— 10. solitary play (LO–10, p. 315)
—— 11. onlooker play (LO–10, p. 315)
—— 12. parallel play (LO–10, p. 316)

a. Use of play to allow a child to work off frustrations and to allow the therapist to analyze the child's conflicts and methods of coping with them
b. Type of play in which the child plays alone and independently of those around him or her
c. Ability to take someone else's point of view
d. Type of play in which the child plays alone, with toys like those other children are using or in a manner that mimics the behavior of other playing children, but does not actually play with the other children
e. Type of play in which the child watches other children playing
f. Type of play in which the child does not engage in ordinary play and may be looking around the room or performing random movements with no goal

____ 13. associative play (LO–10, p. 316)
____ 14. cooperative play (LO–10, p. 316)
____ 15. ritual (LO–10, p. 316)
____ 16. pretend play (LO–11, p. 317)
____ 17. semiotic function (LO–12, p. 320)

a. Type of play in which children transform the physical environment into a symbol and try out many different roles
b. Type of play in which children play together but with little or no organization
c. Ability to assign meaning to arbitrary sound patterns, gestures, or images
d. A form of spontaneous play involving controlled repetition
e. Children playing together with a sense of group identity and organized activity

____ 18. humanism (LO–16, p. 327)
____ 19. global self-concept (LO–16, p. 327)
____ 20. phenomenological approach (LO–16, p. 327)
____ 21. self as knower (LO–16, p. 328)
____ 22. moral development (LO–23, p. 336)
____ 23. moral realism (LO–24, p. 336)

a. How an individual generally perceives the self; seen as a key organizing principle of personality in the humanistic view
b. View of psychology that places a strong emphasis on the role of the self and self-concept as central to understanding the child's development
c. A view of the self as the active observer
d. Development that concerns rules and conventions about what people should do in their interactions with other people
e. Piaget's term for the first stage of moral development; rightness or goodness of behavior judged by considering the consequences of behavior, not intentions; rules are believed to be unchangeable and handed down by all-powerful authorities; there is a belief that, if a rule is broken, punishment will be meted out immediately
f. View that the individual's perception of the world is more important in understanding an individual's development than actual behavior

_____ 24. moral autonomy (LO–24, p. 336)

_____ 25. immanent justice (LO–26, p. 336)

_____ 26. empathy (LO–26, p. 339)

_____ 27. guilt (LO–26, p. 339)

_____ 28. altruism (LO–27, p. 339)

_____ 29. role-taking or perspective-taking skills
(LO–27, p. 339)

a. Belief that, if a rule is broken, punishment will be meted out immediately, that somehow punishment is mechanically linked to the violation

b. Ability to feel the distress of another

c. Piaget's term for the second stage of moral development; right or good behavior is judged by the intention of the actor, not by the consequences of the act; this view recognizes that rules are socially agreed upon conventions that can be changed by consensus

d. In the psychoanalytic perspective, the feeling of anxiety that comes from transgressing; responsible for harnessing the drives of the id

e. Abilities that allow the understanding that other people have feelings and perceptions different from one's own

f. Performance of behaviors designed to help another individual without regard for potential external reward

Answers to Key Terms Matching Exercise

1. e	6. d	11. e	16. a	21. c	26. b
2. f	7. c	12. d	17. c	22. d	27. d
3. c	8. a	13. b	18. b	23. e	28. f
4. b	9. f	14. e	19. a	24. c	29. e
5. a	10. b	15. d	20. f	25. a	

Self-Test A

Choose the best alternative.

1. Timmy finds it difficult to initiate activity, is very anxious about social comparison, and is ineffective in social interactions. His parents most likely are (LO–1, p. 301)
   a. authoritarian.
   b. authoritative.
   c. permissive-indulgent.
   d. permissive-indifferent.

2. Which of the following is not mentioned in the text as an important aspect of divorce that influences the child's behavior? (LO–6, pp. 307–9)
   a. family conflict
   b. the child's relationship with both parents
   c. the age of the child
   d. the birth order of the child

3. Which of the following statements concerning the development of the children of divorced parents is true? (LO–6, pp. 308–9)
   a. Sons benefit from being in the custody of the father.
   b. Daughters benefit from being in the custody of the mother.
   c. It makes little difference with which parent a child lives after a divorce.
   d. Both a and b are correct.

4. Which of the following characterizes interactions with peers, not interactions with both peers and family? (LO–8, p. 312)
   a. rough-and-tumble play
   b. smiling
   c. touching
   d. vocalizing

5. Jimmy is playing with a cup and is pouring water out of the cup and watching the water spill into the sink. He then refills the cup and repeats this again and again. Which function of play is best represented in Jimmy's activity? (LO–9, p. 314)
   a. affiliation with peers
   b. tension release
   c. coping with conflict
   d. exploration

6. Karen is drawing a picture. Next to her, Susan is also drawing a picture, while across the room Nancy and Ellen are playing with dolls together. Karen and Susan are engaging in what kind of play? (LO–10, p. 316)
   a. solitary play
   b. onlooker play
   c. parallel play
   d. associative play

7. Pretend play appears at about what age? (LO–11, p. 317)
   a. 18 months
   b. two years
   c. four years
   d. five years

8. Which of the following is thought to be the relationship between pretend play and language development? (LO–12, p. 320)
   a. Pretend play is a prerequisite for language development.
   b. Language development is a prerequisite for pretend play.
   c. Pretend play and language development are concurrent developments.
   d. Precise correspondence between pretend play and language is unlikely.

9. The interest in the effects of self-generation and self-reference in memory is an important aspect of understanding (LO-16, p. 328)
   a. the self-concept.
   b. the self as knower.
   c. self-esteem.
   d. personality.

10. At what age do children primarily focus on external characteristics when asked to describe themselves? (LO–16, p. 329)
    a. 3 to 6 years
    b. 6 to 9 years
    c. 8 to 12 years
    d. 10 to 17 years

11. The "anatomy is destiny" explanation of sex-role differences is attributed to (LO–17, p. 329)
    a. Freud.
    b. Piaget.
    c. Erikson.
    d. Kohlberg.

12. The two developmental periods during which sex hormones are produced and influence development are (LO–18, pp. 329—30)
    a. the prenatal period and early infancy.
    b. the prenatal period and adolescence.
    c. infancy and adolescence.
    d. infancy and early childhood.

13. The theorist who argues that cognitive development—specifically, the ability to categorize objects and behaviors—is related to sex-role development is (LO–19, p. 330)
    a. Bem.
    b. Freud.
    c. Erikson.
    d. Kohlberg.

14. Janet Hyde has shown that children who hear a sentence describing good job performance with the pronoun *he* or *they* usually will not say that a woman can do the job well, but if the sentence contains *she,* they usually will say that a woman can do the job well. This demonstrates which of the following? (LO-19, pp. 332–33)
    a. Sexism in thought is primary and produces sexism in language.
    b. Sexism in thought can in some instances produce sexism in language.
    c. Sexism in language can in some instances produce sexism in thought.
    d. Sexism in language is primary and produces sexism in thought.

15. Research has shown that parents respond differently to boys and girls in all of the following except (LO–21, p. 331)
    a. gross motor activities.
    b. physical activity.
    c. dependence.
    d. aggression.

16. Peers influence each other's sex-role development in all of the following ways except (LO–21, pp. 332–33)
    a. playing in cross-sexed groups.
    b. playing in same-sexed groups.
    c. rewarding sex-appropriate activities.
    d. criticizing cross-sex activities.

17. Which of the following statements regarding how elementary teachers influence sex-typing in children is false? (LO–21, p. 334)
    a. Most teachers are female and present female models of behavior.
    b. Female teachers tend to reinforce feminine behavior.
    c. Girls are given more disapproval and other forms of negative attention than boys.
    d. Boys and girls get about the same amount of positive attention.

18. Which two areas of psychology have developed treatment programs for gender-deviant children? (LO–22, pp. 334–35)
    a. behavioral and cognitive
    b. behavioral and psychoanalytical
    c. cognitive and psychoanalytical
    d. cognitive and biological

19. Moral development involves all of the following domains except (LO–23, p. 336)
    a. reasoning.
    b. behavior.
    c. feeling.
    d. situations.

20. Which of the following best characterizes Piaget's view of the moral realist? (LO–24, p. 336)
    a. The child judges behavior based on the consequences of the actions.
    b. The child sees rules as changeable by consensus.
    c. The child believes that punishment is a socially mediated event.
    d. The child believes that punishment for a transgression is not inevitable.

Answers to Self-Test A

1. a	5. d	9. b	13. d	17. c
2. d	6. c	10. a	14. c	18. b
3. d	7. a	11. c	15. d	19. d
4. a	8. d	12. b	16. a	20. a

Self-Test B

Choose the best alternative.

21. Dora is very easygoing and self-reliant and takes on social responsibility easily. Her parents most likely are (LO-1, p. 301)
    a. authoritarian.
    b. authoritative.
    c. permissive-indulgent.
    d. permissive-indifferent.

22. Which of the following statements about sibling rivalry is true? (LO–4, p. 304)
    a. There is more sibling rivalry between opposite-sexed siblings in the toddler years and more between same-sexed siblings in the elementary years.
    b. There is more sibling rivalry between same-sexed siblings in the toddler years and more between opposite-sexed siblings in the elementary years.
    c. There is more sibling rivalry between opposite-sexed siblings than between same-sexed siblings at all ages.
    d. There is more sibling rivalry between same-sexed siblings than between opposite-sexed siblings at all ages.

23. What percentage of children are expected to spend some part of their childhood in a single-parent family? (LO–5, p. 306)
    a. 10 to 20 percent
    b. 20 to 30 percent
    c. 40 to 50 percent
    d. 50 to 60 percent

24. For children, what is an advantage of having a working mother? (LO–5, pp. 306–7)
    a. The quality of time together is better, even if the actual amount of time is less.
    b. Children are exposed to less rigid sex-role stereotypes.
    c. Children have more free time away from adult supervision.
    d. Children have more time with their fathers than in other families.

25. What are the findings on perspective-taking tasks with children who have frequent peer contact and children who have little peer contact? (LO–7, p. 311)
    a. Children with frequent peer contact are more advanced in perspective-taking skills.
    b. Children with infrequent peer contact are more advanced in perspective-taking skills.
    c. Children do not differ in perspective-taking skills as a function of peer contact.
    d. Children with infrequent peer contact are initially less advanced in perspective-taking skills, but catch up and surpass children with frequent peer contact.

26. Betty and Jane are playing together, digging a hole in the backyard to reach China. Which function is play serving for them? (LO–9, p. 314)
    a. affiliation with peers
    b. tension release
    c. advances in cognitive development
    d. exploration

27. Matthew is building a tower of blocks. He is oblivious to anything going on around him. Matthew is engaged in what kind of play? (LO–10, p. 315)
    a. unoccupied play
    b. solitary play
    c. onlooker play
    d. parallel play

28. What kind of play involves transforming the physical environment into a symbol? (LO–11, p. 317)
    a. play therapy
    b. cooperative play
    c. pretend play
    d. parallel play

29. A psychologist who emphasizes the role of the self and self-concept as central in understanding the child's development is most likely (LO–16, p. 327)
    a. a humanist theorist.
    b. a trait theorist.
    c. a situational theorist.
    d. a behavioral theorist.

30. The view that sexuality is essentially unlearned and instinctual comes from the work of (LO–17, p. 329)
    a. Freud.
    b. Erikson.
    c. Bem.
    d. Piaget.

31. According to Ehrhardt, if a woman received androgen during pregnancy and subsequently had a daughter from that pregnancy, what is likely to be true of the daughter? (LO–18, pp. 330–31)
    a. She probably will be androgynous in her sex-role orientation.
    b. She probably will be more energetic in play and will play with boys more than girls.
    c. She probably will be very feminine, enjoying doll play and wearing dresses.
    d. She probably will be very concerned with her appearance and will be quiet and shy.

32. What accounts for sex-role development, according to Kohlberg? (LO–19, p. 330)
    a. identification with the same-sexed parent
    b. imitation of same-sexed models
    c. reinforcement of sex-appropriate behavior
    d. categorizing oneself as male or female

33. Which parent appears to be more important for sex-typing children? (LO–20, p. 331)
    a. mothers
    b. fathers
    c. Mothers and fathers appear to be equally important.
    d. The relative importance of the parents in sex-typing depends upon the parenting style used.

34. Children who play in cross-sex activities are likely to receive which of the following from their peers? (LO–21, pp. 332–33)
    a. criticism
    b. affection
    c. positive reinforcement
    d. acceptance

35. Female teachers tend to reinforce what kinds of behaviors? (LO–21, p. 334)
    a. feminine behavior in both boys and girls
    b. feminine behavior in girls only
    c. masculine behavior in boys
    d. androgynous behavior in both sexes

36. Which children are the most likely to meet with attempts to actively change their sex-typed behavior? (LO–22, pp. 334–35)
    a. androgynous boys
    b. androgynous girls
    c. gender-deviant girls
    d. gender-deviant boys

37. At what age do children first show sex-typed play? (LO–22, p. 335)
    a. 18 months to 3 years
    b. 3 to 7 years
    c. 7 to 12 years
    d. after 12 years

38. At what age do children first acquire gender constancy? (LO-22, p. 335)
    a. 1 to 3 years
    b. 3 to 7 years
    c. 7 to 12 years
    d. after 12 years

39. Which of the following best characterizes Piaget's view of moral autonomy? (LO–24, pp. 336–37)
    a. The child judges behavior based on consequences of actions.
    b. The child believes in immanent justice.
    c. The child sees rules as changeable by consensus.
    d. The child believes that rules are handed down by authorities.

40. Altruistic behavior is most closely tied to which of the following emotions? (LO–27, pp. 339–40)
    a. guilt
    b. empathy
    c. love
    d. shame

Answers to Self-Test B

21. b	25. a	29. a	33. b	37. a
22. a	26. a	30. a	34. a	38. b
23. c	27. b	31. b	35. a	39. c
24. b	28. c	32. d	36. d	40. b

Questions to Stimulate Thought

1. What effect does the style of parenting have on the child's developing personality?
2. Is the effect of divorce on the child's development better, worse, or no different than having parents who do not get along?
3. What is a peer?
4. Compare the relationships formed with peers and parents.
5. What is play?
6. Is television good?
7. Are the differences between boys and girls genetic?
8. Is the English language sexist? Would or does it matter?
9. Is the child who Piaget characterized as a moral realist really thinking morally?
10. What supports altruism?

Research Project

This project is an observational study of children's play. Pick a partner from the class and go to a neighborhood playground to observe two children—one about three years old, the other about five years old—for 10 minutes each. One of you should act as the observer, the other as the recorder. Record on the data sheet for each child the amount of time spent in each of Parten's categories of play. Then calculate the percentage of time spent in each category for the time period. Compare the differences as a function of age, using the data sheet that follows, and then answer the questions.

Data Sheet

Category	Child 1 Sex _____ Age _____		Child 2 Sex _____ Age _____	
Unoccupied Play				
Solitary Play				
Onlooker Play				
Parallel Play				
Associative Play				
Cooperative Play				

Questions

1. In what category of play did the three-year-old child spend the largest amount of time? In what category of play did the child spend the least amount of time?
2. In what category of play did the five-year-old child spend the largest amount of time? In what category of play did the child spend the least amount of time?
3. What were the differences between the children in the kinds of play they engaged in? To what do you attribute these differences? (Use information about cognitive, physical, and social development to answer this question.) Are there variables besides age that could account for the differences you observed?
4. How do your findings compare with those of Parten and Barnes?

9 Physical and Cognitive Development in Middle and Late Childhood

Learning Objectives

After studying this chapter, you should be able to:

1. Describe endomorphic, mesomorphic, and ectomorphic body builds. (p. 349)
2. Describe the patterns of growth in general and the improvement of gross and fine motor skills in particular during middle and late childhood. (pp. 349–50)
3. Describe the changes in health and ideas about health during middle and late childhood. (pp. 350–51)
4. Explain the concept of handicapped and describe its incidence in the middle and late childhood population. (pp. 351–52)
5. Explain the relationship between handicapped children and the concepts of labeling and mainstreaming. (pp. 353–55)
6. Explain the concept of learning disabilities. (pp. 355–57)
7. Describe hyperactivity and its management. (p. 357)
8. Describe the characteristics of concrete operational thought. (pp. 358–60)
9. Describe the conservation of liquid task and explain the meaning of the results. (p. 359)
10. Explain the constraints on concrete operational thought. (p. 360)
11. List and explain three general principles of education implicit in Piaget's ideas. (pp. 360–61)
12. Describe four of Piaget's contributions to the study of child development and four criticisms of or limits to his theory. (pp. 361–63)
13. Describe and explain five control processes or strategies used to promote long-term memory and their relationship to the development of memory during middle and late childhood. (pp. 365–66)
14. Describe the impact of acquired knowledge on memory. (pp. 366–69)
15. Define metamemory and explain its impact on memory. (pp. 368–69)
16. Describe the relationship of development of inferencing to schemata and scripts. (pp. 370–72)
17. Explain Sternberg's componential analysis of intelligence. (pp. 372, 376)
18. Explain the relevance of the structure/process dilemma to the study of intellectual development. (pp. 376–77)
19. Describe the implications of information processing theory for the reform of American schools. (pp. 371–81)

Summary

During middle and late childhood, children grow two to three inches and gain three to five pounds per year. They develop distinctive body builds: endomorphic (rounded, somewhat chubby), mesomorphic (athletic, muscular), or ectomorphic (skinny, thin). Motor behavior becomes smoother and more coordinated at this time. Sensory mechanisms continue to mature, with binocular vision becoming well-developed and hearing acuity increasing.

Elementary school children recognize that health requires almost continual work and that nutrition and fitness are important in its maintenance. They do not define health as an absence of illness. There is, however, a gap between their apparent knowledge and their behavior since many children are in rather poor physical shape by the time they enter first grade. There has been concern recently about the effects of stress on children, stimulated by the study of the effects of the Type A behavioral pattern in adults. Approximately 10 to 16 percent of the children between 5 and 18 years of age have an identifiable handicap. The federal government has ordered mainstreaming—the education of these children in the same setting as nonhandicapped children. One issue is the potential damage done by labeling some children as handicapped.

Dyslexia, minimal brain dysfunction, and hyperactivity are examples of learning disabilities. Learning disabled children are more likely to have any one of a series of problems than are children without the disability. Hyperactive children are often treated with amphetamine-like drugs, such as Ritalin.

The concrete operational period extends from about seven years of age to the beginning of adolescence. During this period, thought is characterized as reversible and decentered but is limited to reasoning about the concrete world as it is. Conservation tasks can be solved: The child realizes that the amount of a substance does not change by changing any of the substance's superficial characteristics. Thought is made up of operations that are mental actions or representations that are reversible. Classification tasks are first correctly solved at this time.

Piaget made four major contributions: (1) brilliant observations of children (his observations have been replicated repeatedly); (2) ideas about what to look for in development; (3) a focus on the qualitative nature of changes in mental development; and (4) imaginative ideas about how change occurs, such as assimilation and accommodation.

Several aspects of Piaget's theory have been criticized. First, stages do not seem to exist empirically in the behavior of the child as they are discussed in the theory. Second, some of the concepts in Piaget's theory, while apparently powerful, are difficult to tie down operationally (for example, assimilation). Third, small changes in procedure have large effects on children's responses, which would affect what stage a child should be assigned to. Fourth, training studies have demonstrated that a child apparently at one Piagetian stage can be taught to respond at the level of a higher stage, something not allowed within Piaget's framework. Fifth, some cognitive abilities seem to emerge earlier than Piaget believed, and their subsequent development may take longer than he thought; that is, the younger child can do more and the older child less than Piaget thought.

Maintenance rehearsal involves the simple repetition of the material to be retained. A study by Flavell and his colleagues found that 7- and 10-year-old children spontaneously move their lips, indicating rehearsal, far more than 5-year-old children. Rehearsal-like processes appear as early as three or four years of age. Organization improves long-term memory. Children of 10 and 11 years of age, but not younger children, have been shown to organize pictures of objects into categories when given a memory task. However, younger children have been trained to produce such groupings, and it improved their retention. Semantic elaboration, which is the encoding of information in a form that preserves the meaning of words and sounds, increases during middle and late childhood and improves long-term memory. Paris and Lindauer demonstrated that 11-year-old children engage in spontaneous inferential processing while 7-year-old children do not. The use of mental imagery also improves long-term memory. Instructions to use imagery during both the learning and the retrieval period have been useful with younger children. Older children spontaneously use imagery during retrieval if they are instructed to do so during learning. Older children also use category information spontaneously during retrieval, although younger children do not.

The learner's knowledge helps to determine the level of memory performance. Mandler and Robinson found that memory for a scene was better than for a meaningless array and that this difference grew larger with age. This suggests that a child's growing knowledge of scenes can be beneficial to his or her memory for scenes. Chess-playing children performed better than novice adults in a study of memory for chessboard displays. Zembar and Naus have shown that both third- and sixth-graders use efficient memory strategies with easy material but not with difficult material. That is, their knowledge of the materials affected their use of efficient memory strategies.

Metamemory has three components: (1) knowledge that learning information is different from perceiving it; (2) knowledge of factors that contribute to performance on memory tasks; and (3) knowledge of when material is mastered. Metamemory improves with age and is related to both the strategies used and performance in learning and memory tasks. Memory monitoring is deficient in young children.

Knowledge about aspects of the world allows us to make inferences about information. Knowledge is thought by some to be organized in structures called schemata. Schemata for events, such as visiting a restaurant or a doctor's office, are called scripts. Scripts emerge early in life, perhaps by one year of age. Nelson showed that four- and five-year-old children had good scripts for eating in different locations (at home, in a day-care center, and at McDonald's). Children also are able to make inferences from their scripts and may categorize objects in a list and remember them better if the categories fit with scripts the child has available.

Sternberg has provided a componential analysis of intelligence that focuses on the availability, accessibility, and ease of execution of metacomponents, performance components, acquisition components, retention components, and transfer components.

The information processing approach raises the question of whether intelligence occurs primarily through a growth in knowledge or through changes in processing. Research indicates that both knowledge and processing are involved.

An analogy is drawn between educational reform and a pendulum that swings back and forth from one extreme in education to another. Possibly, the fields of education and psychology have not interacted sufficiently to allow new understandings of children to affect education.

Guided Review

You may want to look at the answers to the "Guided Review" statements as you read, or you may want to use the exercise as a form of self-test by covering up the answers below the statements with a sheet of paper and not consulting them until you have attempted to fill in the blanks of each statement.

1. Elementary school children grow an average of _____ to _____ inches per year. At 11 years of age, the average girl is _____ inches tall and weighs _____ pounds, and the average boy is _____ inches tall and weighs _____ pounds. There is a noticeable _____ of the trunk during middle and late childhood.
   two, three, 58, 88.5, 57.5, 85.5, slimming

2. Children who are more rounded and perhaps a bit chubby are sometimes referred to as _____ . Children who develop skinny, thin body builds are sometimes known as _____ . Children with athletic, muscular builds are sometimes known as _____ .
   endomorphs, ectomorphs, mesomorphs

3. Motor coordination _____ with age. There appear to be sex differences in _____ motor skills, with boys outperforming girls. In _____ motor skills, girls generally outperform boys. During middle and late childhood, the _____ systems continue to mature.
   improves, gross, fine, sensory

4. Elementary school children seem to understand health but are in _____ physical condition. One way in which they exercise is through _____ sports. Of all the activities in which children participate, _____ presents the greatest risk of injury.
   poor, competitive, football

5. The _____ _____ behavioral pattern is correlated with cardiovascular disease in adults. The person with this pattern is always _____ with the slow pace of events, is _____ , has an _____ pace, and shows _____ .
   Type A, impatient, competitive, accelerated, hostility

6. In a recent study, children who were rated high in Type A behavior were found to have more physical _____ of stress but did not differ on visits to the _____ from children who were rated low in Type A behavior. They were more likely to have _____ _____ _____ fathers and low _____ - _____ . Also, their parents were more likely to be _____ of failure.
   symptoms, doctor, high Type A, self-esteem, critical

7. Approximately _____ to _____ percent of the U.S. population of children ages 5 to 18 are estimated to be handicapped. Federal regulations now require that these children be educated in the same _____ as nonhandicapped children.
   10, 15, setting

8. The assignment of a term used to describe a handicapped child's condition is called _____ . The label creates _____ in others for the child's _____ and may actually make the handicapped child's behavior _____ . The current trend is to refer to _____ and levels of _____ rather than _____ .
   labeling, expectations, behavior, worse, skills, functioning, labels

9. The attempt to educate handicapped children in the normal school setting is called _____ . One advantage of mainstreaming is that it eliminates the _____ associated with being in a separate class.

   mainstreaming, stigma

10. A learning disabled child has _____ in some educational area, a normal score on a standardized _____ test, no primary _____ - _____ disturbances, no uncorrected _____ deficits, and no history of severe _____ deprivation.

    deficits, intelligence, emotional-behavioral, sensory, emotional

11. Many children labeled learning disabled are experiencing a _____ _____ . They do not have less ability than other children; their ability is simply developing more _____ .

    developmental lag, slowly

12. As many as _____ percent of all American children are diagnosed as hyperactive. This syndrome includes _____ activity and an impaired _____ of _____ _____ .

    5, increased, span, focused attention

13. Hyperactivity is frequently treated with _____ . The most common kinds are the _____ , particularly _____ . One problem with these drugs is that their effectiveness _____ with time so that the dosage must be _____ . The data on the effectiveness of this therapy are _____ .

    drugs, amphetamines, Ritalin, decreases, increased, mixed

14. The child is presented with two identical beakers, each filled to the same level with liquid. The child is asked if these beakers have the same amount of liquid, and he or she usually says "yes." Then the liquid from one beaker is poured into a third beaker, which is taller and thinner than the first two. The child is then asked if the amount of liquid in the tall, thin beaker is equal to that which remains in one of the original beakers. If the child now says "yes," then _____ has been demonstrated. The solution of this task is the Piagetian test of entry into the stage of _____ _____ .

    conservation, concrete operations

15. According to Piaget, concrete operational thought is made up of _____—that is, mental actions or representations that are _____ .

    operations, reversible

16. The ability to _____ is an operation that allows one to divide things into different sets and subsets. This ability enables the child to create or understand the relationships in a _____ _____ .

    classify, family tree

17. The concrete operational thinker needs to have objects and events _____ in order to think about them. For example, this thinker cannot _____ the steps to complete an _____ equation.

    present, imagine, algebraic

18. Piaget's theory contains information about the young person's _____ in the areas of math, science, and logic. From the Piagetian perspective, the most important problem of education is _____ . According to Piaget, the child's mind is not _____ , and we must learn to understand what children are saying and respond in the same _____ .

    reasoning, communication, empty, mode

19. According to Piaget, the child comes to school with _____ about space, time, causality, and so forth and with an _____ to learn. The child has not _____ his or her ideas, nor has the child been _____ them. The ideas were acquired through _____ _____ with the environment. School must not dull the _____ to learn with a _____ curriculum.

    ideas, enthusiasm, inherited, taught, spontaneous interaction, eagerness, rigid

20. Piaget showed us some important things to look for in development, including the shift to _____ _____ in infancy and the change from thinking in a _____ manner during the elementary school years to thinking in a more _____ way during adolescence.

    object permanence, concrete, abstract

21. Piaget's theory has been criticized for a lack of _____ in development, that is, similarity and cross-linkages among aspects of stages. This weakens support for his notion that development follows a series of _____ .

    synchrony, stages

22. A criticism of Piagetian concepts is that many of them have only loose ties to _____ procedures. Small _____ in procedure have large effects on a child's _____ .

    experimental, changes, cognition

23. It has been possible to _____ children to pass tasks at a cognitive level above theirs. Gelman trained _____ children to solve _____ problems.

    train, preoperational, conservation

24. Certain cognitive abilities may appear _____ and develop _____ than Piaget believed.

    earlier, slower

25. Case believes that the _____ of cognitive structures at any point in development is limited by the current size of _____ - _____ _____ . He conceives of short-term memory as being divided into _____ space and _____ space. While the total space for short-term memory does not change, as the child's operations become more _____ during development, the space available for the former increases. Case's work adds the concept of automatization from _____ _____ to Piaget's ideas.

    complexity, short-term memory, storage, operating, automatized, information processing

26. Rehearsal, organizational processing, semantic elaboration, mental imagery, and the retrieval or search processes are learning activities that fit under the category of control processes that are _____ . They are under the learner's _____ control and are appropriately referred to as _____ .

    effortful, conscious, strategies

27. Extended processing of to-be-remembered material after it has been presented is called _____ . Simple repetition is _____ rehearsal. Rehearsal that attempts to link the to-be-remembered material to other known or understood material is called _____ rehearsal.

    rehearsal, maintenance, elaborative

28. Given the task of remembering from two to five pictures of nameable objects for 15 seconds, _____ percent of the 5-year-olds, _____ percent of the 7-year-olds, and _____ percent of the 10-year-olds made _____ movements, indicating some sort of _____ process. There was a _____ _____ between this measure of rehearsal and _____ . If those who did not rehearse were taught rehearsal, recall _____ .
10, 60, 85, lip, rehearsal, positive correlation, recall, improved

29. When presented with pictures from four different categories and told to study them for a recall test, 10- and 11-year-old children showed evidence of _____ processing, while younger children did not. Training in _____ grouping enabled the younger children to follow this strategy and _____ their memory.
organizational, semantic, improved

30. A process by which information is encoded in a way that preserves meaning but not necessarily the form of words and sounds is called _____ _____ . This skill increases between the ages of _____ and _____ . This suggests that the use of spontaneous _____ processing increases from _____ to _____ years of age.
semantic elaboration, 7, 11, inferential, 7, 11

31. A control process that makes use of mental—usually visual—associations is called _____ . In a study of children from grades _____ and _____ , _____ groups usually benefited from the imagery instructions. However, when the words were difficult to image or the rate of presentation was _____ , the _____ -graders did not.
imagery, 2, 6, both, fast, second

32. If a control process has effects at the time of recall, it is said to be influencing _____ . In a study by Pressley and Levin using paired-associate learning, first- and sixth-grade students were instructed to use imagery only during learning or during both learning and recall. For the _____ students, the different instructions made no difference in performance. However, for the _____ students, those not specifically instructed to use imagery during recall had _____ recall scores.
retrieval, older, younger, lower

33. Mandler and Robinson compared memory for meaningful scenes and for disorganized arrays of objects in first-, third- and fifth-grade children. _____ were recognized better than _____ , and this difference _____ with age. In a study comparing the memory for chessboard arrangements of chess-playing children and novice adults, the chess-playing children were _____ than the adults. These data indicate a role for _____ in memory.
Scenes, arrays, increased, better, knowledge

34. Knowledge that learning is different from _____ information, knowledge of memory _____ , and the ability to _____ memory are components of _____ . Metamemory _____ with age and appears to be a predictor. of children's memory _____ .
perceiving, techniques, monitor, metamemory, improves, skill

35. The understanding of when one has studied enough to have mastered a body of information is the result of _____ _____ . In one study, children were shown a number of pictures equal to their predetermined memory spans and given as much time as they thought they needed to learn the pictures perfectly. When tested, the older children recalled _____ than the younger children.
memory monitoring, more

36. A relationship between two events that is not directly stated requires an _____ . Inferences may be based on _____ or on prior _____ . The ability to make inferences _____ with age.

inference, logic, knowledge, improves

37. Active organizations of past experiences that provide a structure from which new information can be judged are called _____ . Schemata for events are often called _____ . Scripts may appear by the age of _____ . Nelson found that _____ - and _____ -year-old children had well-developed scripts for what happens in different types of eating places. Children will falsely recognize objects from a story they have heard if that story follows a script with which they are familiar because they make _____ based upon the script.

schemata, scripts, one, four, five, inferences

38. Categories based upon classification by common characteristics are called _____ categories. Categories based upon schemata and scripts emerge _____ than taxonomic categories. In a recent memory study, _____ children showed higher recall and more clustering in a scriptal condition than in a taxonomic condition.

taxonomic, earlier, preschool

39. Apparently, many very early scripts are actually _____ from an evolving fund of general knowledge. One study found that, by the _____ grade, the scripts for _____ activities were the same for children who both had and had not attended preschool.

reconstructed, third, preschool

40. A _____ in Sternberg's analysis is an elementary information process that operates on internal representations of objects. Sternberg has identified _____ information processing components.

component, five

41. _____ are higher-order control processes used for making _____ and _____ . _____ components are used to _____ a problem-solving strategy. _____ components, also called _____ components, are used in learning new information. _____ components, also called _____ components, access information in _____ - _____ memory. _____ components are used in _____ knowledge to new situations.

Metacomponents, plans, decisions, Performance, execute, Acquisition, storage, Retention, retrieval, long-term, Transfer, applying

42. Frank Keil calls the question of whether intellectual development is the result of older children's greater knowledge or of changes in information processing abilities the _____/_____ issue.

structure/process

43. An information processing criticism of American education is that what is typically taught is _____ , not _____ ; that is, we do not systematically teach children to _____ .

content, process, think

Key Terms Matching Exercise

Match the Key Term on the left with the correct definition on the right.

—— 1. endomorphic body build (LO–1, p. 349)
—— 2. mesomorphic body build (LO–1, p. 349)
—— 3. ectomorphic body build (LO–1, p. 349)
—— 4. Type A behavioral pattern (LO–2, p. 350)
—— 5. Type B person (LO–2, p. 351)
—— 6. labeling (LO–5, p. 350)

a. Assignment of a child to a category and the effects that category may then have on the child
b. Typified by a person who is excessively competitive, has an accelerated pace of ordinary activities, and is impatient with the rate at which most events occur
c. Thin, skinny body build, with neither a predominance of fat nor muscle
d. Rounded, chubby body build, with more fat tissue than muscle tissue
e. Muscular body build, with more muscle tissue than fat tissue
f. Person who is not excessively competitive, does not have an accelerated pace of ordinary activities, and is not impatient with the rate at which most events occur

—— 7. mainstreaming (LO–5, p. 354)
—— 8. learning disabilities (LO–6, p. 355)
—— 9. developmental lag (LO–6, p. 357)
—— 10. hyperactivity (LO–7, p. 357)
—— 11. amphetamines (LO–7, p. 357)
—— 12. operation (LO–8, p. 359)

a. Increase in purposeless physical activity and a significantly impaired span of focused attention
b. Term used to describe slow-developing ability in some children
c. Category that includes children diagnosed as dyslexic, children with minimal brain dysfunction, and children who are hyperactive
d. Process by which children in need of special education are placed in regular classrooms rather than special classrooms
e. Internalized set of actions that allow a child to do mentally what before was done physically
f. Synthetic stimulants used to maintain high levels of performance for short periods

_____ 13. concrete operation (LO–8, p. 360)
_____ 14. automatization (LO–12, p. 362)
_____ 15. control processes (LO–13, p. 365)
_____ 16. rehearsal (LO–13, p. 365)
_____ 17. maintenance rehearsal (LO–13, p. 365)
_____ 18. elaborative rehearsal (LO–13, p. 365)

a. Control process that involves repeating the material over and over

b. Use of processes that are not under conscious control and that do not draw substantially on information processing capacity

c. Reversible mental action on real, concrete objects

d. Learning and memory strategies that draw heavily on information processing capacities and are under the learner's conscious control

e. Extended processing of to-be-remembered material after it has been presented; a control process used to facilitate long-term memory

f. Extended processing of to-be-remembered material that uses organization, imaging, and making connections with other material in memory

_____ 19. organizational processing (LO–13, p. 365)
_____ 20. semantic elaboration (LO–13, p. 365)
_____ 21. mental imagery (LO–13, p. 366)
_____ 22. retrieval (LO–13, p. 366)
_____ 23. metamemory (LO–15, p. 368)
_____ 24. inference (LO–16, p. 370)

a. Active grouping of information into higher-order units or "chunks" to retain it more completely

b. Control process that makes use of the formation of mental images of pictures

c. Knowledge of one's own memory

d. Process by which information is encoded in such a form that preserves the meaning of words and sounds

e. Control process that uses certain search strategies to recover items from memory

f. Relationship noted between one event and another that is not directly stated

_____ 25. schemata (LO–16, p. 371)
_____ 26. scripts (LO–16, p. 371)
_____ 27. componential analysis (LO–17, p. 376)
_____ 28. component (LO–17, p. 376)
_____ 29. metacomponents (LO–17, p. 376)
_____ 30. performance components (LO–17, p. 376)

a. Processes used to carry out a problem-solving strategy; a cognitive framework or a way in which knowledge is organized in long-term memory

b. Elementary information process that operates on internal representation of objects

c. Schemata for events

d. Higher-order control processes used for executive planning and decision making when problem solving is required

e. Sternberg's information processing model of intelligence

f. Structures of knowledge about aspects of the world, such as objects, events, and the spatial layout

_____ 31. acquisition or storage components (LO–17, p. 376)

_____ 32. retention or retrieval components (LO–17, p. 376)

_____ 33. transfer components (LO–17, p. 376)

a. Processes involved in accessing previously stored information

b. Processes used in learning new information

c. Processes used in generalization, such as using information learned on one task to help solve another task

Answers to Key Terms Matching Exercise

1. d	6. a	11. f	16. e	21. b	26. c	31. b
2. e	7. d	12. e	17. a	22. e	27. e	32. a
3. c	8. c	13. c	18. f	23. c	28. b	33. c
4. b	9. b	14. b	19. a	24. f	29. d	
5. f	10. a	15. d	20. d	25. f	30. a	

Self-Test A

Choose the best alternative.

1. A tall, thin body build is termed (LO–1, p. 349)
   a. endomorphic.
   b. mesomorphic.
   c. ectomorphic.
   d. endomorphic and ectomorphic.

2. In the performance of gross motor skills, (LO–2, p. 350)
   a. boys outperform girls.
   b. girls outperform boys.
   c. sex differences do not emerge until puberty.
   d. girls outperform boys initially, but boys surpass the girls by puberty.

3. The item of concern about children's health to which the Type A behavior pattern is relevant is (LO–3, pp. 350–51)
   a. infection.
   b. physical fitness.
   c. fat intake and heart disease.
   d. stress.

4. The percentage of handicapped school-aged children in the United States is (LO–4, p. 351)
   a. 10 to 15 percent.
   b. 5 to 7 percent.
   c. 3 to 5 percent.
   d. 1 to 2 percent.

5. Handicapped and nonhandicapped children must be educated in the same classrooms. (LO–5, pp. 354–55)
   a. This is mainstreaming but is not yet required.
   b. This is federally mandated mainstreaming.
   c. This has been shown to be disadvantageous to both handicapped and nonhandicapped children.
   d. This does not permit special services for handicapped children.

6. Low performance in a specific educational area, combined with normal intelligence and no behavioral problems, is a definition of (LO–6, p. 355)
   a. learning disability.
   b. mental retardation.
   c. slow learning.
   d. developmental lag.

7. The approximate number of hyperactive children in kindergarten through the eighth grade being treated by drugs is (LO–7, p. 357)
   a. 100,000.
   b. 500,000.
   c. 1,000,000.
   d. over 2,000,000.

8. One characteristic of concrete operational thought is (LO–8, p. 359)
   a. reversibility.
   b. centration.
   c. abstract reasoning.
   d. the personal fable.

9. A child is given the conservation of liquid task. The child argues that the liquid in the two containers is the same because, although one container is taller, the other is fatter. This is an example of (LO–9, p. 359)
   a. decentration.
   b. reversibility.
   c. egocentrism.
   d. classification.

10. A logical child who requires real objects for the basis of his or her reasoning is (LO–10, p. 360)
    a. sensorimotor.
    b. preoperational.
    c. concrete operational.
    d. formal operational.

11. Which of the following is consistent with Piaget's ideas on education? (LO–11, pp. 360–61)
    a. the use of immediate reinforcement
    b. punishment
    c. practice in automatization
    d. allowing discovery by the child

12. One of Piaget's contributions to the study of child development was (LO–12, p. 361)
    a. suggesting a cognitive interpretation of reinforcement.
    b. casting doubt on the unitary nature of the stages of thought.
    c. describing development as a continuous and gradual process.
    d. simple but insightful descriptions of child behavior.

13. A child hears the following sentence, "The boy unlocked the door." The child later identifies the word *key* as having appeared in the sentence. This is an example of which of the following? (LO–13, p. 365)
    a. maintenance rehearsal
    b. organizational processing
    c. semantic elaboration
    d. mental imagery

14. A child is trying to learn a list of words. The child places all of the words of animals in one pile, the words of school subjects in a second pile, and the words of tools in a third pile. This is an example of which of the following? (LO–13, p. 365)
    a. maintenance rehearsal
    b. organizational processing
    c. semantic elaboration
    d. mental imagery

15. Knowledge relevant to a task (LO–14, pp. 366–69)
    a. provides a better filter.
    b. allows shallower processing of information.
    c. totally explains age differences in performance on information processing tasks.
    d. makes information processing more efficient.

16. Which of the metamemory functions is most crucial from a practical standpoint? (LO–15, pp. 368–69)
    a. recognition that learning information is different from perceiving information
    b. knowledge of factors that contribute to performance on memory tasks
    c. knowledge of memory strategies to use
    d. knowledge of how to monitor memory during learning

17. Given the text information about scripts, which of the following lists would be easiest for a preschool child to learn? (LO–16, p. 372)
    a. cat, pig, deer
    b. hamburger, pizza, steak
    c. ball, bat, glove
    d. couch, desk, table

18. In Sternberg's componential analysis, which component would be used to generalize previously learned information to a new task? (LO–17, p. 376)
    a. transfer components
    b. metacomponents
    c. retrieval components
    d. performance components

19. Which of the following involves process as opposed to structure? (LO–18, pp. 376–77)
    a. learning the proper steps in fixing a car
    b. passing an anatomy test
    c. memorizing the bones of the body for a test
    d. learning faster than the others in the class

20. How may the "swinging pendulum solution" to educational reform be converted to the "spiral staircase solution" to educational reform? (LO–19, pp. 377–78)
    a. by applying science and technology to education
    b. by taking a fad approach to education
    c. by lax enforcement of standards in education
    d. by providing tough standards in education

Answers to Self-Test A

1. c	5. b	9. b	13. c	17. c
2. a	6. a	10. c	14. b	18. a
3. d	7. b	11. d	15. d	19. d
4. a	8. a	12. d	16. d	20. a

Self-Test B

Choose the best alternative.

21. A short, chubby body build is called (LO–1, p. 349)
    a. endomorphic.
    b. mesomorphic.
    c. ectomorphic.
    d. blastomorphic.

22. The age at which motor coordination is sufficient that most children can learn to play tennis is (LO–2, pp. 349–50)
    a. 4.
    b. 7.
    c. 11.
    d. 13.

23. High Type A children (LO–3, pp. 352–53)
    a. go to the doctor more than low Type A children.
    b. have more chronic illnesses than low Type A children.
    c. do not notice the stress even though it is damaging them.
    d. are able to report the high level of stress.

24. What percentage of children between the ages of 5 and 18 have speech handicaps? (LO–4, p. 351)
    a. 1 percent
    b. 3 to 4 percent
    c. 6 percent
    d. 0.1 percent

25. The technical term used to describe the categorizing of children by handicap is (LO–5, pp. 353–54)
    a. mainstreaming.
    b. labeling.
    c. stereotyping.
    d. handicapping.

26. If a child is doing poorly in reading, which of the following conditions must be met before diagnosing a learning disability? (LO–6, p. 355)
    a. showing a normal intelligence level
    b. demonstrating behavior problems
    c. demonstrating a sensory or perceptual deficit
    d. finding a history of emotional deprivation

27. Besides the obvious increase in general activity, what characteristic distinguishes the hyperactive child? (LO–7, p. 357)
    a. subclinical brain damage
    b. a poor attachment bond with the mother
    c. an impaired span of focused attention
    d. a reading problem

28. Which of the following is not characteristic of concrete operational thought? (LO–8, pp. 359–60)
    a. reasoning
    b. reversibility
    c. the ability to classify
    d. animism

29. A child is given the conservation of liquid task. The child argues that the liquid in the two containers is the same because you only poured it, and you could pour it back. This argument is an example of (LO–9, pp. 359–60)
    a. animism.
    b. reversibility.
    c. egocentrism.
    d. classification.

30. The concrete operational thinker (LO–10, p. 360)
    a. can consider all the possible social structures that might evolve.
    b. is able to mentally reverse an action.
    c. is concerned about being the center of everyone's attention.
    d. can form and consider a hypothesis.

31. One of the important goals for teaching children should be _____ , according to Piaget. (LO–11, pp. 360–61)
    a. rewarding correct responses
    b. eliminating punishment from the schools
    c. redesigning the curriculum so that children learn more useful content
    d. learning how to communicate with the child

32. Which of the following is a criticism that has been leveled at Piaget's work and theory? (LO–12, pp. 361–63)
    a. The stages of thought turned out to be unitary.
    b. Children cannot be prematurely pushed from one stage to another by training.
    c. Small procedural changes appear to change the child's cognitions.
    d. Some cognitive abilities appear much later than Piaget described.

33. Who is most likely to do well on a memory task for a set of bird songs? (LO–14, pp. 366–67)
    a. an individual who processes information rapidly
    b. an individual who is familiar with many bird songs
    c. an individual who has a large information processing capacity
    d. an individual who has good strategies for organizing information

34. A child is given the task of memorizing the states and their capitals. The child repeats over and over, "New York, Albany; California, Sacramento; Oregon, Salem...." This is an example of which of the following? (LO–13, p. 365)
    a. semantic elaboration
    b. organizational processing
    c. imagery
    d. maintenance rehearsal

35. What characteristic of the learner contributes the most on memory tasks? (LO–14, pp. 366–67)
    a. attitudes
    b. motivation
    c. prior knowledge
    d. intelligence

36. An example of metamemory is (LO–15, pp. 368–69)
    a. writing down a long series of numbers.
    b. listening carefully when a name is said.
    c. the increase in memory skill with age.
    d. the effect of knowledge on memory.

37. Jimmy, age four, knows that, when you go to the store, you walk around, pick up something, stand in a line at the front of the store, give a cashier some money, and then leave with the item you picked up. This is an example of (LO–16, p. 371)
   a. short-term memory.
   b. long-term memory.
   c. a script.
   d. metamemory.

38. In Sternberg's componential analysis, which component would be used to carry out a problem-solving strategy? (LO–17, p. 376)
   a. transfer components
   b. metacomponents
   c. retrieval components
   d. performance components

39. Which of the following involves structure as opposed to process? (LO–18, pp. 376–77)
   a. Sternberg's analysis
   b. measuring speed of thinking
   c. passing an anatomy test
   d. testing pure problem solving

40. Patricia Cross argues that the swinging pendulum in educational reform is caused by (LO–19, p. 377)
   a. getting caught up in educational fads in education.
   b. applying advances in science and technology to education.
   c. staying with educational plans too long.
   d. All of the above are correct.

Answers to Self-Test B

21. a	25. b	29. b	33. b	37. c
22. c	26. a	30. b	34. d	38. d
23. d	27. c	31. d	35. c	39. c
24. b	28. d	32. c	36. a	40. a

Questions to Stimulate Thought

1. Are learning disabilities failures to learn?
2. In what way is concrete operational thought not adult?
3. What is the highest level of intellectual achievement you would expect for one who never gets beyond concrete operational thought?
4. Compare and contrast the schema and the operation.
5. What would a school be like if recommendations based on the Piagetian approach to cognitive development were implemented?
6. How are memory and metamemory related?
7. How do control processes aid memory (retention)?
8. What would a school be like if recommendations based on the information processing approach to cognitive development were implemented?

Research Project

For this exercise, you pair up with another class member to test two children—a four- to five-year-old child and an eight- to nine-year-old child—using several of Piaget's tasks. You will administer two conservation and two classification tasks to each child and then compare the children's responses and attempt to interpret those responses in view of Piaget's theory. To test the two children, you will need permission from the human subjects review board at your school and a signed informed consent form from the children's parents. A description of the tasks, the data sheet for recording the observations, and a list of questions you are to answer follow.

Conservation Task 1: Conservation of number task. Make two sets of 10 identical items, with each set a different color; for example, one set of 10 blue poker chips and a second set of 10 white poker chips. Place one row of 10 in front of the child and ask the child to make an identical row with the other set. Ask the child if the two rows have the same number of items or if one row has more. Do not go on until the rows are identical in number and arrangement and the child agrees that the two rows are the same. Now spread one row out and push the other row together so that the display looks as follows:

OOOOOOOOOO

O O O O O O O O O O

Ask the child if the rows have the same number of items or if one row has more. Ask the child why the rows are the same or why one row has more and which row, if either, has more. If the child says that one row has more, ask the child where the more came from. Record all responses.

Conservation Task 2: Conservation of liquid task. Pour an identical amount of juice into two identical glasses. Ask the child if the two glasses have the same amount and adjust the volume in each glass until the child agrees that both have the same. Now pour the liquid from one glass into a taller, thinner glass. Ask the child if the amount of juice is the same in both glasses or if one glass has more. If the child thinks that one glass has more, ask which one. Have the child justify the judgment of same or different amount. Record all responses.

Classification Task 1: Classification of groups. Present the child with cutouts of big and small triangles, circles, and squares. Some of the shapes should be red, some blue, and some green. Ask the child to put together those things that go together. Record how the child sorts the objects. Now ask the child if there is another way to put the objects together. Record the second sort.

Classification Task 2: Present the child with a set of 10 red and 2 blue wooden beads. (You could also use poker chips or M & Ms of two different colors for this task.) Ask the child if there are more red beads or more blue beads. If the child were to make a train with the red beads and another train with the blue beads, which train would be longer? Now ask the child if there are more red beads or more wooden beads. If the child were to make a train with the red beads and another train with the wooden beads, which train would be longer? Record all responses.

Data Sheet

Task	Child One Sex _____ Age	Child Two Sex _____ Age
Conservation task 1 Creation of row Response Justification		
Conservation task 2 Response Justification		
Classification task 1 First ordering Second ordering		
Classification task 2 Response: red/blue? Response: red/wooden?		

Questions

1. Which tasks did the four- to five-year-old child solve? How would you characterize the nature of the child's responses to the questions?
2. Which tasks did the eight- to nine-year-old child solve? How would you characterize the nature of the child's responses to the questions?
3. How would you characterize the differences between the performances of the younger child and older child on these tasks?
4. What do these observations tell you about Piaget's theory? How would the children be classified into Piaget's stages, based on their responses to your tasks?

---

10 Intelligence and Achievement

Learning Objectives

After studying this chapter, you should be able to:

1. Describe the contributions of Binet and explain the concept of general intelligence. (pp. 389–91)
2. Explain Wechsler's view of intelligence. (p. 391)
3. Describe the views of Spearman, Thurstone, Cattell, and Guilford with regard to intelligence. (pp. 393–94)
4. Define cultural bias and describe the use of criterion sampling, culture-fair tests, and social intelligence tests to supplement standardized intelligence tests and SOMPA. (pp. 394–97)
5. Describe the assessment of infant intelligence and the stability of intelligence during development. (pp. 397–98)
6. Describe the substance of Arthur Jensen's view of the heredity-environment issue with respect to intelligence. (p. 399)
7. Describe the impact of family size and structure, sibling order, and intervention programs on the development of intelligence. (p. 401)
8. Describe the impact of institutionalization and school on the development of intelligence. (p. 401)
9. Describe the relationship between genetic and cultural background and intelligence. (p. 401)
10. Explain the relationship of mental retardation to intelligence. (pp. 402–3, 405)
11. Explain the relationship of giftedness to intelligence. (pp. 403–5)
12. Explain the relationship between creativity and intelligence, including Guilford's contribution to the issue. (pp. 404, 406–7)
13. Describe the evolution of writing. (pp. 407, 409)
14. Compare and contrast the ABC, whole-word, and phonics methods of teaching reading to the method devised by Rozin and Gleitman. (pp. 409–11)
15. Define bilingualism and explain why it is currently important. (pp. 412–14)
16. Compare and contrast the learning of first and second languages. (pp. 412–14)
17. Compare and contrast the status of mathematical achievement in American and Japanese children and give three reasons for the differences in achievement. (pp. 414–17)
18. Explain the importance of motivation in children's development. (pp. 418–19)
19. Describe the achievement motivation views of McClelland and Atkinson. (pp. 419–21)
20. Describe the roles of the attribution process and locus of control in explaining the importance of achievement. (pp. 422–23)
21. Describe the relationship of delay of gratification to achievement. (pp. 423–26)
22. Describe the cultural standards of achievement in American society. (p. 427)
23. Describe parental and peer effects on the development of an achievement orientation. (p. 428)
24. Describe the role of teachers and schools in developing an achievement orientation. (pp. 428–30)
25. Explain the relationship of reinforcement to the development of achievement motivation. (pp. 430–31)

Summary

Binet devised the first intelligence test in 1905 to identify children in French schools who should be placed in special classes. The initial formation of the test was empirical. Many items were tested, and those answered differently by good and poor students were retained. "Higher" mental abilities, such as memory, attention, and comprehension, were better predictors of success in school than items that measured such things as reaction time and speed of hand movement. Binet developed the idea of mental age. The ratio of mental age to chronological age eventually developed into the formula for calculating IQ. Standardization of the Binet showed that scores on this test followed a normal distribution in the population. The Stanford-Binet has a mean of 100, with a standard deviation of 16. The current version can be administered to people from the age of two years through adulthood. In the latest edition, responses can be analyzed into four separate area scores: verbal reasoning, quantitative reasoning, abstract/visual reasoning, and short-term memory.

Like Binet, Wechsler views intelligence as general in nature. However, the Wechsler scales are divided into verbal and nonverbal categories, which are further subdivided to reflect specific aspects of intelligence. Wechsler devised the WAIS (for adults), the WISC-R (for children), and the WPPIS (for children ages 4 to 6½).

In his two-factor theory of intelligence, Spearman suggested that intelligence was composed of general intelligence and a specific factor. Spearman believed that, together, these two factors could account for performance on an intelligence test. Thurstone presented the view that a number of specific factors, rather than one general and one specific factor, make up intelligence. Cattell proposed that there are two different forms of intelligence: fluid intelligence and crystallized intelligence. Guilford proposed a model of 120 mental abilities, composed of all possible combinations of five operations, four contents, and six products.

Alternatives and supplements to standardized intelligence tests have been proposed. Many critics of standardized intelligence tests believe that the tests are not valid; that is, that they do not measure what they are intended to measure. Some psychologists have attempted to develop culture-fair intelligence tests, with little success. Mercer has devised a battery of tests called SOMPA, which includes measures of verbal and nonverbal intelligence, the family's social and economic background, the child's social adjustment to school, and the child's physical health. This may provide a more comprehensive view of the child than a single intelligence test score.

IQ tests still do not provide a correlation between intelligence measured in infancy and intelligence measured at five years of age. Correlations improve after about six years of age.

Genetic and environmental influences on intelligence are complex. Jensen has reported a high heritability (.80) for intelligence, based on twin and family-of-twins studies. Henderson, however, has argued that an estimate of .50 seems more reasonable. Institutionalized children who receive intensive interaction from an adult, such as an "adoptive mother," do much better on an IQ test than institutionalized children who do not receive such interaction. Intervention programs have shown some environmental effects on performance on intelligence tests. Children from intact families, the firstborn, and those from small families perform better than their less-fortunate counterparts. Social class differences are also found in intellectual performance.

Mental retardation is indicated by subaverage general intellectual functioning existing concurrently with deficits in adaptive behavior and manifested during the developmental period. Some forms of mental retardation, such as Down's syndrome and cretinism, are biologically based. Other forms, such as cultural-familial, may be environmental in origin.

Gifted children are often identified by well-above-average performances on IQ tests. Terman's longitudinal study of gifted children has found that gifted people have more intellectual accomplishments, more satisfying personal lives, and better health than a control group.

Sternberg has proposed that there are two facets to intelligence: coping with novelty and automatization. This view of intelligence implies that giftedness can be understood in terms of the ability to think in novel ways, particularly in an insightful manner, and that mental retardation may, in part, involve inadequate automatization of processes.

Creativity and intelligence are not identical, although a certain level of intelligence appears to be necessary to be creative. Guilford has proposed that creativity may involve divergent thinking, rather than convergent thinking. Two techniques to encourage creativity in the classroom are brainstorming and playing with improbabilities.

There are three different kinds of writing systems: alphabetic, syllabic, and logographic. Rozin and Gleitman have developed a method of teaching reading in which children begin with logographic or pictographic representations. After mastering this, the children are taught to read by a syllabic system and finally by the alphabetic system of ordinary English. Research does not clearly demonstrate that this procedure makes reading English any easier for children to master, but it does motivate them to read. The three traditional methods of teaching children to read are the ABC method, the whole-word method, and the phonics method. A combination of the whole-word method and the phonics method is usually taught in American schools.

Bilingualism is an issue in language development that has implications for education and public policy. Children who acquire two languages simultaneously go through three stages. First, the vocabulary is mixed, with a single utterance consisting of words from both languages. Second, the vocabularies are separated, but the child uses the same syntactic rules for both languages. Third, the languages are differentiated in both vocabulary and syntax. Aside from phonology, there is no strong evidence that children acquire a second language any easier than an adult, if motivation and exposure are controlled.

The National Assessment of Educational Progress suggests striving for the following mathematical objectives: mathematical knowledge, mathematical skills, making measurements, reading graphs and tables, mathematical understanding, and mathematical applications. A third-grader should be able to identify the plus and minus signs, describe how to add and subtract, actually do the addition and subtraction, arrange sets of numbers for addition or subtraction, and explain the use of addition and subtraction outside of school (applications).

The level of mathematical skills in Japanese schoolchildren appears substantially higher than in American schoolchildren. The difference has been explained in terms of the amount of time spent on the activities, the amount of practice, and the children's level of attention.

Motivation involves the question of why people behave, feel, or think the way they do. In behavioral theories, rewards in the environment are important to motivation, and in psychoanalytic theories, motivation is biological and instinctive. Cognitive and information processing theories assume that the child is motivated by the desire for knowledge and information.

McClelland has argued for the importance of need for achievement, and Atkinson has introduced the concepts of hope for success and fear of failure. Fear of failure can result in trait anxiety or state anxiety.

Attribution theorists have analyzed the achievement situation in terms of internal and external factors; that is, whether the control is perceived to be within the person or external to the person. An individual with an external locus of control feels that others dictate events, while an individual with an internal locus of control feels that the self dictates events. Weiner believes that we tend to attribute success and failure to ability, effort, task difficulty, and luck.

Mischel has investigated delay of gratification in children. Situational variables, such as whether the desired item is visually present, affect whether gratification can be delayed. Cognitive variables, such as whether the child thinks about the desirable attributes or the neutral attributes of the object, also contribute to the length of delay tolerated. Longitudinal research has shown that preschool children who are able to delay gratification are more likely to become adolescents who are attentive, able to concentrate, and more competent in a number of ways than children who as preschoolers were less able to delay gratification.

Middle-class American adolescents are more achievement oriented than lower-class adolescents or adolescents from other cultures. The parents' model, expectations, and requirements are important determinants of achievement motivation. Elkind has worried that perhaps we are hurrying our children into striving for achievement.

Schools that effectively promote achievement have a strong sense of involvement and commitment on the part of teachers and administrators, appreciation for individual differences, and a knowledge of child development. Getting children to attribute success and failure to effort rather than to external factors has been shown to increase achievement orientation. Observational learning (modeling) is also important.

Intrinsic motivation is behavior that is motivated by an underlying need for competence and self-determination. Extrinsic motivation refers to behavior that is influenced by external rewards. Incentives are external cues that stimulate motivation. However, care must be exercised in the use of incentives because, for example, extrinsic rewards can weaken the performance of intrinsically motivated behavior.

Guided Review

You may want to look at the answers to the "Guided Review" statements as you read, or you may want to use the exercise as a form of self-test by covering up the answers below the statements with a sheet of paper and not consulting them until you have attempted to fill in the blanks of each statement.

1. A California court has ruled, in the case of one black student, that IQ tests are _____ _____ . However, in another court case in _____ , a judge ruled that they were not.
   culturally biased, Illinois

2. The approach to psychology that uses various measurement instruments called _____ is called the _____ approach.
   tests psychometric

3. The first intelligence test was constructed by _____ _____ and _____ _____ . They believed that the best predictions of success in school were made using the "higher" mental abilities (_____ , _____ , and _____) rather than the so-called "lower" mental abilities, which were largely based on _____ skills.
   Alfred Binet, Theodore Simon, memory, attention, comprehension, motor

4. Binet called the concept of describing the level of a child's intellectual functioning the child's _____ _____ . It was based on the _____ of _____ that a child of a given age could answer correctly.
   mental age, number, items.

5. The formula for calculating IQ from the mental age was:
   (_____ age ÷ _____ age) × _____ .
   mental, chronological, 100

6. Assuming that the distribution of intelligence in the population is _____ , the revised Binet (now called the _____ - _____) has been standardized with a mean of _____ and a standard deviation of _____ .
   normal, Stanford-Binet, 100, 16

7. The most recent revision of the Stanford-Binet is the _____ . It provides for the analysis of the individual's responses into _____ separate area scores.
   fourth, four

8. _____ _____ defined intelligence as "the global capacity of the individual to act purposefully, to think rationally, and to deal effectively with the environment." The scales that he developed are divided into verbal and nonverbal _____ .
   David Wechsler, categories

9. The WISC-R is the _____ _____ _____ _____ _____ , the WAIS is the Wechsler _____ _____ - _____ , and the WPPIS is the Wechsler _____ _____ _____ _____ _____ . The first of these is used with children between the ages of _____ and _____ . The last is used with children between the ages of _____ and _____ .
   Wechsler Intelligence Scale for Children, Adult Intelligence Scale, Preschool and Primary Intelligence Scale, 5, 18, 4, 6½

10. A two-factor theory of intelligence was proposed by _____ , and Thurstone developed a _____ - _____ theory.

    Spearman, multiple-factor

11. Raymond Cattell conceptualized the primary mental abilities described by Thurstone as being influenced by two forms of intelligence, which he labeled _____ and _____ intelligence. The first was thought to be _____ , while the second was believed to be determined by the _____ .

    fluid, crystallized, innate, environment

12. Howard Gardner has developed a theory of intelligence based on _____ different kinds of intelligences. He believes that each of these intelligences can be destroyed by specific _____ _____ and that each shows up in both the _____ and in _____ .

    seven, brain damage, gifted, idiot savants

13. J. P. Guilford's _____ of _____ model was composed of combinations of five _____ , four _____ , and six _____ of intellectual functioning.

    structure, intellect, operations, contents, products

14. The concept that expresses the extent to which a test measures what it is intended to measure is called _____ . To evaluate the _____ _____ of a test, the scores on the test are compared with the scores on some other measure, called the _____ . Intelligence tests are reasonably good at predicting _____ (which makes grades the _____) and are not bad at predicting _____ success.

    validity, criterion validity, criterion, grades, criterion, occupational

15. A test that gives no advantage to people with a particular social background is called a _____ - _____ test. There are no _____ items in the Raven Progressive Matrices Test. It is also possible to devise a test with items _____ to the members of the group being tested.

    culture-fair, verbal, familiar

16. The _____ is a battery of measures designed to be used with children from an impoverished background. This battery adds _____ , _____ , and _____ measures to the usual information gathered with the WISC-R.

    SOMPA, social, behavioral, health

17. The correlation between the results of very early estimates of IQ and later estimates is _____ . However, recent work has suggested that _____ during infancy may be a good predictor of later IQ.

    very low, dishabituation

18. A datum that appears to support Jensen's view of intelligence is that there is a _____ correlation between the intelligence scores of identical twins than of fraternal twins. Using some complex calculations, Jensen places the heritability estimate for intelligence at _____ .

    higher, .80

19. Some criticize Jensen's work because his definition of intelligence is based upon a _____ and because the environments sampled were too _____ .

    test, similar

20. Current programs have shown that the intelligence of children of low-income families can be increased by intervening with the _____ . Also, children tend to perform better if they are _____ and come from _____ and/or _____ families. However, many child developmentalists believe that the nature of the _____ in the family is more important than any particular detail of the family's _____ .

mother, firstborn, intact, small, interaction, structure

21. Harold Skeels removed children from an _____ orphanage and placed them in an institution in which they received _____ _____ . The change in treatment _____ intellectual functioning. Although criticized on _____ grounds, this kind of finding has been supported by Brackbill and Bronfenbrenner in work in the _____ _____ that looked at the _____ of child care in _____ .

unstimulating, individual attention, improved, methodological, Soviet Union, quality, institutions

22. In a study of 63 disadvantaged black children, Breitmayer and Ramey found that _____ educational day-care experiences remediated the effects of _____ on _____ .

enriched, poverty, intelligence

23. "Significantly subaverage general intellectual functioning existing concurrently with deficits in adaptive behavior and manifested during the developmental period" is a definition of _____ _____ . This term is a _____ that describes a child's cognitive performance, usually on an _____ test, relative to other children. Many experts caution that one should consider the terms *trainable* and *educable*, as well as the term *mental retardation* itself, as labels that describe _____ performance only.

mental retardation, label, IQ, current

24. _____ to the central nervous system, an extra chromosome (_____ syndrome), or a _____ deficiency (_____) can cause _____ _____ . Retardation can also be caused by damage to the fetus before or during _____ .

Damage, Down's, thyroid, cretinism, mental retardation, birth

25. Cases of mental retardation that do not have a known organic cause are called _____ - _____ . Children with this type of retardation frequently come from _____ environments.

cultural-familial, impoverished

26. A child with a well-above-average intellectual capacity is called _____ . _____ did the classic study of gifted children. The children in his study had remarkable _____ and _____ success, and their overall feeling about their private, social lives was _____ .

gifted, Terman, academic, material, positive

27. The gifted children in Bloom's study who became stars devoted _____ amounts of time to training and practice.

enormous

28. The two facets of Sternberg's conception of intelligence are skill at coping with _____ tasks and situations and skill at _____ information processing. Coping with novelty can be assessed in tests of _____ problems. Automatization of an information processing task can be measured with the _____ task.

novel, automatizing, insight, synonyms

29. Sternberg explains giftedness in terms of the ability to think in _____ ways and in an _____ manner. In Sternberg's view, retardation is the result of inadequate _____ of processes or other similar deficits in the efficiency of information processing.
novel, insightful, automatization

30. The definition and measurement of creativity is _____ . Creativity appears to be only weakly related to _____ .
difficult, intelligence

31. In Guilford's model of intelligence, creativity is most closely related to _____ thinking. This type of thinking produces _____ _____ to one question. _____ thinking, on the other hand, involves moving toward one _____ answer.
divergent, many answers, Convergent, correct

32. _____ is a group effort to produce possible solutions to a problem. _____ are not allowed, only _____ are. A second technique for encouraging creativity is the technique called _____ with _____ . The teacher must foster a _____ _____ in the classroom to encourage the development of creativity.
Brainstorming, Criticisms, suggestions, playing, improbabilities, creative atmosphere

33. The current systems of writing have evolved from systems originated in _____ and _____ . A system that uses individual symbols to correspond roughly to the phonemes in a language is an _____ system. A system in which each written symbol corresponds to a spoken syllable is called a _____ system. A system in which each written symbol corresponds to a word is called a _____ system. The historical trend in the development of writing systems has been toward symbolizing _____ segments of sound.
China, Egypt, alphabetic, syllabic, logographic, smaller

34. _____ and _____ have developed a system of teaching reading that parallels the evolution of writing. In the _____ stage, the child is taught that meaning can be represented visually. Next, in the _____ stage, the child is taught that pictures can stand for words. The third stage is one in which the child learns that _____ _____ can correspond to sounds. It is called the _____ stage. The stage in which the child is taught that symbols can correspond to syllables is called the _____ stage. Finally, the child is taught that syllables can be broken into _____ and that a symbol can roughly correspond to this sound. This is the _____ stage.
Rozin, Gleitman, semasiographic, logographic, written symbols, phoneticization, syllabary, phonemes, alphabet

35. Identifying and responding to the phonemes contained in syllables is called _____ _____ . It is _____ for children to attain and is important for _____ .
linguistic awareness, difficult, reading

36. The _____ method of teaching reading stresses the sounds that letters make when they are in words. When children learn to read with the _____ - _____ method, they learn associations between words and their meanings. The now obsolete _____ method emphasizes the memorization of the _____ of the letters of the alphabet. The current approach is to use some combination of the _____ and _____ - _____ methods.
phonics, whole-word, ABC, names, phonics, whole-word

37. According to Volterra and Taeschner, the first stage of learning two languages simultaneously is the creation of _____ vocabulary. In the second stage, the child has developed _____ _____ vocabularies but _____ syntax. Finally, in the third stage, the languages are _____ .

one, mixed, two separate, one, differentiated

38. The issue of _____ is a current practical education problem that concerns the _____ acquisition of a second language.

bilingualism, successive

39. Young children (do/do not) _____ acquire a second language more quickly and easily than an adult. They (are/are not) _____ more skilled in acquiring a second language. The process of second-language acquisition (is/is not) _____ qualitatively different from first-language acquisition. The exception to these conclusions concerns the acquisition of _____ .

do not, are not, is not, phonemes

40. The variable that is not controlled in comparisons of adults and children who are learning languages is _____ .

time

41. The National Assessment of Educational Progress suggests that the following are appropriate objectives for mathematics education: _____ , _____ , _____ , and _____ .

knowledge, skills, understanding, application

42. Generally, American children are very _____ oriented. However, specifically with respect to mathematics, they are clearly being surpassed by _____ children.

achievement, Japanese

43. It appears that the most likely explanations for the apparent differences in math achievement between American and Japanese children are the differences in the amounts of _____ and _____ that children in the two countries get in mathematics. The _____ of the different educational systems did not differ. The _____ mothers had a generally higher level of schooling. The _____ children are not more intelligent. The Japanese teachers do not have _____ experience than the American teachers. The Japanese school week is _____ , as is the school _____ . Japanese teachers spend approximately _____ percent of the time on mathematics, as opposed to approximately _____ percent for American teachers. Japanese children are _____ likely to be paying attention to the teacher. Japanese children get _____ homework .

time, practice, curricula, American, Japanese, more, longer, year, 25, 12, more, more

44. _____ focuses on the issue of how behavior occurs, while the question of why people behave, think, and feel is one of _____ .

Learning, motivation

45. From the cognitive perspective, motivation comes from the person's _____ for _____ and _____ .

desire, information, knowledge

46. According to the behavioral perspective, arranging the _____ so that it is _____ provides motivation. Thus, motivation is seen as _____ to the child.

environment, rewarding, external

47. According to the psychoanalytic view, motivation is primarily _____ and part of the _____ . This means that, for psychoanalysts, motivation is an _____ .

unconscious, id, instinct

48. _____ view of achievement motivation is that it is a property of the individual's psychological makeup and need system. It is thought to develop out of interactions between the child and _____ and from the cultural standards in which the child lives. _____ training and _____ foster its development.

McClelland's, parents, Independence, democracy

49. The need for achievement concept has been criticized for not being _____ and for being too _____ .

stable, global

50. Atkinson added the idea that _____ in success or failure is an important component of achievement motivation. He suggested that _____ _____ _____ is the same as achievement motivation. _____ _____ _____ is the child's anxiety about doing poorly.

belief, hope for success, Fear of failure

51. Atkinson believes that _____ level and _____ should be assessed to measure motivation. Aspiration level refers to the level of one's _____ ; persistence refers to the _____ of _____ one works on a task.

aspiration, persistence, expectations, length, time

52. Children whose hope for success is _____ than their fear of failure have a healthy achievement orientation. _____ of _____ can interfere with achievement behavior because extreme _____ inhibits this form of motivation.

greater, Fear, failure, anxiety

53. _____ _____ is the consistent tendency to experience anxiety across situations. _____ _____ is anxiety that is specific to a particular situation.

Trait anxiety, State anxiety

54. _____ anxiety is linked to school performance. Moderate levels of this form of anxiety _____ performance; that is, the relationship between state anxiety and performance is _____ .

State, maximize, curvilinear

55. Both _____ and _____ levels of anxiety _____ behavior. There is an interaction between the level of _____ and the _____ of the task. For _____ - _____ or simple tasks, the optimal level of anxiety is _____ . For _____ or _____ tasks, the optimal level is much _____ .

low, high, inhibit, anxiety, difficulty, well-learned, high, new, difficult, lower

56. Attribution theory addresses people's tendency to _____ causes to the behavior of others. Personality traits or motives are _____ causes; environmental or situational factors are _____ causes. A child who thinks that he or she failed because the test was too hard is employing an _____ cause. One who thinks that he or she did well because he or she is smart is employing an _____ cause.

infer, internal, external, external, internal

57. Weiner believes that people attribute success or failure to _____ , _____ , _____ _____ , and _____ . People tend to feel _____ after success and _____ after failure.

ability, effort, task difficulty, luck, good, bad

58. The child's sense of personal _____ is closely linked to the way the child views achievement. If the child feels in control, he or she has an _____ locus of control. The feeling that one is powerless to control his or her own destiny reflects an _____ locus of control. _____ are much more likely to grow up with an internal locus of control than _____ are.

responsibility, internal, external, Boys, girls

59. Postponing an immediate reward in favor of a later, more desired reward is called _____ _____ _____ . Children can delay gratification for a _____ period of time if they do not think about the reward or, instead, think about its "cool" features, rather than its hot ones. Mischel has found that the ability to delay gratification in the preschool period predicts _____ during _____ .

delay of gratification, longer, competence, adolescence

60. _____ -class children are more likely to be able to _____ _____ than _____ -class children. They show more _____ _____ when asked to tell stories about achievement-related situations.

Middle, delay gratification, lower, achievement motivation

61. Children _____ the standards of reward that they see their _____ adopt. They also model the achievement standards of _____ and _____ at school.

imitate, parents, peers, teachers

62. Both _____ _____ and _____ also work in the peer situation. Recently, it has been found that both of these factors can result in _____ _____ - _____ and the sort of _____ effort behavior that produces _____ performance. Even if schools take steps to assure a cooperative atmosphere in the classroom, the parents of _____ -ability students may undermine the efforts.

social comparison, competitiveness, negative self-esteem, low, ineffective, high

63. Schools that are effective in fostering motivation in their students take _____ _____ seriously and have teachers and administrators who have a strong sense of _____ and who are willing to spend _____ to make the work _____ .

individual differences, caring, time, interesting

64. When students learn to modify their achievement attributions, there are changes in _____ . Training sixth-grade students to make _____ evaluations _____ the time the students spent trying to solve an unsolvable task.

persistence, effort, increased

65. Gagne warns that such attribution training requires great _____ . The child may also have a self-image of _____ _____ . Given the behavioral principle of _____ , it may be best to start with tasks that require only a small amount of _____ and then gradually increase the amount required for _____ .

patience, low ability, shaping, effort, success

66. If students are going to imitate the teacher, that teacher must make a good _____ .
Effective teachers use a variety of _____ , signal _____ behavior, maintain
_____ contact, and state the desired _____ . They also are _____ -
_____ ; value _____ , work, and effort; and are self-_____ .
They maintain a classroom climate of _____ and mutual respect.
impression, rewards, appropriate, eye, attitudes, well organized, achievement, disciplined, warmth

67. The person in the class most likely to be imitated is the most _____ student. This means that there
are at least _____ important models in each class.
popular, two

68. Motivation that is based upon an underlying need is called _____ motivation. Extrinsic motivation
refers to behavior supported by _____ .
intrinsic, rewards

69. External cues that stimulate motivation are called _____ . One recent study showed that the
application of _____ incentives and rewards can decrease _____ if the task
was already _____ motivated.
incentives, external, performance, intrinsically

70. Schunk found that either _____ cues (information about peer performance) or
_____ cues (goals) improved performance in a math problems task. Children who received
_____ produced the highest level of performance.
external, internal, both

Key Terms Matching Exercise

Match the Key Term on the left with the correct definition on the right.

____ 1. psychometricians (LO–1, p. 389)
____ 2. Mental age (MA) (LO–1, p. 389)
____ 3. IQ (LO–1, p. 389)
____ 4. normal distribution (LO–1, p. 390)
____ 5. mean (LO–1, p. 390)

a. Symmetrical frequency distribution, with a majority of the cases falling in the middle of the possible range of scores and fewer scores appearing toward the ends of the range

b. Those who use measurement techniques to assess a concept of psychology

c. Binet's measure of the level of the child's intellectual functioning

d. Originally defined as (MA/CA) $\times$ 100; however, now defined in statistical terms as a deviation score

e. Sum of the scores divided by the number of scores (also the arithmetic average)

_____ 6. standard deviation (LO–1, p. 390)
_____ 7. two-factor theory (LO–3, p. 393)
_____ 8. multiple-factor theory (LO–3, p. 393)
_____ 9. fluid intelligence (LO–3, p. 393)
_____ 10. crystallized intelligence (LO–3, p. 393)
_____ 11. structure of intellect model (LO–3, p. 393)

a. Spearman's theory of intelligence, which proposes that intelligence is composed of a general factor and a specific factor
b. Measure of the amount of variation in a set of scores
c. Aspect of intelligence that is independent of education and experience in Cattell's theory
d. Thurstone's argument that a number of specific factors, rather than one general and one specific factor, make up intelligence
e. Guilford's model that proposes 120 mental abilities, composed of all possible combinations of operations, contents, and products
f. Aspect of intelligence affected by schooling and environment in Cattell's theory

_____ 12. operations (LO–3, p. 394)
_____ 13. contents (LO–3, p. 394)
_____ 14. products (LO–3, p. 394)
_____ 15. validity (LO–4, p. 394)
_____ 16. criterion validity (LO–4, p. 394)
_____ 17. culture-fair test (LO–4, p. 396)

a. Forms in which information occurs: units, classes, relations, systems, transformations, or implications
b. Intelligence tests that attempt to eliminate cultural bias
c. Extent to which a test measures what it is intended to measure
d. Extent to which a measure of a test can be correlated to another measure or can accurately predict another measure or criterion
e. Kinds of information being operated upon: figural, symbolic, semantic, or behavioral
f. According to Guilford, intellectual activities or processes carried out on information

_____ 18. SOMPA (LO–4, p. 396)

_____ 19. institutionalization (LO–8, p. 401)

_____ 20. mental retardation (LO–10, p. 402)

_____ 21. cretinism (LO–10, p. 403)

_____ 22. cultural-familial retardation (LO–10, p. 403)

_____ 23. gifted child (LO–11, p. 403)

a. Severe form of mental retardation caused by thyroid insufficiency

b. Form of mild retardation with no detectable brain abnormality but at least one parent or sibling who is also mentally retarded

c. Child with well-above-average intellectual capacity or a superior talent

d. The process of placing a person in group living facilities for corrective or therapeutic purposes

e. System of Multicultural Pluralistic Assessment; battery of tests that provides information about the child's verbal and nonverbal intelligence, social and economic background, social adjustment to school, and physical health

f. Significantly subaverage general intellectual functioning existing concurrently with deficits in adaptive behavior and manifested during the developmental period

_____ 24. creativity (LO–12, p. 404)

_____ 25. divergent thinking (LO–12, p. 406)

_____ 26. convergent thinking (LO–12, p. 406)

_____ 27. brainstorming (LO–12, p. 406)

_____ 28. playing with improbabilities (LO–12, p. 406)

_____ 29. syllabic writing system (LO–13, p. 407)

a. Many-faceted phenomenon, involving, among other things, the production of unique ideas or products

b. Writing system in which each written symbol corresponds to a spoken syllable

c. Type of thinking that produces many different answers to a single problem

d. Technique used to encourage creativity in which unlikely occurrences are presented and people generate possible events that might follow those occurrences

e. Type of thinking wherein attention is directed toward finding one correct answer to a question

f. Technique for fostering creativity in which a topic is suggested, ideas are freewheeling, criticism is withheld, and combination of suggested ideas is encouraged

_____ 30. logographic writing system (LO–13, p. 407)
_____ 31. ABC method (LO–14, p. 411)
_____ 32. whole-word method (LO–14, p. 411)
_____ 33. phonics method (LO–14, p. 411)
_____ 34. motivation (LO–18, p. 418)
_____ 35. *n* achievement (LO–19, p. 419)

a. Need and motivation to strive for success; viewed as a property of the individual, remaining constant over different domains and time

b. Writing system in which each visual symbol corresponds to a word or phrase

c. Method of teaching reading that emphasizes memorizing the names of the letters of the alphabet

d. Desires, needs, or interests that energize the organism and direct it toward a goal

e. Method of teaching reading that stresses the sounds that letters make when in words

f. Method of teaching reading that is based on learning direct associations between words and their meanings

_____ 36. hope for success (LO–19, p. 420)
_____ 37. fear of failure (LO–19, p. 420)
_____ 38. trait anxiety (LO–19, p. 421)
_____ 39. attribution theory (LO–20, p. 422)
_____ 40. internal locus of control (LO–20, p. 423)
_____ 41. external locus of control (LO–20, p. 423)

a. Adolescent's anxiety about doing well; relevant to achievement motivation

b. Individual's perception that others or events have more control over the individual than that person has over himself or herself

c. Stable and permanent tendency to experience a certain level of anxiety across time and circumstances

d. Theory that views individuals as cognitive beings who attempt to understand the causes of their own and others' behavior

e. Equivalent of achievement motivation; the adolescent's underlying drive for success

f. Individuals' perception that they are in control of their world, can cause things to happen, and can command their own rewards

_____ 42. delay of gratification (LO–21, p. 423)
_____ 43. intrinsic motivation (LO–24, p. 430)
_____ 44. extrinsic motivation (LO–25, p. 430)
_____ 45. incentives (LO–25, p. 431)
_____ 46. self-efficacy (LO–25, p. 431)

a. Indexes judgments of how well one can execute courses of action required in situations

b. External cues that stimulate motivation

c. Refers to behavior influenced by external rewards

d. Refers to behavior influenced by underlying needs for competence and self-determination

e. Purposely deferring immediate gratification for more desired future gratification

1. b	9. c	17. b	25. c	33. e	41. b
2. c	10. f	18. e	26. e	34. d	42. e
3. d	11. e	19. d	27. f	35. a	43. d
4. a	12. f	20. f	28. d	36. e	44. c
5. e	13. e	21. a	29. b	37. a	45. b
6. b	14. a	22. b	30. b	38. c	46. a
7. a	15. c	23. c	31. c	39. d	
8. d	16. d	24. a	32. f	40. f	

Self-Test A

Choose the best alternative.

1. What was the task required of Alfred Binet? (LO–1, p. 389)
   a. He was asked to come up with a general theory of intelligence.
   b. He was asked to design a test that would identify students who would not benefit from regular classes.
   c. He was asked to determine the relationship between intelligence and creativity in French schoolchildren.
   d. He was asked to design achievement tests that measured the reading and mathematical abilities of schoolchildren.

2. Jonathan has a mental age of 10 and a chronological age of 8. Jonathan's IQ would be (LO–1, p. 389)
   a. 125.
   b. 113.
   c. 100.
   d. 80.

3. How does the Wechsler scale differ from the Binet? (LO–2, p. 391)
   a. The Binet provides a measure of general intelligence; the Wechsler does not.
   b. The Wechsler provides a measure of general intelligence; the Binet does not.
   c. The Wechsler measures both verbal intelligence and performance; the Binet does not.
   d. The Binet measures both verbal intelligence and performance; the Wechsler does not.

4. Which theorist is associated with the theory that intelligence consists of a general and a specific factor? (LO–3, p. 393)
   a. Guilford
   b. Cattell
   c. Thurstone
   d. Spearman

5. Intelligence that focuses on the individual's adaptability and capacity to perceive and integrate things and that is independent of education and experience is called (LO–3, p. 393)
   a. general intelligence.
   b. specific intelligence.
   c. fluid intelligence.
   d. crystallized intelligence.

6. Jenny teaches Jill how to use a screwdriver by picking one up and demonstrating its use. According to Guilford, what content is being used? (LO–3, p. 394)
   a. figural
   b. symbolic
   c. semantic
   d. behavioral

7. Dr. Smith uses the Stanford-Binet to measure Donna's IQ. She then looks at several performance measures: how quickly Donna learns a game, how well Donna can shop in a store, and whether Donna reads any books or magazines. Dr. Smith finds that Donna's performance on the test and her performance on the other measures are strongly related. The use of both measures is a kind of (LO–4, p. 394)
   a. developmental scale.
   b. criterion validity.
   c. transfer component.
   d. normal distribution of behavior.

8. Which of the following is an example of a culture-fair test? (LO–4, p. 396)
   a. Stanford-Binet
   b. WAIS
   c. Chitling Test
   d. Kaufman Assessment Battery for Children

9. An attempt to incorporate social intelligence into the assessment of IQ is illustrated by the use of (LO–4, p. 396)
   a. the WISC-R.
   b. culture-fair tests.
   c. the SOMPA battery of tests.
   d. repeated testing.

10. The proponent of the position that intelligence is largely inherited was (LO–6, p. 399)
    a. Kamin.
    b. Piaget.
    c. Jensen.
    d. Spearman.

11. Which of the following statements is true? (LO–7, p. 401)
    a. Later-born children generally have higher IQs than earlier-born siblings.
    b. Children from large families generally have higher IQs than children from small families.
    c. Children from father-absent families usually score lower on IQ tests than children from intact families.
    d. Firstborn siblings generally have lower IQs than second-born siblings.

12. In a classic study, intelligence as measured by IQ scores of institutionalized children was raised by (LO–8, p. 401)
    a. improving the nutrition in the institution.
    b. assigning each infant to an "adoptive mother"—a mentally retarded young woman who cared for the infant.
    c. providing trips for the children outside of the institution.
    d. coaching the children on Piagetian tasks.

13. Cretinism is caused by (LO–10, p. 403)
    a. an extra chromosome.
    b. a defect in metabolizing a certain amino acid.
    c. brain damage during delivery.
    d. a defect in the functioning of the thyroid gland.

14. According to Sternberg's model of intelligence, gifted children are better at _____ than nongifted children. (LO–11, p. 405)
    a. automatization
    b. thinking in insightful ways
    c. developing transfer components
    d. retrieval components

15. A group of children are asked to think of as many different solutions to the question "How can our school raise money for athletic equipment?" They are told not to criticize ideas, just to produce them. Which technique is being used? (LO–12, p. 406)
    a. brainstorming
    b. enrichment
    c. grouping
    d. playing with improbabilities

16. In the study by Rozin and Gleitman, the use of pictographic representations corresponds to which of the following? (LO–14, p. 410)
    a. ABC method
    b. alphabetic writing system
    c. logographic writing system
    d. syllabic writing system

17. In teaching children to read, what is the currently accepted method? (LO–14, p. 411)
    a. ABC method alone
    b. whole-word method with phonics method
    c. whole-word method alone
    d. phonics method alone

18. According to Volterra and Taeschner, what is the first stage in children's simultaneous acquisition of two languages? (LO–16, p. 412)
    a. single, mixed vocabulary
    b. two sets of syntactic rules, but mixed vocabulary
    c. two completely separated languages
    d. two vocabularies, one set of syntactic rules

19. The force that energizes and directs behavior, thoughts, and feelings is (LO–18, p. 418)
    a. incentive.
    b. cognition.
    c. reinforcement.
    d. motivation.

20. According to Elkind, exposing very young children to achievement motivation situations (LO–23, p. 428)
    a. is good for them because, when they are older, they will have a healthy achievement motivation.
    b. actually has the opposite effect; that is, the children give up.
    c. has no effect until the child is well into elementary school.
    d. is not a good idea.

Answers to Self-Test A

1. b	5. c	9. c	13. d	17. b
2. a	6. d	10. c	14. b	18. a
3. c	7. b	11. c	15. a	19. d
4. d	8. d	12. b	16. c	20. d

Self-Test B

Choose the best alternative.

21. Which of the following tasks did Binet find best discriminated between children who did well in school and those who did not? (LO–1, p. 389)
    a. reaction time
    b. comprehension
    c. block design
    d. picture assembly

22. Thomas has a mental age of 7 and a chronological age of 14. What is Thomas's IQ? (LO–1, p. 389)
    a. 200
    b. 103
    c. 78
    d. 50

23. For what population is the WPPIS designed? (LO–2, p. 391)
    a. adults
    b. normal school-aged children
    c. preschool-aged children
    d. infants

24. Which theorist is associated with the position that intelligence does not involve a general factor, but rather, many different specific factors? (LO–3, p. 393)
    a. Thurstone
    b. Binet
    c. Wechsler
    d. Spearman

25. Tania is given the problem 8 + 9 = ? to solve. This task requires which of Guilford's operations? (LO–3, p. 394)
    a. memory
    b. convergent thinking
    c. divergent thinking
    d. evaluation

26. To be sure a test measures what it is supposed to measure, we must evaluate the test's (LO–4, p. 394)
    a. reliability.
    b. validity.
    c. practical applications.
    d. theoretical implications.

27. A test that is standardized on one group and then used to evaluate a group that is substantially different from the standardization group could be said to have (LO–4, p. 395)
    a. cultural bias.
    b. validity.
    c. cultural fairness.
    d. test-retest reliability.

28. Which psychologist is responsible for developing the SOMPA for testing children's intellectual functioning? (LO–4, p. 396)
    a. Jensen
    b. Piaget
    c. Mercer
    d. Sternberg

29. Which of the following measures of infants has proven to be positively correlated with IQ at five years of age? (LO–5, p. 398)
    a. age of onset of walking
    b. the development of object permanence
    c. measures of dishabituation
    d. reactions to strangers

30. Jensen argues for which of the following positions for intelligence? (LO–6, p. 399)
    a. It is primarily genetically determined.
    b. It is primarily environmentally determined.
    c. It has both a strong genetic and strong environmental component.
    d. It has a strong environmental and a moderate genetic component.

31. What criticism has been leveled at heritability studies? (LO–6, p. 399)
    a. Some data from heritability studies have been fraudulent.
    b. Most heritability studies have not included environments that differ from one another in radical ways.
    c. They do not adequately control for genetic similarity.
    d. Very little data on heritability have been published.

32. Sarah is the third of seven children from an upper-class family. Dorothy is the only child in a lower middle-class family. What is most likely to be their relative scores on an IQ test? (LO–7, p. 401)
    a. They will probably score the same because social class will balance birth order and family size.
    b. Sarah will probably score better than Dorothy because upper-class children generally do better than lower-class children.
    c. Dorothy will probably score better than Sarah because firstborn children and children from small families generally do better than later-born children and children from large families.
    d. A prediction cannot be made in this case.

33. What procedure could be implemented to prevent long-term negative effects on the intelligence of institutionalized children? (LO–8, p. 401)
    a. an "adoptive mother" program
    b. a concentrated enrichment program
    c. adequate physical care of the children
    d. adequate medical care of the children

34. In which of Sternberg's facets of intelligence are mentally retarded individuals lower than normal individuals? (LO–10, p. 405)
    a. skill at coping with novel tasks
    b. ability to generate insightful solutions to tasks
    c. the automatization of information processing skills
    d. All of the above are correct.

35. What is the probable order of development, from earliest to most recent, of the following writing systems? (LO–13, p. 409)
    a. logographic to syllabic to alphabetic
    b. alphabetic to syllabic to logographic
    c. syllabic to logographic to alphabetic
    d. logographic to alphabetic to syllabic

36. According to Volterra and Taeschner, what is the second stage in children's simultaneous acquisition of two languages? (LO–16, p. 412)
    a. single, mixed vocabulary
    b. two sets of syntactic rules, but mixed vocabulary
    c. two completely separated languages
    d. two vocabularies, but one set of syntactic rules

37. According to research by Mischel, preschoolers who are able to delay gratification will become adolescents who (LO–21, pp. 425–26)
    a. go to pieces under stress.
    b. are restless and fidgety.
    c. use and respond to reason.
    d. think of themselves as bad.

38. Children in the United States trail children in Japan in mathematical skills because (LO–17, p. 417)
    a. the Japanese children get more practice in math.
    b. Japanese teachers are better prepared in math.
    c. Japanese parents in the study had more education than the American parents.
    d. the Japanese children have a higher intellectual level (IQ).

39. John blames his lack of preparation for his poor test score, while Bill complains that the questions were tricky and that there was not enough time. John's orientation is _____ , and Bill's is _____ . (LO–20, p. 422)
    a. internal/internal
    b. internal/external
    c. external/internal
    d. external/external

40. In cartoons, you sometimes see the rider of a donkey dangling a carrot in front of the beast. In the language of this chapter, the carrot is (LO–25, p. 431)
    a. a motive.
    b. a reinforcement.
    c. an incentive.
    d. a controller.

Answers to Self-Test B

21. b	25. b	29. c	33. a	37. c
22. d	26. b	30. a	34. c	38. a
23. c	27. a	31. b	35. a	39. b
24. a	28. c	32. c	36. d	40. c

Questions to Stimulate Thought

1. Is intelligence process or content?
2. Is intelligence inherited or acquired? Is the issue of whether intelligence is process or content related to this answer?
3. How fair are intelligence tests both in principle and in practice? Explain.
4. Is intelligence stable throughout life? Why or why not?
5. Can mental retardation and giftedness be defined in terms of intelligence alone? Why or why not?
6. There are parts of the United States where English is not the dominant language. If English is to be maintained as the national language, how should it be done? How should the problem of teaching English as a second language be dealt with?
7. What is involved in teaching reading? Which method of teaching reading should be used and why?
8. Is achievement motivation learned?
9. Why do some children have high achievement motivation?

Research Project

In this exercise, you present two creativity tasks to each of two children—one age 6, the other age 10. You should evaluate the children's responses with regard to the hypothesis that there may be both age differences and individual differences in creativity. Be sure to keep a "straight face" during each child's response period and to treat both children the same. Use the following data sheet and data summary sheet for collecting and summarizing your data. Then answer the questions that follow.

Data Sheet

Child 1: Age _____   Sex _____

Task 1: What are some unusual ways to use a spoon?

Task 2: How many objects can you name that are red?

Child 2: Age _____   Sex _____

Task 1: What are some unusual ways to use a spoon?

Task 2: How many objects can you name that are red?

Data Summary Sheet

1. Enter the number of responses for each child for each task into the following table:

Task	Child 1	Child 2
One		
Two		

2. Without looking at the data first, create a scale measuring the originality of the responses and score the responses for originality.

Questions

1. Which child had the larger number of responses for Task 1? for Task 2?
2. Which child had more original responses for Task 1? for Task 2?
3. Overall, which child seemed to provide more creative responses? To what would you attribute this? How does your finding fit with information on creativity presented in the text? Do you think that your particular tasks were appropriate for eliciting creative responses in children? Why or why not?

11 Social and Personality Development in Middle and Late Childhood

Learning Objectives

After studying this chapter, you should be able to:

1. Describe the changes in parent-child interactions in middle and late childhood, including the transition from caregiving and support activities to chores, material reinforcement, self-entertainment, monitoring of activities, and school-related issues. (p. 441)
2. Describe the use of discipline during middle and late childhood and the transfer of control from the parent to the child. (p. 442)
3. Explain the impact of the changes in the child during middle and late childhood on the parents. (pp. 442–43)
4. Explain the impact of growing up in a stepparent family. (pp. 443–44)
5. Explain the issues concerning latchkey children. (p. 444)
6. List and explain the factors that promote peer popularity. (p. 445)
7. Explain the importance of social cognition in peer relationships in middle and late childhood. (pp. 446, 449)
8. Define friendship and describe the changes in friendships and their importance in middle and late childhood. (pp. 449–52)
9. Explain the role of classroom structure on social development during middle and late childhood. (pp. 452–54)
10. Describe a good teacher. (pp. 454–55)
11. Define and explain the importance of Aptitude-Treatment Interaction. (pp. 455–56)
12. Explain the implications of the assertion that schools have a middle-class bias. (pp. 457–58)
13. Describe the development of the self in middle and late childhood and the possible relationship to perspective taking. (pp. 460–62)
14. Compare and contrast self-concept and self-esteem. (pp. 462–63)
15. Define social competence and explain its measurement and importance. (pp. 464–66)
16. Describe the two major changes in sex typing that occur during middle and late childhood. (p. 466)
17. Define the concept of sex or gender roles and explain the importance of the concept of androgyny. (pp. 466–68)
18. What are sex-role stereotypes? Explain their effect on social development during middle and late childhood. (pp. 469–70)
19. List and explain at least four actual differences between men and women. (pp. 470–72, 475)
20. Describe Kohlberg's theory of moral development and explain the criticisms of his work and theory. (pp. 476–84)
21. Compare and contrast moral reasoning and social conventional reasoning. (p. 484)
22. Describe the relationship between socioeconomic status and the report of problems and disturbances in middle and late childhood. (p. 488)
23. Describe the two major reasons for referring children for clinical help during middle and late childhood. (pp. 488–89, 491–92)
24. Describe the resilient child. (p. 492)

Summary

Children mature, and parents respond by adjusting demands and expectations in accordance with the changes in the child. The issues of early childhood include modesty, bedtime, temper, fighting, eating, manners, autonomy in dressing, and attention seeking. During the elementary school years, new issues, such as chores, self-entertainment, and monitoring, appear. In middle and late childhood, school-related matters take on a central importance.

Discipline changes during elementary school as the child becomes easier to reason with. There is less physical punishment. Deprivation of privileges, appeals to self-esteem, and guilt are more likely to be used. During these years, there is a coregulation process as control shifts from parent to child. The parents of elementary school children are more experienced than they were during the child's infancy.

Remarriage after divorce is common and can result in many different kinds of families, with attending complications and conflicts. In the 1990s, almost 30 percent of all children will be part of a stepfamily before their 18th birthday. Relationships within the stepfamily are frequently conflict-ridden, strained, and distant.

Latchkey children are those whose parents work and who, after school, use their own key to let themselves into their empty house. They are unsupervised for two to four hours a day. This unsupervised time may provide the child with an impetus for development, or it may be a negative experience, resulting in the child getting into trouble.

Peer interaction increases during elementary school. By 7 to 11 years of age, children are spending 40 percent of their time with peers. Peer popularity in school is related to reinforcing others' behaviors, listening carefully to peers' conversations, being happy, showing enthusiasm and concern for others, and having self-confidence without conceit. Neglected children are not actively disliked but have no friends; rejected children are disliked by their peers.

Social information processing skills can affect peer relations. Intention or motive is attributed to others' behavior, and misinterpretation can lead some children to respond aggressively. Social knowledge, or availability of scripts for developing friendships, also affects a child's ability to develop peer relations.

Friendships are specific attachments to a peer and have similarities to parent-infant attachment. However, they often are not permanent. Intimacy in friendship develops with age, with adolescents knowing more intimate things about their friends than elementary school children. Friends are similar to one another in interests, values, and attitudes. Friendships involve sharing, and this shared support appears early in development. Girls' friendships appear to be characterized by more intimacy than boys' friendships. Having a best friend is positively associated with self-esteem, but the direction of causality is uncertain. Friendships also involve much shared knowledge about one another, and this clearly develops with age. The research suggests that good communication skills are important in developing friendships.

A group exists when children interact with one another on an ongoing basis, sharing values, goals, norms, and guidelines. A leader is also an important characteristic of a group.

Competition between groups breeds hostility and distrust, whereas situations that require cooperation breed intergroup friendship and understanding.

By the time they graduate from high school, children have spent more that 10,000 hours in school. During middle childhood, the classroom is still the major context, although it is more likely to be experienced as a social unit than in the preschool.

Some classrooms are open or flexible, and others are highly structured and traditional. Some students may do better in structured environments, while others may perform better in a flexible classroom. A meta-analysis has revealed that some of the components of a flexible classroom may be important individually. Teachers also may function better in one environment than the other.

Positive teacher traits are enthusiasm, planning ability, poise, adaptability, and awareness of individual differences. Erikson believes that good teachers have the ability to produce a sense of industry, rather than inferiority, in their students.

Teachers can be classified as challenging and demanding, or as encouraging good performance. Teachers working with high-socioeconomic-status/high-ability students are more successful if they are challenging and demanding, while teachers who are successful with low-socioeconomic-status/low-ability students are warm and encouraging. This is a reflection of Aptitude-Treatment Interaction.

Teachers and administrators are predominantly white and middle class and may have lower expectations for children who are lower class or nonwhite. Teachers with lower-class origins appear to perceive their lower-class students more positively than do middle-class teachers.

In middle and late childhood, the child's ability to understand how he or she is viewed by others increases, as does differentiation, individuation, and stability. Selman proposed a developmental sequence of perspective taking that involves understanding the viewpoint of another and realizing that others can take our view. In Selman's view, self-awareness develops along with perspective-taking skills.

Self-concept and self-esteem are sometimes used interchangeably. They can be assessed with Harter's Perceived Competence Scale for Children, the Piers-Harris Scale, or Coopersmith's Self-Esteem Inventory.

Social competence is defined as the ability to make use of environmental resources to achieve a good developmental outcome. The developmental tasks differ at different ages. Therefore, what constitutes social competence differs at different ages. To adequately assess social competence, broad, rather than narrow, assessments in ecologically valid contexts are necessary. Assessments should emphasize the coordination of affect, cognition, and behavior.

The issue of androgyny challenges the view that well-adjusted children behave in sex-appropriate ways. The androgyny view claims that masculinity and femininity, rather than being polar opposites, are independent dimensions and that an individual can and should have characteristics of each. Androgyny can be assessed with the Bem Sex-Role Inventory and a number of other scales.

Relating androgyny to competence is hampered by the difficulties in specifying the dimensions. Some researchers have suggested the concepts of assertiveness and integration. If assertiveness and integration are the determining characteristics, then androgynous children would be expected to be superior in situations requiring those characteristics.

Stereotypes are used as verbal shorthand, and stereotypical labels, whether accurate or not, have effects on people. The terms *masculine* and *feminine* both have stereotypes associated with them.

Males and females exhibit a number of sex differences in abilities. In their analysis of the literature, Maccoby and Jacklin reported that women are more verbal, while men are more mathematical and aggressive. Baumrind has distinguished between instrumental competence and incompetence. There is some evidence that boys are socialized to be instrumentally competent, while girls are socialized to be instrumentally incompetent. Girls also attribute failure to uncontrollable factors more than boys do. Females have lower expectations for success across many tasks, and the tendency to think in this way begins early in development.

Kohlberg's theory of moral development can be seen as an extension of Piaget's view. In Kohlberg's scheme, there are three levels of moral reasoning, with two stages at each level. At the preconventional level, the child's reasoning about moral issues is based on punishments or rewards expected from the environment. At the conventional level, the child's reasoning about moral issues stems from the standards of other people, such as parents, or from the rules of society. At the postconventional level, the individual's reasoning about moral issues is based on an internal moral code. Kohlberg found that higher levels of moral reasoning appear with age, and he accepted a conflict-equilibrium model to account for change from one stage to the next. General cognitive development is a necessary but not a sufficient condition for the child to change his or her level of moral reasoning. The modeling of more advanced arguments is one way to provide conflict, and according to research, to achieve more advanced reasoning. Like Piaget, Kohlberg believed that peer interaction is critical in providing cognitive conflict for adolescents. The effectiveness of transactive discussion in advancing moral reasoning in adolescents indicates the importance of communication skills in peer discussion.

Kohlberg's theory has been criticized on a number of grounds. First, moral thought is not the same as moral behavior, and some argue that Kohlberg has placed too much emphasis on reasoning, thereby neglecting moral action. Second, Kohlberg's research methods have been criticized, in part for being limited in scope, for being exceedingly difficult to score, and for focusing on limited issues that may not be the issues with which children and adolescents are primarily concerned. Third, Gilligan has criticized Kohlberg for only interviewing males in developing his theory and has also suggested that his view omits a concern for caring and relationships as key ingredients in moral reasoning. Fourth, many critics view moral development as more culture-specific than Kohlberg believed. It is argued that morality should be construed as a matter of the individual's accommodation to the values and requirements of society.

Social conventional reasoning regulates social interactions and appears to be independent of moral reasoning. Even young children seem to believe that social conventional rules can be changed so that behaviors previously unacceptable can become acceptable, while moral transgressions are unacceptable even if there is no rule prohibiting them.

A number of attempts have been made to introduce moral education into schools. John Dewey argued that school organization is such that schools present an authoritarian rather than a democratic model to students and that obedience is one of the prime messages. He called this the "hidden curriculum." Debate exists over exactly what should be taught in moral education—whether the focus should be on specific values or on ways of reasoning about moral issues.

There is a general decline in the number of reported problems for children from 4 to 16 years of age. Parents of lower-socioeconomic-status children report more problems than parents of middle-socioeconomic-status children.

A number of different behaviors, such as aggression, school failure, anxiety, antisocial behavior, and poor peer relations, can be related to childhood depression, which makes it difficult to diagnose. Another problem that appears during middle and late childhood is underachievement in school. Some children seem to be extraordinarily resilient at exhibiting normal development in spite of poor developmental background and environment. Some children who have everything against them and are exposed to much stress still thrive and become extremely competent. The critical variable may be the quality of their attentional processes.

Guided Review

You may want to look at the answers to the "Guided Review" statements as you read, or you may want to use the exercise as a form of self-test by covering up the answers below the statements with a sheet of paper and not consulting them until you have attempted to fill in the blanks of each statement.

1. As children move into the elementary school years, parents spend _____ time with them. The size in the drop in attention seems to be inversely correlated with parental _____ .
    less, education

2. During the early childhood period, the focus of parent-child interaction is on such issues as _____ , _____ regularities, _____ of temper, _____ with siblings and peers, _____ behavior, _____ in dressing, and attention-_____ behavior. During the elementary school years, new issues emerge, such as _____ and the possible _____ for them, self-_____ , and _____ outside the home.
    modesty, bedtime, control, fighting, eating, autonomy, seeking, chores, pay, entertainment, monitoring

3. During middle and late childhood, _____-related matters become prominent. Problems in this area are the main reason for _____ help.
    school, clinical

4. In some ways, discipline is easier from the elementary years on because the child can _____ . The child can understand the reason for _____ rules. The incidence of _____ punishment decreases after the beginning of elementary school.
    reason, disciplinary, physical

5. The transition between the _____ parental control of the preschool years and the reduced supervision of the _____ years has been called _____ . During this time, parents should _____ , _____ , and _____ the child, effectively use all direct contacts, and strengthen the child's self-_____ skills.
    strong, adolescent, coregulation, monitor, guide, support, monitoring

6. Parents of elementary school children have more _____ than when the children were younger. The reduction in child-rearing demands that occurs during _____ and _____ childhood may be accompanied by the mother's decision to return to a _____ .
    experience, middle, late, career

7. It is estimated that, during the 1990s, _____ to _____ percent of all children will be part of a stepfamily before their 18th birthday. In the _____ _____ , both the stepparent and the biological parent bring children to the marriage. In a _____ _____ , the stepparent brings no children to the marriage.
25, 30, complex stepfamily, simple stepfamily

8. Relationships with the _____ are more strained than those with the _____ parent. Those with the stepfather tend to be _____ and _____ ; relationships with the stepmother tend to be _____ but _____ .
stepparent, biological, distant, unpleasant, extensive, abrasive

9. Children who return to an empty home after school are called _____ children. Elkind worries that latchkey children have too much _____ . They are more likely to get into _____ .
latchkey, responsibility, trouble

10. The proportion of peer interaction at age 2 is _____ percent; by age 4, it is _____ percent; and between the ages of 7 and 11, it increases to more than _____ percent. These interactions involve _____ and _____ -focused issues. Boys, more than girls, prefer _____ sports, but both list _____ _____ , _____ , and _____ as important. Groups tend to be _____ -sexed. In one study, children spent more than twice as much time with peers as with _____ .
10, 20, 40, play, dominance, team, general play, going places, socializing, same, parents

11. Giving _____ enhances children's popularity, as does _____ to others, showing _____ , being _____ , and having self-_____ . Popularity is also facilitated by physical _____ , being _____ - class, and being _____ .
reinforcements, listening, enthusiasm, yourself, confidence, attractiveness, middle, intelligent

12. _____ children have few friends, but _____ children, who are more likely to be _____ and _____ , are overtly disliked by their peers.
Neglected, rejected, disruptive, aggressive

13. Dodge's analysis of children's understanding of social situations reflects an _____ _____ approach. According to Dodge, inappropriate aggression is frequently the result of a deficit in _____ - _____ detection. In Dodge's research, socially rejected and neglected children had _____ intention-cue detection scores than popular and average children. Dodge's work shows that aggressive children incorrectly attribute hostile _____ to peers.
information processing, intention-cue, lower, intentions

14. Inability to interact appropriately with peers may mean that a child does not have a _____ for forming a friendship. Further, it has been found that boys without peer adjustment problems are better at a number of _____ _____ skills than maladjusted boys.
script, social cognitive

15. One of the most important components of a friendship is _____ . Friendships involve specific attachments that have several characteristics not unlike those found in _____ - _____ . Friendships begin to be prevalent when the child is _____ to _____ years old.
intimacy, parent-child attachment, 8, 10

16. Diaz and Berndt found that eighth-grade children knew _____ intimate things about their friends than did fourth-grade children. The majority of the evidence suggests that _____ have more intimate friendships than does the opposite sex.

    more, girls

17. Friends tend to have _____ characteristics and _____ and can provide _____ in coping with conflict. By the middle of the elementary school years, friendships involve a considerable amount of _____ information about each other's personal and social characteristics.

    similar, attitudes, support, reciprocal

18. Parker and Gottman found that children who were exposed to a conversationally skilled doll showed _____ signs of friendship formation than those children who were exposed to a conversationally unskilled doll. This identifies the importance of _____ skills in the formation of friendships.

    more, conversational

19. The distinguishing characteristic of a group is the differentiation of _____ and _____ . According to Sherif, intergroup hostility is increased by _____ between the groups and is decreased by _____ between the groups.

    leaders, followers, competition, cooperation

20. The 13 years of education that the typical American child gets amounts to over _____ hours of school. Concerning the social context at school, the _____ is still the major context for the elementary school child; however, it is more likely to be perceived as a _____ _____ than it was in preschool.

    10,000, classroom, social unit

21. _____ classrooms provide a wide variety of learning materials, are characterized by space flexibility, and allow students to assume responsibility for their learning. In _____ classrooms, specific sequences of tasks are followed most of the time.

    Open, traditional

22. Giaconia and Hedges performed a complex analysis called a _____ - _____ . They found that, when the open classroom had a large effect on the child's _____ - _____ , the role of the child was a criterion in all investigations. Otherwise, the effects of manipulating classroom structure have generally been found to be _____ .

    meta-analysis, self-concept, small

23. According to Erikson, good teachers can produce a sense of _____ rather than _____ in their students. They promote _____ with those who know things and know how to do things. They are _____ .

    industry, inferiority, identification, flexible

24. Recently, educational experts such as Cronbach and Snow have argued that teaching effectiveness should be studied by looking at the Aptitude-Treatment _____ . In an Aptitude-Treatment Interaction, _____ refers to academic potential. Treatment refers to the _____ _____ . Students with high-achievement orientation do well in a _____ classroom, while those with low-achievement orientation do better in a _____ classroom.

    Interaction, aptitude, teaching method, flexible, traditional or structured

25. _____ poor work is not a good way to motivate low-socioeconomic-status students. These students respond best when _____ _____ is praised. High-socioeconomic-status students respond best to a _____ pace and enforced _____ .

Criticizing, good work, quicker, standards

26. Schools have a _____-class bias. The teaching climate in the low-income school described by Clark would be expected to lead to _____ performance. Middle-class teachers have _____ expectations for children from low-income families than children from middle-class families. It appears that teachers with _____ - _____ backgrounds might make better teachers in low-income schools.

middle, poorer, lower, lower-class

27. _____ by itself is not sufficient to promote understanding between different races. Within the schools, multi-ethnic curricula, projects focused on racial issues, and mixed work groups lead to _____ changes in racial sensitivity and understanding.

Desegregation, positive

28. According to Maccoby, an important part of the development of self-concept is the child's ability to understand how others _____ him or her. Children develop a more _____ view of themselves as they get older. They also develop a more _____ view of themselves. They tend to describe themselves in terms of how they are _____ from peers. With age, the self-concept is more _____ . Children display more ability to integrate new _____ into a _____ sense of who they are.

perceive, differentiated, individuated, different, stable, information, stable

29. Selman's views on the development of the self are related to the development of _____ _____ . In Selman's Stage 0 of perspective taking, very young children are not able to conceive of an inner self separate from external _____ . In Stage 1, children believe that a person's inner life is reflected by his or her _____ . In Stage 2, children realize that the inner life of the self may not be reflected in the person's _____ . Children at Stage 3 take a _____ - _____ perspective. Individuals at Stage 4 understand that mutual perspective taking does not always lead to _____ _____ .

perspective taking, appearances, behavior, behavior, third-person, complete understanding

30. The sense that each person develops of who he or she is is called the _____ - _____ . A closely related concept that reflects the value that children place on themselves is called _____ - _____ .

self-concept, self-esteem

31. The Piers-Harris Scale consists of items designed to measure a child's _____ - _____ as a stable and consistent aspect of personality. Harter's Perceived Competence Scale for Children assesses the child's competence across _____ , _____ , and _____ subscales. It includes one general subscale that is supposed to reflect _____ - _____ independent of any particular skill. Harter and Pike have also developed a pictorial version for _____ _____ .

self-concept, cognitive, social, physical, self-worth, young children

32. For Waters and Sroufe, the _____ _____ child is "one who is able to make use of environmental resources to achieve a good developmental outcome." _____ of _____ , ego _____ , and ego _____ are important strengths of the socially competent child. _____ for _____ is also an important dimension.

socially competent, Delay, gratification, resiliency, control, Need, achievement

33. The assessment of social competence should consider both _____ and _____-_____ aspects. The psychologist should be concerned with the _____ validity of the results obtained. A third issue in the assessment of social competence involves how the child coordinates _____ , _____ , and _____ . The assessment of social competence should also plug into the _____/_____ capacities of the child in dealing with critical events or transactions in his or her world.

global, fine-grained, ecological, affect, cognition, behavior, integrative/adaptive

34. In middle childhood, _____ show a strong increase in sex-typed behavior, while many girls (do/do not) _____ begin to show a stronger preference for _____ interests and activities.

boys, do not, girls'

35. The term _____ refers to the extent to which a person's psychological makeup includes both masculine and feminine characteristics. The aspects of masculinity and femininity that our culture _____ are the ones that comprise androgyny. The individual who scores low on both masculinity and femininity is labeled as _____ .

androgynous, values, undifferentiated

36. The core items on scales designed to measure androgyny are _____ - _____ for the masculine characteristics and _____ for the feminine characteristics.

self-assertion, integration

37. The _____ child should be the most competent if self-assertion and integration are the criteria for competence. However, if the criteria focus on self-assertion alone, both _____ and _____ children ought to perform well, and if the criteria focus on integration alone, both _____ and _____ children ought to be superior.

androgynous, masculine, androgynous, feminine, androgynous

38. _____ - _____ _____ are broad categories that reflect impressions about people, events, and ourselves relative to gender. The terms _____ and _____ are both adjectives reflecting stereotypes.

Sex-role stereotypes, masculine, feminine

39. According to Maccoby and Jacklin, females are more _____ , and males are more _____ and _____ . However, Maccoby and Jacklin do not find evidence that girls are more _____ or _____ than boys. Tieger argues that consistent sex differences do not appear until the age of _____ .

verbal, mathematical, aggressive, social, suggestible, six

40. _____ _____ means performing behaviors that are socially responsible and purposeful. Baumrind has suggested that women are socialized to assume roles of _____ _____ . The expectation that boys will become _____ and girls will become nurses is consistent with this assertion.

Instrumental competence, instrumental incompetence, doctors

41. Boys are more likely to attribute success to _____ , while girls tend to attribute it to _____ and _____ . Moderate parental permissiveness and attempts to accelerate achievement promote _____ _____ in girls.

ability, effort, luck, achievement motivation

42. If one believes that one's behavior does not control the outcome of an attempt, then a state of _____ _____ may develop. According to Dweck and Eliot, even when girls outperform boys on a task, they do not feel that they did as well. This is evidence that girls have formed a _____ expectancy for success. Apparently, the _____ girls underestimate their skills the most.
    learned helplessness, lower, brightest

43. During adolescence, both boys and girls focus on the integration of _____ and _____-_____ choices. Gifted girls perceive a conflict between _____ and _____. However, an intervention program developed by Kerr produced an _____ in the high-prestige career choices made by gifted girls.
    vocational, life-style, career, family, increase

44. Kohlberg used the _____ for much of his research on the moral reasoning of children. In his view, a child without internalized moral values and who bases moral judgments on consequences is operating at the _____ level, one who has internalized authorities' standards of moral behavior is operating at the _____ level, and one who has developed a personal moral code after exploring alternative moral options is operating at the _____ level.
    interview, preconventional, conventional, postconventional

45. In the first stage of Kohlberg's theory, moral judgments are based on the presence or absence of _____. In the second stage, moral judgments are based on the presence or absence of _____. In the third stage, judgments are based on other people's _____, such as those of the _____, while in the fourth stage, judgments are based on the _____ _____. A person operating at the highest stages of moral reasoning bases judgments on a _____ moral code accepted by the community or one that is _____.
    punishments, rewards, standards, parents, rules of society, personal, individualized

46. Kohlberg has found that advancement through his stages of moral development is related to _____ and to _____.
    age, intelligence

47. Exposure to a model who is operating at a more advanced level of moral reasoning than the child has been shown to _____ the level of the child's moral reasoning. Presenting arguments slightly above the functioning level of the child produces cognitive _____.
    advance, conflict

48. One benefit of the mutual give-and-take of peer interactions is the opportunity to take the _____ of another person. Berkowitz and his associates found that _____ discussion was most effective for affecting change in the adolescent's moral reasoning. Transactive discussion can take two forms, of which _____ transaction is the more effective in advancing moral reasoning.
    perspective, transactive, operational

49. Some critics of Kohlberg's work have argued that he did not pay enough attention to moral _____. One critic has argued that the Kohlberg protocols are very _____ to score. It is possible that the Kohlberg stories are too _____ in scope.
    behavior, difficult, narrow

50. Gilligan has argued that the Kohlberg data are very _____ - _____ . Gilligan suggests that there are two perspectives in moral reasoning: the _____ perspective, which focuses on the rights of the individual, and the _____ perspective. However, a literature review by Walker revealed that only 8 out of 108 studies showed sex differences favoring _____ .
sex-biased, justice, care, males

51. Some critics argue that moral development is more _____ - _____ than Kohlberg's approach suggests. According to Bronfenbrenner and Garbarino, a child who is exposed to multiple social _____ and multiple _____ views is more likely to be morally _____ and less likely to be _____ oriented. The view that society, not the individual, is the source of all values is referred to as _____ . In this view, moral development is a process of _____ to the values and requirements of society.
culture-specific, agents, sociopolitical, sophisticated, authority, societalism, accommodation

52. _____ _____ rules exist to control behavioral irregularities. They are _____ , while _____ rules are not.
Social conventional, arbitrary, moral

53. The _____ _____ refers to the implicit teaching of values in the schools. It was Dewey's view that, in school, the student learns about _____ and _____ of _____ rather than about democratic principles. Teachers' rules and peer relations transmit attitudes about _____ issues.
hidden curriculum, obedience, defiance, authority, democratic

54. Kohlberg argues for teaching _____ - _____ _____ rather than any particular value system. Recent evidence shows that students from _____ alternative high schools are more willing to act responsibly than students from traditional, _____ high schools.
moral-reasoning skills, democratic, authoritarian

55. Achenbach and Edelbrock found a general _____ in reported behavior problems with age. They also found that _____-socioeconomic-status parents reported more problems than _____ - socioeconomic-status parents.
decrease, low, middle

56. Such symptoms as aggression, school failure, anxiety, antisocial behavior, and poor peer relations are often related to _____ during childhood. The array of depressive symptoms seen in childhood is _____ than that seen in adults.
depression, broader

57. Problems in _____ are the largest cause of referrals for clinical treatment during childhood. A child who earns grades that are lower than what would be predicted by IQ scores is called an _____ , while an _____ earns higher grades than an IQ test predicts. A child who is purposely inactive in order to keep school grades low may be described as _____ - _____ . Passive-aggressive underachieving children usually have a low tolerance for _____ .
school, underachiever, overachiever, passive-aggressive, criticism

58. Children who flourish despite terrible home environments have been described as _____ . According to Garmezy, resilient children have superior _____ capabilities.
resilient, attention

Key Terms Matching Exercise

Match the Key Term on the left with the correct definition on the right.

____ 1. peer sociotherapy (LO–1, p. 440)

____ 2. coregulation process (LO–1, p. 442)

____ 3. complex stepfamily (LO–4, p. 443)

____ 4. simple stepfamily (LO–4, p. 443)

____ 5. latchkey children (LO–5, p. 444)

____ 6. neglected children (LO–6, p. 445)

a. Gradual transfer of control from parent to child; a transition period

b. Children who carry a house key and return from school to an empty house and are unsupervised for a period of time

c. Result when both stepparent and biological parent bring children to the marriage

d. Result when the stepparent does not bring children to the newly formed family

e. Children who are ignored by their peers

f. Therapy program designed to help individuals improve their peer relations in classroom settings, group activities, and sports by training peers to provide support and encouragement to each other in group settings

____ 7. rejected children (LO–6, p. 445)

____ 8. intention-cue detection (LO–7, p. 447)

____ 9. intimacy in friendship (LO–8, p. 450)

____ 10. open classroom (LO–9, p. 453)

____ 11. Classroom Environment Scale (LO–9, p. 453)

a. Measure that assesses teacher-student and peer relationships, as well as the organization of the classroom

b. Children who are disliked by their peers

c. Classroom climate that offers free choice of activities, space flexibility, varied learning materials, individual instruction, self-responsibility by students, multi-age grouping of children, team teaching, and classrooms without walls

d. Ability to interpret social cues to determine the reason for a behavior

e. Self-disclosure and the sharing of private thoughts

____ 12. meta-analysis (LO–9, p. 454)

____ 13. Aptitude-Treatment Interaction (LO–11, p. 455)

____ 14. aptitude (LO–11, p. 455)

____ 15. treatment (LO–11, p. 455)

____ 16. Perceived Competence Scale for Children (LO–15, p. 462)

a. Hypothetical academic potential and personality dimensions in which students differ

b. Application of statistical techniques to already existing studies

c. Idea that the outcome of a particular educational intervention might depend upon the level of the students and vice versa

d. Educational technique adopted in the classroom

e. Measure of self-concept that emphasizes the assessment of the child's sense of competence across different domains

_____ 17. androgyny (LO–17, p. 467)

_____ 18. undifferentiated (LO–17, p. 467)

_____ 19. sex-role stereotypes (LO–18, p. 469)

_____ 20. learned helplessness (LO–19, p. 473)

_____ 21. preconventional moral reasoning (LO–20, p. 476)

a. Lack of motivation and negative affect associated with the belief that the rewards one receives are beyond personal control

b. Level in Kohlberg's theory of moral development in which the child shows no internalization of moral values but bases moral thinking on punishments and rewards

c. Term used to describe an individual who does not perceive himself or herself as either masculine or feminine

d. Sex-role orientation that describes an individual whose psychological makeup includes both masculine and feminine aspects of behavior

e. Personality characteristics attributed to people on the basis of their sex without regard for their individuality

_____ 22. conventional moral reasoning (LO–20, p. 476)

_____ 23. postconventional moral reasoning (LO–20, p. 476)

_____ 24. transactive discussion (LO–20, p. 480)

_____ 25. justice perspective (LO–20, p. 483)

_____ 26. care perspective (LO–20, p. 483)

_____ 27. societalism (LO–20, p. 484)

a. Reasoning that operates on the reasoning of another individual

b. Level in Kohlberg's theory of moral development characterized by morality that is internalized and based on the development of a moral code derived from an active exploration of alternative moral courses and options

c. View of morality that argues that society, not the individual, is the source of all values

d. Level in Kohlberg's theory of moral development in which the child internalizes externally generated standards, that is, abides by the standards of the family or society

e. An approach to moral development proposed by Gilligan in which people are viewed in terms of their involvement with other people; the focus is on their communication with others

f. An approach to moral development proposed by Gilligan in which people are differentiated from one another and seen as standing alone; the focus is on the rights of the individual

Answers to Key Terms Matching Exercise

1. f	5. b	9. e	13. c	17. d	21. b	25. f
2. a	6. e	10. c	14. a	18. c	22. d	26. e
3. c	7. b	11. a	15. d	19. e	23. b	27. c
4. d	8. d	12. b	16. e	20. a	24. a	

Self-Test A

Choose the best alternative.

1. Which of the following statements about the relationship between stepchildren and stepparents is true? (LO–4, pp. 443–44)
   a. The relationship between stepfather and child is distant and somewhat unpleasant.
   b. The relationship between stepmother and child is distant and somewhat unpleasant.
   c. The relationship between stepfather and child involves an extensive but abrasive set of interactions.
   d. The relationship between stepmother and child is warm and affectionate.

2. Which of the following is not a potential problem for latchkey children? (LO–5, p. 444)
   a. They may get into trouble without limits and parental involvement during latchkey hours.
   b. They may be forced to grow up too fast.
   c. They may be required to take on responsibilities before they are ready for them.
   d. They may thrive on the responsibility and become more mature and independent.

3. Which of the following has not been associated with peer popularity? (LO–6, p. 445)
   a. using reinforcement
   b. showing conceit
   c. showing enthusiasm
   d. showing concern for others

4. Deficiencies in which of the following information processing strategies can lead to inappropriate aggression in some boys? (LO–7, p. 447)
   a. intention-cue detection
   b. response search
   c. selecting an optimal response
   d. enactment

5. How do friendships differ from the parent-child bond? (LO–8, p. 449)
   a. Parents are a source of security in upsetting circumstances; friends are not.
   b. Separation from parents arouses anxiety; separation from friends does not.
   c. The parent-child bond is permanent; friendships are not.
   d. Children develop a sense of trust in their parents, but not in their friends.

6. When are intimate friendships first formed? (LO–8, p. 450)
   a. early childhood
   b. early adolescence
   c. late childhood
   d. late adolescence

7. All of the following traits in a teacher relate positively to the student's intellectual development except (LO–10, p. 454)
   a. impulsiveness.
   b. enthusiasm.
   c. adaptability.
   d. awareness of individual differences.

8. Which of the following situations will produce the best outcome? (LO–11, pp. 455–56)
   a. a low-ability student with a challenging and demanding teacher
   b. a high-achievement oriented student in a flexible classroom
   c. a high-ability student with a warm and encouraging teacher
   d. a low-achievement oriented student in a flexible classroom

9. Ed describes himself primarily in terms of how he is different from his peers. Ed is most likely in what age group? (LO–13, p. 461)
   a. infancy
   b. early childhood
   c. middle childhood
   d. adolescence

10. Which of the following leads to high self-esteem? (LO–14, p. 462)
   a. very strict rules at home
   b. varying the rules to fit the situation
   c. allowing unlimited freedom
   d. parental expression of affection

11. Which of the following positions reflects Waters and Sroufe's position on assessment of social competence? (LO–15, pp. 465)
   a. The focus in assessment needs to be narrow and particular, rather than broadband.
   b. There needs to be a stronger emphasis on ecologically valid assessment in real-life circumstances.
   c. Affect, cognition, and behavior need to be assessed individually, rather than assessing the coordination of the dimensions.
   d. There need to be more tightly controlled studies in laboratories, away from the complexities of the real world.

12. Jimmy is a sympathetic, warm, affectionate, analytical, forceful, little boy. His sex-role orientation is best labeled as (LO–17, p. 467)
   a. masculine.
   b. feminine.
   c. undifferentiated.
   d. androgynous.

13. Two currently used androgyny scales were developed by (LO-17, p. 467)
   a. Bem and Spence.
   b. Freud and Erikson.
   c. Skinner and Watson.
   d. Maccoby and Jacklin.

14. Broad categories that reflect our impressions about people, events, and ourselves are (LO–18, p. 469)
   a. sex-role stereotypes.
   b. gender identity.
   c. gender constancy.
   d. gender.

15. Which of the following is a way in which males differ from females, according to research evaluated by Maccoby and Jacklin? (LO–19, p. 470)
   a. Males are more verbal.
   b. Males are more competitive.
   c. Males are more dominant.
   d. Males are more mathematical.

16. When an individual believes that the rewards he or she receives are beyond personal control, the individual experiences (LO–18, p. 473)
   a. learned helplessness.
   b. instrumental competence.
   c. instrumental incompetence.
   d. fear of failure.

17. Kohlberg's theory of moral development concentrates primarily on which of the following? (LO–20, p. 476)
    a. moral feeling
    b. moral reasoning
    c. moral behavior
    d. moral action

18. If a child is presented with a moral dilemma and responds by arguing that the person should choose a course of action that avoids punishment, which of Kohlberg's stages of moral development would be represented? (LO–20, p. 476)
    a. Stage 1
    b. Stage 2
    c. Stage 3
    d. Stage 4

19. If a child is presented with a moral dilemma and responds by arguing that the person should choose a course of action so that people will not think badly of him or her, which of Kohlberg's stages of moral development would be represented? (LO–20, p. 476)
    a. Stage 1
    b. Stage 2
    c. Stage 3
    d. Stage 4

20. Which of the following problems is found more in children who have been referred to clinics than in those who have not been referred to clinics? (LO–23, pp. 488–89)
    a. bed-wetting
    b. poor schoolwork
    c. fear of certain animals
    d. fear of certain places

Answers to Self-Test A

1. a	5. c	9. d	13. a	17. b
2. d	6. b	10. d	14. a	18. a
3. b	7. a	11. b	15. d	19. c
4. a	8. b	12. d	16. a	20. b

Self-Test B

Choose the best alternative.

21. In a stepparent family, the child's relationship with the stepmother is frequently (LO–4, p. 444)
    a. the same as with the stepfather.
    b. warm and accepting.
    c. distant and unpleasant.
    d. extensive but abrasive.

22. Wally comes home from school every day and takes care of himself until his parents come home from work at six o'clock. During the summer, he is home alone all day. This is a description of (LO–5, p. 444)
    a. an abandoned child.
    b. permissive-indulgent parenting.
    c. insecure attachment.
    d. a latchkey child.

23. Knowledge of a script that will allow one to become friends with another is an aspect of (LO–7, p. 446)
    a. social information processing.
    b. social knowledge.
    c. perspective-taking skills.
    d. communicative skills.

24. Friends are often similar in all of the following except (LO–8, p. 450)
    a. age.
    b. sex.
    c. attitudes toward school.
    d. ability.

25. Research on the formation of children's groups has found all of the following except which? (LO–8, p. 452)
    a. Norms develop in all groups.
    b. Frustration and competition contribute to hostility between groups.
    c. Hierarchical structures emerge, with the middle positions filled first.
    d. Intergroup hostility can be reduced by setting up a goal that requires cooperation from both groups.

26. Which of the following children is likely to do better in a traditional classroom than in an open classroom? (LO–11, pp. 455–56)
    a. Jane, who has a high-achievement orientation
    b. Bill, who has a low-achievement orientation
    c. Terry, who has high ability and enjoys challenges
    d. Don, who motivates himself

27. Which of the following adjectives is likely to be used by a teacher with lower-class origins to characterize a lower-class student? (LO–12, p. 457)
    a. lazy
    b. rebellious
    c. happy
    d. fun-loving

28. The Piers-Harris Scale has been criticized for all of the following reasons except which? (LO–14, p. 462)
    a. Children's self-perception changes according to the situation, but the Piers-Harris Scale measures a stable aspect of personality.
    b. It relies on self-report, which can be distorted by the reporter.
    c. It takes too long to administer and is impractical.
    d. There is no assurance that children will respond honestly.

29. A child who is able to use environmental resources to achieve a good developmental outcome is (LO–15, p. 464)
    a. socially competent.
    b. low in ego control.
    c. low in ego resiliency.
    d. identity achieved.

30. For what area of development do Waters and Sroufe advocate broadband assessments in ecologically valid contexts? (LO–15, p. 465)
    a. self-concept
    b. social competence
    c. delay of gratification
    d. identity

31. Karen is a sensitive, compassionate, individualistic, self-reliant, little girl. Karen's sex-role orientation is best labeled as (LO–17, p. 467)
    a. masculine.
    b. feminine.
    c. undifferentiated.
    d. androgynous.

32. An androgynous individual is one whose psychological makeup (LO–17, p. 467)
    a. includes both masculine and feminine aspects.
    b. is masculine if the individual is female.
    c. is feminine if the individual is male.
    d. is low on both masculine and feminine aspects.

33. Timmy is going to see the doctor, and he expects that the doctor will be a strong man who will know how to make him better. Timmy is using _____ to generate his expectations. (LO–18, pp. 469–70)
    a. gender constancy
    b. gender identity
    c. sex-role stereotypes
    d. person constancy

34. According to research evaluated by Maccoby and Jacklin, which of the following is a way in which females differ from males? (LO–19, pp. 470–71)
    a. Females are more verbal.
    b. Females are more sensitive.
    c. Females are more compliant.
    d. Females are more suggestible.

35. Behavior that is socially responsible and purposeful is called (LO–18, p. 472)
    a. instrumental incompetence.
    b. instrumental competence.
    c. learned helplessness.
    d. dominant.

36. In Kohlberg's view, which of Piaget's stages of cognitive development is a prerequisite for Stage 5 moral reasoning? (LO–20, pp. 476–78)
    a. sensorimotor
    b. preoperational
    c. concrete operational
    d. formal operational

37. Research by Eliot Turiel has found that children show a preference for a response _____ their level of moral reasoning. (LO–20, p. 478)
    a. one stage below
    b. two stages below
    c. one stage above
    d. two stages above

38. Which of the following criticisms of Kohlberg's theory of moral development is most strongly associated with Carol Gilligan? (LO–20, p. 481)
    a. sex bias
    b. a coding scheme that is too difficult
    c. cultural specificity
    d. lack of concern with moral behavior

39. Reasoning about a dress code in a school is an example of a problem requiring (LO–21, p. 484)
    a. moral reasoning.
    b. moral performance.
    c. transactive discussion.
    d. social conventional reasoning.

40. Which of the following statements about childhood depression is true? (LO–23, pp. 488–89)
    a. It occurs as early as the third month of life.
    b. It is more common in girls than boys.
    c. It is more common in boys than girls.
    d. The frequency declines during puberty.

Answers to Self-Test B

21. d	25. c	29. a	33. c	37. c
22. d	26. b	30. b	34. a	38. a
23. b	27. c	31. d	35. b	39. d
24. d	28. c	32. a	36. d	40. b

Questions to Stimulate Thought

1. What is the relationship, if any, between parenting styles and discipline techniques?
2. Is the family the same institution it was in the past (10, 20, 30, 50, or 100 years ago)?
3. Can the skills for popularity be learned? Are there factors in popularity that are beyond the child's control?
4. When is a peer a friend?
5. What is the impact of the school experience on the development of the child?
6. What teacher characteristics or teaching styles are the best or most effective?
7. How is sex-role orientation related to psychological competence?
8. Should moral reasoning be taught in the schools? How or why not?
9. Is social conventional reasoning the same as moral reasoning?

Research Project

In this project, you evaluate three prime-time television shows for sex-role stereotyping. Pick three shows between 8:00 and 9:00 in the evening that children might watch. For each show, record the following information: (1) number of males and females as main characters, (2) occupations of main males and females, and (3) thematic connections between males and females (for example, is the female in distress and the male the rescuer?). Use the data sheet that follows to record your information and then answer the questions that follow.

Data Sheet

Program _____   **Male**   **Female**

Number

Occupations

Connections

Program _____	Male	Female
Number		
Occupations		
Connections		

Program _____	Male	Female
Number		
Occupations		
Connections		

Questions

1. In the shows you watched, were more main roles taken by males or females? What kinds of occupations did the males have? What kinds of occupations did the females have? Were there status differences in the occupations of the males and females? What were they?
2. What kinds of themes connected the males and females in the television programs you watched? Were the themes stereotyped for male-female relationships?
3. Was the overall impression one of strong sex typing on television? Did the programs you watched support the data presented in the text? If not, to what do you attribute the difference?
4. What do you think these models are teaching children about what it means to be a male or a female in our society? Do you think that these models are a fair representation of the way women and men act in the real world?

Section 5 Adolescence

12 Physical and Cognitive Development in Adolescence

Learning Objectives

After studying this chapter, you should be able to:

1. Present G. Stanley Hall's view of adolescence. (pp. 503–4)
2. Describe the factors that went into the molding of the concept of adolescence between 1890 and 1920. (pp. 504–5)
3. Explain how the use of stereotypes has influenced popular notions about the nature of adolescence. (p. 505)

4. Define puberty and menarche. (pp. 506–8)
5. Define the hypothalamic-pituitary-gonadal axis and endocrine system. (pp. 508–9, 511)
6. Define gonadotropin. (pp. 508, 510)
7. List and give the functions of the sex steroids. (pp. 510–11)
8. Describe the physical changes, in terms of both growth and sexual maturation, associated with puberty in both boys and girls. (pp. 511–16)
9. Describe the effects that going through puberty has on adolescent body image. (pp. 516–17)
10. Describe how the timing of puberty can affect the social development of both boys and girls. (pp. 517–21)
11. List and explain the characteristics of formal operational thought. (pp. 522–28)
12. Describe the egocentrism of adolescence. (pp. 529–32)
13. Explain implicit personality theory. (p. 532)
14. Describe social monitoring during adolescence. (pp. 533–34)
15. Explain the importance of vocational orientation and work during adolescence. (pp. 534–37)

Summary

Several different views of adolescence have been proposed. G. Stanley Hall proposed the turbulent "storm and stress" view of adolescence. Hall, who was strongly influenced by Darwin, believed that adolescence was primarily biological. According to Cohen, adolescence is a social-cultural construct, and schools, work, and economics have all played important parts in this construct. The view of adolescence as a time of conflict may be a misrepresentation based on observations of disturbed adolescents, rather than the normal group. The current view is that both biological and cultural influences operate on the adolescent.

Adolescence is marked by the onset of puberty. Sexual maturation and growth spurts are the most prominent signs of the pubertal process. The endocrine system is responsible for both growth and sexual maturation through the release of hormones. Androgens are male sex hormones, and estrogens are female sex hormones. The hormones most prominent in puberty are testosterone and estradiol. For males, puberty involves an increase in the size of the testicles and penis, the appearance of body hair, voice changes, and the first ejaculation. For females, puberty involves the development of breasts, the appearance of body hair, widening of the hips, development of fatty tissue over the body, and the onset of menstruation. The growth spurt begins for girls at about age 10½ and at about age 12½ for boys. During the growth spurt, females grow about 3½ inches a year, males about 4 inches a year.

The timing of puberty can have consequences for the psychological well-being of the individual. Early-maturing boys perceive themselves more positively and are more successful in peer relations than later-maturing boys. For girls, early maturation is not necessarily a benefit. Early-maturing girls do better in heterosexual relationships and show more independence than later-maturing girls. However, they tend to get lower grades and achievement test scores than later-maturing girls. Early-maturing girls are more satisfied with their bodies in early adolescence, while later-maturing girls are more satisfied with their bodies in late adolescence.

The last stage of Piaget's theory of cognitive development is formal operational thought. This stage, which is usually present in adolescents and adults, is characterized by abstractness, hypothetical-deductive reasoning, perspective taking, idealism, and advanced understanding of language. Thought is no longer limited to the real and concrete but can be applied to the possible and to abstract propositions. Scientific reasoning appears. The adolescent is able to generate possible hypotheses and to systematically test them to discover a correct answer. Understanding of metaphor and changes in the pragmatics of language also characterize this period. Formal operational thinkers are better than concrete operational thinkers at perspective taking, such as considering and understanding another person's point of view.

Piaget emphasized universal and consistent patterns of formal operational thought. However, individual differences that were not explained by Piaget's theory characterize the cognitive development of adolescents and adults. One finding is that the same individual may reason formally in one domain but not in others.

During adolescence, egocentrism is reflected in two types of adolescent thinking—construction of the imaginary audience and the personal fable. The imaginary audience is the adolescent's belief that others are as preoccupied with the adolescent's behavior as he or she is. The personal fable refers to the adolescent's sense of personal uniqueness and indestructibility.

Adolescents become implicit personality theorists, according to Carl Barenboim. They think more abstractly about the behavior of others and try to verify assumptions. They look for more complex causes of behavior. Although these abilities may be present, they are not always used when appropriate.

The ability to use cognitive strategies to monitor social behavior increases during adolescence, which is an application of adolescents' new reasoning abilities to social situations. Adolescents also become able to reflect on their opinions of others and to realize that these opinions may be influenced by such factors as fatigue, illness, or prejudice.

Adolescents become more interested in career exploration. Super and his colleagues found that, from the end of high school to the mid-20s, many individuals floundered and made unplanned changes in their jobs. Youths are not a large part of the full-time work force. However, about three-fourths of high school seniors work part-time. Working helps adolescents to understand how to get and keep a job and how to manage money and budget time. It does not help them to get along better with adults. Overall, unemployment does not appear to be high among adolescents who want jobs, although a disproportionate number of unemployed adolescents are black.

Guided Review

You may want to look at the answers to the "Guided Review" statements as you read, or you may want to use the exercise as a form of self-test by covering up the answers below the statements with a sheet of paper and not consulting them until you have attempted to fill in the blanks of each statement.

1. The father of the scientific study of adolescence was _____ _____ _____ . He was influenced by _____ , who believed that _____ influences on development were more important than _____ ones.

    G. Stanley Hall, Darwin, genetic, environmental

2. Hall believed that the stages of development were _____ , _____ , _____ , and _____ . He saw adolescence as full of turmoil, a period of _____ and _____ .

    infancy, childhood, youth, adolescence, storm, stress

3. According to Cohen, adolescence is a concept that was _____ . Society created adolescence as a transition between _____ and _____ .

    invented, childhood, adulthood

4. One view of the creation of adolescence has it linked to the drive for _____ _____ _____ . From this view, schools are seen primarily as vehicles for transmitting _____ skills to youth. Others see the schools as having _____ purposes.

    compulsory public education, intellectual, economic

5. Compulsory education laws in the early 1900s resulted in decreased adolescent _____ and increased adolescent _____ _____ . In the period from 1910 to 1930, there was a _____ percent increase in high school enrollments.

    employment, school attendance, 450

6. Yankelovich found little difference between adolescents and their parents in attitudes toward such things as _____ - _____ , _____ _____ , and _____ _____ . However, only _____ percent of adolescents, as opposed to _____ percent of their parents, said that religion was important. Hill blames the stereotype of the adolescent on the visible adolescents of the _____ .

    self-control, hard work, saving money, 66, 89, 1960s

7. Adolescence is influenced by the interaction of _____ and _____ factors. Bronfenbrenner's _____ model involves _____ experiences; that is, the interaction of the _____ setting with such social agents as _____ , _____ , and _____ . It also involves a consideration of _____ and _____ present in the culture.

biological, cultural, ecological, sociocultural, social, family, peers, teachers, attitudes, ideologies

8. The extent to which adolescence is determined by heredity or past experiences is called _____ in development. New experiences may be the stimulus for _____ .

continuity, discontinuity

9. The first menstruation is called _____ . In the last 100 years, its age of occurrence has _____ . Currently, it occurs at about _____ years of age. Apparently, a higher level of _____ and _____ are the cause. The occurrence of menarche is associated with the individual's _____ . About _____ percent of the body weight must be fat. Starvation can lead to _____ , the delay or cessation of menstruation. _____ can be defined as the rapid change to maturation.

menarche, dropped, 12.5, health, nutrition, weight, 17, amenorrhea, Puberty

10. _____ glands release their secretions, called _____ , directly into the bloodstream rather than through ducts, as the _____ glands do. The hormones regulate _____ .

Endocrine, hormones, exocrine, organs

11. The part of the endocrine system that is crucial in puberty involves the _____ - _____ - _____ axis. The _____ is a part of the brain that interacts with the master gland or _____ . The term _____ refers to the testes or the ovaries. The pituitary secretes a _____ that stimulates the testes or the ovaries.

hypothalamic-pituitary-gonadal, hypothalamus, pituitary, gonadal, gonadotropin

12. Male sex hormones are called _____ , and female sex hormones are called _____ . The most important male sex hormone is _____ , while the hormone most responsible for female puberty is _____ .

androgens, estrogens, testosterone, estradiol

13. Nottelmann, Susman, and colleagues have studied the association of _____ development and _____ characteristics with _____ , _____ _____ , and _____ _____ in adolescence. Competent adolescent adjustment was associated with higher _____ _____ levels and lower _____ _____ levels. The effect was stronger in _____ .

physical, behavioral, gonadotropins, sex steroids, adrenal androgens, sex steroid, adrenal androgen, boys

14. In boys, the growth spurt begins at about _____ years of age; it begins at about _____ years of age in girls. Girls grow about _____ inches in _____ years. Boys grow about _____ inches in _____ years. Boys tend to surpass girls in size by about age _____ .

12½, 10½, 7, two, 8, two, 14

15. The most conspicuous changes brought by sexual maturation in boys are _____ elongation, development of the _____ , and growth of _____ _____ . The most conspicuous changes in girls are the growth of _____ _____ , development of the _____ , and _____ .

penis, testes, pubic hair, pubic hair, breasts, menarche

16. Pubertal girls appear to fantasize about the _____ , while boys fantasize about _____ _____ . _____ occurs in almost all boys by the age of _____ . By the age of 15, only _____ percent of girls have masturbated. Masturbation is higher among the _____ active.

future, sexual activity, Masturbation, 15, 25, sexually

17. Homosexual contact is more frequent before the age of _____ and is more common in _____ . Participation in homosexual relationships has _____ _____ during recent years.

15, boys, remained constant

18. The percentage of adolescents reporting intercourse has _____ during the last 80 years. The increase for females is _____ than that for males. Currently, the proportions of males and females reporting intercourse are _____ . Males engage in intercourse _____ than females.

increased, greater, equal, earlier

19. A boy's fear of being seen as homosexual for failing to engage in intercourse is called _____ .

homophobia

20. Two emotions that may accompany the changes of puberty are _____ and _____ . Early studies showed that both girls and boys who mature early in adolescence perceive themselves in a more _____ way than do those who mature later. The effect for girls was _____ than that for boys. More recently, the results for boys were _____ , but it appears that early-maturing girls have more _____ at school than later-maturing girls. When young women were interviewed, those expressing the most satisfaction with their figures were the ones who had matured _____ .

pride, embarrassment, positive, smaller, confirmed, problems, later

21. Physical attractiveness is associated with _____ in young girls. In one study, unattractive girls rated themselves as less _____ and scored lower in _____ - _____ . However, _____ girls in the middle of pubertal change had higher self-esteem than the _____ girls.

popularity, popular, self-esteem, unattractive, attractive

22. In females, the onset of _____ development but not growth of _____ _____ is linked to social development. This is an example of the importance of the _____ of maturational events.

breast, pubic hair, timing

23. According to Piaget, _____ _____ thought appears during adolescence. It involves _____ thinking, one indication of which is the adolescent's increased tendency to think about _____ itself. Adolescents also think in _____ ways and generate all the _____ in a given situation.

formal operational, abstract, thought, idealistic, possibilities

24. The problem-solving strategy in which one generates and tests hypotheses is called _____ - _____ reasoning. When presented with a game like "Twenty Questions," the formal operational thinker will implicitly or explicitly formulate a _____ composed of hypotheses to test.

hypothetical-deductive, strategy or plan

25. Adolescents are more sophisticated in their ability to understand _____ . They become able to understand _____ , an implied comparison between two ideas. They also show an increased understanding of _____ . Such understanding is exemplified by the increased popularity of _____ *Magazine* at this age.

words, metaphor, satire, *Mad*

26. Adolescents are better able to _____ than children. This requires understanding the _____ and _____ ideas. Adolescents also have a better understanding of _____, the social rules of conversation. To understand the full _____ of a speaker's message, the listener must be sensitive to the speaker's _____ and _____. Children confuse _____ and _____, but adolescents are able to distinguish them.
write, audience, organizing, pragmatics, meaning, belief, purpose, sarcasm, deception

27. The _____ formal operational thinker begins to see many of the possible combinations of events and situations necessary to solve a problem, but is less able to generate a _____. The late formal operational thinker is interested in what is _____ and _____ to account for what has occurred.
early, plan, necessary, sufficient

28. The adolescent's belief that others are as preoccupied with the adolescent's behavior and appearance as he or she is is called the _____ _____. It is an example of formal operational _____. The adolescent's sense of personal uniqueness and indestructibility is called the _____ _____.
imaginary audience, egocentrism, personal fable

29. Elkind called the permanent features of the person, such as intelligence, the _____ self. He called temporary features, such as a haircut, the _____ self. Young adolescents are _____ inclined to reveal aspects of either self than children or older adolescents. Also, they are _____ likely to reveal aspects of the _____ self than of the _____ self.
abiding, transient, less, less, abiding, transient

30. Some have explained the imaginary audience in terms of the development of _____ perspective, rather than in terms of egocentrism.
social

31. _____ _____ refers to a person's ability to interpret the intentions of other people's social behavior.
Social monitoring

32. One future-oriented task of adolescence is _____ selection. Apparently, adolescents are neither _____ nor _____ in their exploration.
career, systematic, intentional

33. The percentage of high school students who report at least some part-time work is _____. The amount that the typical adolescent works has _____ in recent years.
75, increased

34. The grades of working adolescents are _____ than those of nonworking ones. On the average, 10th-graders who work more than _____ hours per week and 11th-graders who work more than _____ hours per week suffer a drop in grades. Work also decreases time spent with _____.
lower, 14, 20, family

35. The percentage of adolescent boys who are not in school, not employed, and looking for work is _____. Most of the unemployed adolescents are high school _____. Unemployment is much higher for _____.
5, dropouts, minorities

Key Terms Matching Exercise

Match the Key Term on the left with the correct definition on the right.

---- 1. storm and stress view (LO–1, p. 503)
---- 2. adolescent generalization gap (LO–3, p. 505)
---- 3. menarche (LO–4, p. 506)
---- 4. amenorrhea (LO–4, p. 507)
---- 5. puberty (LO–4, p. 507)
---- 6. hormones (LO–5, p. 508)

a. Development of widespread conclusions and stereotypes about adolescents that are based on information about a limited set of adolescents due to a weak research base
b. Period of rapid change to physical maturation, including sexual maturation
c. First menstruation in pubertal females
d. Abnormal absence or suppression of menstruation
e. View that sees adolescence as a turbulent time charged with conflict, contradictions, and wide swings in mood and emotion
f. Powerful chemical substances that regulate the body; secretions of endocrine glands

---

---- 7. hypothalamic-pituitary-gonadal axis (LO–5, p. 508)
---- 8. hypothalamus (LO–5, p. 508)
---- 9. pituitary gland (LO–5, p. 508)
---- 10. gonadal (LO–5, p. 508)
---- 11. gonadotropin (LO–6, p. 508)
---- 12. androgens (LO–7, p. 508)
---- 13. estrogens (LO–7, p. 508)

a. Small endocrine gland located at the base of the brain that secretes hormones that control growth and the other endocrine glands
b. Aspect of the endocrine system that involves the interaction of the hypothalamus, pituitary gland, and the gonads; involved in sexual development and behavior
c. Brain structure believed to be important in the regulation of hunger, temperature, emotion, and other visceral functions
d. Hormone released by the pituitary that stimulates the gonads
e. Referring to the sex glands
f. Hormones that mature primarily in males
g. Hormones that mature primarily in females

---- 14. testosterone (LO–7, p. 508)
---- 15. estradiol (LO–7, p. 508)
---- 16. sex steroids (LO–7, p. 510)
---- 17. adrenal androgens (LO–7, p. 510)
---- 18. thyroid gland (LO–7, p. 511)

a. Hormones secreted by the adrenal glands that are associated with male functions and behaviors
b. Gland that interacts with the pituitary gland to influence growth
c. Androgen or male sex hormone; plays an important part in puberty and all male sexual functions
d. Hormones, including testosterone and estradiol, that mature differently in males and females
e. Female sex hormone; important for pubertal development and other sexual functions in females

_____ 19. goodness-of-fit model (LO–10, p. 520)
_____ 20. hypothetical-deductive reasoning (LO–11, p. 523)
_____ 21. metaphor (LO–11, p. 525)
_____ 22. pragmatics (LO–11, p. 526)
_____ 23. egocentrism in adolescence (LO–12, p. 529)

a. Thinking characteristic of 11- to 14-year-olds, including the imaginary audience and the personal fable
b. Rules pertaining to the social context of language and how people use language in conversation
c. Implied comparison between two ideas that is conveyed by the abstract meanings contained in the words used to make the comparison
d. Aspect of formal operational thought; ability to entertain many possibilities and test many solutions in a planful way when faced with having to solve a problem
e. Lerner's theory that the adolescent may be at risk when the demands of a particular social context and the adolescent's physical and behavioral characteristics are mismatched

_____ 24. imaginary audience (LO–12, p. 529)
_____ 25. personal fable (LO–12, p. 529)
_____ 26. abiding self (LO–12, p. 530)
_____ 27. transient self (LO–12, p. 530)
_____ 28. implicit personality theory (LO–13, p. 532)

a. Elkind's term for the characteristics of the self that are believed to be permanent or stable over time
b. Individuals' ideas about what their own and other people's personalities are like
c. Elkind's concept describing the type of adolescent egocentrism that refers to the adolescent's uniqueness and indestructibility
d. Elkind's concept describing the type of adolescent egocentrism that refers to the adolescent's inaccurate belief that he or she will be the center of everyone's attention
e. Elkind's term for the characteristics of the self that are believed to vary over time.

Answers to Key Terms Matching Exercise

1. e	5. b	9. a	13. g	17. a	21. c	25. c
2. a	6. f	10. e	14. c	18. b	22. b	26. a
3. c	7. b	11. d	15. e	19. e	23. a	27. e
4. d	8. c	12. f	16. d	20. d	24. d	28. b

Self-Test A

Choose the best alternative.

1. The first important scientist to study adolescence was (LO–1, p. 503)
   a. Jean Piaget.
   b. G. Stanley Hall.
   c. Sigmund Freud.
   d. Charles Darwin.

2. An important influence on the thinking about adolescence in the period from 1890 to 1920 was (LO–2, p. 504)
   a. Erikson's development of the Eight Stages of Man.
   b. Freud's psychoanalysis.
   c. the discovery of the functioning of the hypothalamic-pituitary-adrenal axis.
   d. compulsory education legislation.

3. An important factor in the development of modern stereotypes about adolescents may have been (LO–3, p. 505)
   a. a series of important studies done in the 1950s and 1960s.
   b. the conspicuous and rebellious adolescents of the 1960s.
   c. the fact that the stereotypes are basically true; that is, adolescents are basically rebellious and under tremendous pressure.
   d. the decrease in the age of puberty.

4. The age of menarche (LO–4, p. 507)
   a. has been declining at an average of about four months per decade for the last 100 years.
   b. has been declining at an average of about one month per decade for the last 100 years.
   c. has been constant for 20 years.
   d. is actually rising now.

5. The testes and the ovaries are controlled by (LO–5, p. 508)
   a. social stimuli, especially those involving the opposite sex.
   b. the adrenal glands.
   c. the cerebral cortex.
   d. the hypothalamus and the pituitary.

6. The pituitary secretes (LO–6, p. 508)
   a. testosterone.
   b. estradiol.
   c. gonadotropins.
   d. adrenal androgens.

7. In males, the growth of facial hair and voice changes are stimulated by (LO–7, p. 508)
   a. estradiol.
   b. gonadotropins.
   c. testosterone.
   d. estrogens.

8. The sex steroids are (LO–7, p. 510)
   a. testosterone and estradiol.
   b. adrenal androgen and gonadotropin.
   c. androgen and estrogen.
   d. exocrine hormones.

9. Generally, the first sexual change during puberty in boys is the (LO–8, p. 513)
   a. growth of the testicles.
   b. onset of the growth spurt.
   c. first ejaculation.
   d. growth of facial hair.

10. The first outward evidence of puberty in girls is (LO–8, p. 513)
    a. the appearance of pubic hair.
    b. breast development.
    c. menarche.
    d. the growth spurt.

11. Compared to attractive girls, unattractive ones (LO–9, p. 519)
    a. have a lower level of self-esteem during puberty.
    b. have a higher level of self-esteem during puberty.
    c. have a lower level of self-esteem before and during puberty but a higher level of self-esteem after puberty.
    d. have a higher level of self-esteem before and after puberty but a lower one during puberty.

12. Girls who have an early onset of puberty are likely to _____ than girls who have a later onset of puberty. (LO–10, p. 518)
    a. be more independent
    b. lag further behind in relationships with the opposite sex
    c. perform better on achievement tests
    d. get better grades in school

13. Girls who have an early onset of puberty are likely to _____ than girls who have a later onset of puberty. (LO–10, p. 518)
    a. be less dominant
    b. have a more difficult transition to high school
    c. end up taller
    d. end up shorter

14. "If fire froze things, could ice be made in an oven?" The age of the youngest child who is likely to be able to effectively deal with questions like this one is (LO–11, p. 528)
    a. 8 years old.
    b. 10 years old.
    c. 12 years old.
    d. 15 years old.

15. A child says to himself, "I think the way to get a good grade on a test is to study hard. Therefore, if I study hard for my next exam, then I will get a good grade." This is an example of (LO–11, p. 523)
    a. idealism.
    b. use of metaphor.
    c. abstractness.
    d. hypothetical-deductive reasoning.

16. "You can't possibly understand what I am feeling!" The age of the youngest child who is likely to make a statement like this is (LO–11, pp. 529, 531)
    a. 6 years old.
    b. 10 years old.
    c. 14 years old.
    d. 18 years old.

17. The permanent characteristics of self are called the (LO–12, p. 530)
    a. transient self.
    b. personal fable.
    c. abiding self.
    d. imaginary audience.

18. The recognition that one's own behavior is not always consistent, but rather depends on the contextual or situational variability one encounters, is a property of (LO–13, p. 532)
    a. becoming an implicit personality theorist.
    b. developing a self-concept.
    c. developing self-esteem.
    d. recognizing that the self is different from others.

19. Flavel argues that the importance of social monitoring is in (LO–14, p. 534)
    a. determining how well you understand a message.
    b. determining whether you should believe or act on a message.
    c. determining who your real friends are.
    d. understanding adults.

20. When does part-time employment interfere with schoolwork? (LO–15, p. 536)
    a. after about 14 hours of work for high school juniors
    b. It's not the time but the type of work that is of primary importance.
    c. after about 20 hours of work for high school sophomores
    d. after about 20 hours of work for high school juniors

Answers to Self-Test A

1. b	5. d	9. a	13. d	17. c
2. d	6. c	10. d	14. d	18. a
3. b	7. c	11. b	15. d	19. b
4. a	8. a	12. a	16. c	20. d

Self-Test B

Choose the best alternative.

21. G. Stanley Hall believed that the most important influence on adolescent development was (LO–1, p. 503)
    a. heredity.
    b. the environment.
    c. attachment to the mother and subsequent identification with the father.
    d. the level of cognitive development.

22. A social or historical occurrence that contributed to the acceptance of adolescence as the transitional time between childhood and adulthood was (LO–2, p. 504)
    a. the always high level of school attendance.
    b. the tendency to start in the work force early.
    c. the increased need for labor.
    d. the decline of the apprenticeship system.

23. One issue on which adolescents differ with their parents, according to one study, is the importance of (LO–3, p. 505)
    a. self-control.
    b. religion.
    c. compromise.
    d. legal authority.

24. The rapid change to maturation (LO–4, p. 507)
   a. is a sudden event.
   b. is called puberty.
   c. is triggered by social stimuli.
   d. is called amenorrhea.

25. Endocrine glands (LO–5, p. 508)
   a. have ducts.
   b. control the hypothalamus.
   c. deliver secretions directly to the blood.
   d. include those that can secrete milk.

26. The hormones important for puberty are _____ in males and _____ in females. (LO–8, p. 508)
   a. gonadotropins/estrogens
   b. progesterone/androgens
   c. androgens/gonadotropins
   d. testosterone/estradiol

27. The testes and the ovaries are stimulated by (LO–6, p. 508)
   a. gonadotropins.
   b. estradiol.
   c. testosterone.
   d. the thyroid gland.

28. Sex steroids are secreted by (LO–7, p. 512)
   a. the pituitary gland.
   b. the adrenal gland.
   c. the ovaries and the testes.
   d. the thyroid gland.

29. All of the sex steroids are (LO–7, p. 512)
   a. androgens and estrogens.
   b. gonadotropins.
   c. exocrine secretions.
   d. secreted by the pituitary.

30. During the growth spurt of puberty, girls grow by _____ per year. (LO–8, p. 511)
   a. 1.5 inches
   b. 2.5 inches
   c. 3.5 inches
   d. 4.5 inches

31. The duration of the growth spurt in both boys and girls is about _____ years. (LO–8, p. 511)
   a. five
   b. two
   c. three
   d. four

32. One reason why attractive girls may have a more difficult adjustment than unattractive ones during the peak of puberty may be (LO–9, p. 519)
   a. because they generally tend to lose their attractiveness.
   b. increased dating pressures from boys.
   c. decreased attention from boys.
   d. increased pressure from girls' groups.

33. Which group experiences the most generally positive psychological results during adolescence from the timing of puberty? (LO–10, p. 517)
    a. late-maturing females
    b. early-maturing females
    c. late-maturing males
    d. early-maturing males

34. The formal operational period is characterized by which of the following? (LO–11, pp. 522–23)
    a. coordination of perception and action
    b. animistic reasoning
    c. logical reasoning about the world as it is
    d. logical reasoning about possibilities

35. Which of the following involves hypothetical-deductive reasoning? (LO–11, p. 523)
    a. solving an algebraic equation
    b. thinking of three possible answers and then testing each to determine the correct one
    c. determining that there are 10 possible ways in which the items in the test can be arranged
    d. understanding metaphor and sarcasm

36. A child says to herself, "I think that the way to get a good grade on a test is to study hard. Therefore, if I study hard for my next exam, I will get a good grade." This child is in which of Piaget's cognitive stages? (LO–11, p. 523)
    a. sensorimotor thought
    b. preoperational thought
    c. concrete operational thought
    d. formal operational thought

37. A boy tries on three outfits in the morning before deciding what to wear. He is very concerned that his clothing be perfect so that no one will criticize him. He expects that, when he goes to school, everyone will be looking at him and evaluating how he looks. Of what stage is this form of egocentrism characteristic? (LO–12, p. 529)
    a. formal operational
    b. concrete operational
    c. preoperational
    d. sensorimotor

38. When in development do the first elements of implicit personality emerge? (LO–13, p. 532)
    a. adolescence
    b. middle childhood
    c. early childhood
    d. adulthood

39. According to Flavell's views, one who is overly _____ has a low level of social monitoring. (LO–14, p. 533)
    a. truthful
    b. untruthful
    c. gullible
    d. consistent

40. The largest number of unemployed adolescents are (LO–15, p. 537)
    a. girls.
    b. boys.
    c. black.
    d. school dropouts.

Answers to Self-Test B

21. a	25. c	29. a	33. d	37. a
22. d	26. d	30. c	34. d	38. c
23. b	27. a	31. b	35. b	39. c
24. b	28. c	32. b	36. d	40. c

Questions to Stimulate Thought

1. What is adolescence?
2. Must the period of adolescence be one of turmoil?
3. Does it matter (within reason) when puberty starts and finishes?
4. How is adolescent thought different from that of children of various ages?
5. What eliminates the egocentrism of adolescence?
6. What is the relationship between egocentrism and social monitoring?
7. Is it good for adolescents who are still in school to work?

Research Project

Pair up with a classmate. One of you is to present the other with Piaget's pendulum task. Then reverse roles, and one of you is to present the other with Piaget's chemical task. Then test an 11-year-old on both tasks.

For the pendulum task, have a frame for a pendulum as well as various lengths of string and a number of weights of equal size. Instruct your subject to assemble the pendulum and to identify the variable(s) that determine the period of the pendulum swing. The possible variables to manipulate are length, weight, height of the drop, and the force of the initial push. Record on the data sheet the variables that the subjects manipulate and the way in which the subjects organize the manipulations.

For the chemical task, have water, hydrogen peroxide, potassium iodine, acid, and thiosulfate in five numbered flasks. All of the chemicals are initially clear liquids. The subjects must determine which combination of chemicals produces a mixture with the color yellow. Record on the data sheet the variables that the subjects manipulate and the way in which the subjects organize the manipulations.

Both tasks present combinatorial problems, which are solved by systematically manipulating each of the variables and all of the possible combinations of variables to identify the correct solution. These tasks test for aspects of formal operational reasoning. After making the observations, answer the questions that follow.

Data Sheet

Task	Subject 1	Subject 2
	Sex _____ Age _____	Sex _____ Age _____
Pendulum Task		
Chemical Task		

Questions

1. How did you and your partner solve the tasks? How would you characterize your responses? Did you and your partner systematically manipulate the variables?
2. How did the 11-year-old solve the tasks? How would you characterize the 11-year-old's responses? Did he or she systematically manipulate the variables?
3. What performance differences did you observe in the younger and older subjects? How would you characterize their performances according to Piaget's theory? Did you find evidence of formal operational reasoning in either, both, or neither of your subjects? How would you account for your findings? What is the nature of the performance difference on these tasks at the two ages?

13 Social Development in Adolescence

Learning Objectives

After studying this chapter, you should be able to:

1. Explain autonomy as a multidimensional concept. (pp. 546–47)
2. Explain the relationship between parenting style and the development of autonomy in adolescence. (pp. 547–48)
3. Explain the aspects of the parent-adolescent association that might be described in terms of attachment or connectedness. (pp. 548–49)
4. Explain the nature of parent-adolescent conflict and its increase in early adolescence. (pp. 551, 553)
5. Describe the changes in the adolescent and the changes in the parents that influence parent-adolescent relationships. (pp. 553–56)
6. Describe the effects of divorce on the adolescent. (pp. 557–59)
7. Describe the development of conformity in adolescence. (pp. 560–61)
8. Explain the role of peers in adolescence. (pp. 561–62)
9. Define the crowd and the clique and explain their importance in adolescence. (pp. 562–63)
10. Compare and contrast the nature of children's and adolescents' groups. (pp. 564–65)
11. Define dating, describe its functions, and explain how relationships with parents, siblings, and peers can affect dating. (pp. 565–68)
12. Describe the functions of the secondary school. (pp. 568–70)
13. Describe the characteristics of schools that are effective for adolescents. (pp. 570–73)
14. Explain the interaction of age of puberty and the organization of middle and junior high schools with regard to the transition from elementary school. (pp. 571, 573–75)

Summary

A number of social forces operate in adolescence, as throughout earlier times in development. Autonomy is an important issue for adolescents, as they attempt to become more independent of the family. Autonomy can exist in some areas, such as buying clothes, but not others, such as choice of occupation. Authoritarian families restrict the adolescent's development of autonomy. Democratic parenting strategies produce more autonomy in adolescents than either authoritarian or permissive parenting strategies.

The adolescent's continuing secure attachment to the parents promotes exploration of the environment (including relationships with others), as well as identity development and secure attachment to peers. Decisions by parents, such as where to live and what church to go to, affect the pool of individuals from which adolescents select friends. Parents who have close relationships with their adolescent children sometimes coach them through relationships.

Parents cope with parent-adolescent conflict in different ways. Some parents clamp down after infractions; others realize that it takes a while for adolescents to become mature and thus are able to deal more calmly with transgressions. Conflict seems to increase during early adolescence, and changes in both the parents and the adolescents may be responsible for the increase. In late adolescence, conflict seems to decrease. Conflicts focus on normal everyday activities like schoolwork and chores. Biological changes, along with pushes for independence and identity, may be part of the cause of conflict. Parents must adapt to the adolescent's physical and cognitive changes. Sexual maturation and size changes are obvious physical changes and contribute to the fact that mother-son relationships are more stressful during this time than father-son relationships. With increases in cognitive abilities, adolescents may challenge parents' decisions more than younger children. Adolescent egocentrism may also lead to misinterpretation of parents' comments. Parents of adolescents are also maturing, and they may compare their lives with their offspring's potential.

Divorce has different effects on adolescents than it has on younger children. Adolescents often fear repeating the divorce in their own marriage. Hetherington found adolescent daughters of widows to be more withdrawn around males and adolescent daughters of divorced women to be more uninhibited around males than daughters of intact families. Hetherington also found that, later in life, the daughters of divorced women married at younger ages than daughters of widows and that both had more sexual adjustment problems than daughters from intact homes.

Peers are another important socializing agent during adolescence, and there is much pressure to conform to the peer group. This conformity peeks by about the ninth grade. Adolescents' behavior is also influenced by peer models. High-status peers are more likely to be imitated than others. One function of the peer group is to provide feedback about such things as one's abilities and talents relative to the group. Peer group relationships can be characterized by the crowd, the clique, or individual friendships. Crowds are larger and more impersonal than cliques, which involve greater intimacy and more group cohesion. Self-esteem may be higher in members of crowds or cliques than in nonmembers.

Dating is an important aspect of adolescent peer relationships and serves various functions, from recreation and status to mate selection. In the United States, most girls begin dating at the age of 14, while most boys begin sometime between the ages of 14 and 15. Males seem to show a stronger sexual motivation in dating relationships than females, while females show more interest in personality exploration and self-disclosure. Adolescents' relationships with parents are thought to be carried forward to influence the construction of dating relationships. Peer relationships, particularly status within a group, may influence frequency of dating.

Schools are another influence in the social world of the adolescent. There has been a controversy about what schools should provide to the adolescent, with the controversy centering around a balance between potential alienation and an academic focus. Research has found that the best schools adapt to individual differences in students' intellectual, biological, and social development. The transition to middle school or junior high can be difficult for adolescents since it occurs at the same time as physical changes and places more demands on students and an increased focus on achievement and performance. Students also move from the top position at their previous school to the lowest status at the new school. Friendships can make the transition easier. Many adolescents are latchkey children after school hours, with no community activities available to them.

Guided Review

You may want to look at the answers to the "Guided Review" statements as you read, or you may want to use the exercise as a form of self-test by covering up the answers below the statements with a sheet of paper and not consulting them until you have attempted to fill in the blanks of each statement.

1. _____ from _____ and _____ to _____ are involved in the adolescent's quest for autonomy. To most people, the term *autonomy* connotes _____-_____ and _____ .

   Independence, parents, conformity, peers, self-direction, independence

2. In a study by Psathas, one dimension of autonomy related to affairs outside the family that emerged was _____ in _____ _____ . The dimension that reflected independence in such items as buying clothes was _____ in _____ - _____ activities. Parental _____ for _____ was reflected in parents asking the adolescent's opinion, and choosing one's career reflected independence in activities with _____ implications.

permissiveness, outside activities, permissiveness, age-related, regard, judgment, status

3. The development of independence is hampered by being raised in an _____ household. _____ parenting involves little parental _____ and few parental _____ . A _____ parenting strategy usually involves the adolescent and the parents _____ ; however, the final authority is with the _____ . When overall competence and adjustment of the adolescent are considered, the _____ strategy is superior to the _____ one.

authoritarian, Permissive, involvement, standards, democratic, equally, parents, democratic, permissive

4. A secure _____ in infancy is carried forward to affect the adolescent's relationships with _____ . Apparently, a secure _____ attachment in adolescence promotes a healthy social exploration of the environment, including relationships with _____ , _____ , and the opposite _____ , and the formation of an _____ . Armsden and Greenberg found that adolescents with secure parental attachments had higher _____ - _____ and _____ _____ than those with insecure attachments.

attachment, parents, parental, peers, friends, sex, identity, self-esteem, life satisfaction

5. Adolescents with secure attachments to the parents are likely to have _____ attachments to peers. Adolescents are influenced more by parents in decisions regarding _____ and _____ orientation.

secure, values, vocational

6. According to Hinde, _____ involve patterns of communications that occur between people who may or may not be intimates. _____ imply enduring bonds between people. The term _____ implies normative _____ for individual behavior.

interactions, Relationships, group, expectations

7. An example of the interaction between parental _____ and peer _____ at the group level involves the choice of a _____ . This partially determines the adolescent's _____ .

behavior, interactions, neighborhood, groups

8. At the interaction level, parents may recommend _____ for peer relationships. This is especially true when _____ relationships exist between _____ and _____ .

strategies, positive, parents, adolescents

9. When the adolescent changes dramatically at _____ , the parents may attempt to force conformity to _____ _____ . The parents may act as if the maturing process—the transition from childhood to adulthood—is a _____ one. Other parents go to the other extreme and are too _____ .

puberty, parental standards, fast, permissive

10. One important area of concern is _____ adolescent activity after school. Steinberg found that latchkey children who were farther from adult supervision were _____ _____ to peer pressure. Those who were raised in an _____ manner and whose parents knew their whereabouts were _____ _____ to peer pressure than those whose parents used other strategies and who did not monitor.

monitoring, more susceptible, authoritative, more resistant

11. Conflicts between the adolescent and the parents are greatest during _____ adolescence, are _____ during high school, and _____ when the adolescent goes away to college.

early, constant, decrease

12. Parental attempts to teach _____ of _____ and _____ to rules are often the stimulus for conflict.

delay, gratification, conformity

13. A recent study found that adolescent identity exploration was positively related to frequency of _____ with parents. Lack of disagreement may signal _____ of _____ .

disagreement; fear; separation, exploration, or independence

14. At puberty, the adolescent gets _____ and matures _____ . Both of these changes alter the way in which parents and child interact. Relationships between _____ and _____ are most stressful during _____ , but relationships between _____ and _____ are less affected. Mothers tend to complain about a lack of participation in _____ activities. Fathers retain influence over family decisions during the son's _____ . By the end of puberty, _____ defer to their _____ . This reduces _____ .

bigger, sexually, mothers, sons, puberty, fathers, sons, family, puberty, mothers, sons, conflict

15. Adolescents develop increased _____ _____ skills. They also think in _____ ways. This results in demands for _____ of rules and comparisons with _____ parents. The adolescent's concern with others' perception of him or her may lead to _____ to parental _____ .

logical reasoning, idealistic, explanations, ideal, overreaction, criticism

16. Adolescent demands for explanations may be incorrectly perceived as _____ because of parental _____ of easy compliance. Changes in _____ lag behind changes in the _____ .

defiance, expectation, expectations, adolescent

17. The adolescent may think that the parent is _____ in comparison with interactions with _____ , where _____ and _____ are normal forms of communication.

repressive, peers, questioning, challenging

18. The _____ world of the adolescent changes with the move to _____ _____, school. The adolescent spends more time with _____ and develops more sophisticated _____.

social, junior high, peers, friendships

19. Adolescence of an offspring is a time of increased _____ for parents. _____ _____ increases, the _____ _____ is higher, and _____ reassessment frequently occurs.

stress, Marital dissatisfaction, economic burden, vocational

20. Both parents and adolescents have concerns about _____ choice, the _____, _____, and sexual _____ at about the same time.

vocational, future, health, attractiveness

21. The average age at marriage has _____ in the last 15 years. If this trend continues, future parents will be the parents of adolescents _____ in _____ age than now.

increased, later, middle

22. Older fathers are _____, _____ better, encourage more _____, and show less _____. However, they are less likely to place _____ on their children and to _____ _____.

warmer, communicate, achievement, rejection, demands, enforce rules

23. Wallerstein and Kelly found that 13-year-old children who experienced parental divorce found the experience _____. Coping was correlated with the adolescent being as _____ as possible in the divorce proceedings and maintaining strong ties to _____.

painful, uninvolved, peers

24. According to Hetherington, girls from widowed homes are more _____ around males than girls from divorced homes. Girls from divorced homes are more likely to be _____ with boys. Hetherington also found that divorced women are more _____ about men and marriage than are widowed women.

withdrawn or passive, aggressive, negative

25. In Hetherington's study, the daughters of divorcees married _____. Their partners were more likely to have _____ problems and poor _____ histories. Daughters of widows tended to marry more _____ men. Both groups reported more _____ problems than women from intact homes.

earlier, drug, work, puritanical, sexual

26. Adolescents spend large amounts of time with _____. One effect of peer groups is the pressure to _____.

peers, conform

27. Conformity to parents' views appears to be relatively strong in the _____ grade, despite conflicting parent and peer influences. During the _____ grade, parent and peer influences are no longer in direct opposition because they operate in _____ situations. The worst grade for parent-child conflict is the _____. Conformity to peer _____ behavior is highest at this time.

third, sixth, different, ninth, antisocial

28. There may be a distinction between two different kinds of _____ . Adolescents may feel less peer pressure for _____ than for peer _____ . However, _____ are more likely to conform to antisocial pressures than _____ .

conformity, misconduct, involvement, males, females

29. Some adolescents are not oriented toward _____ . Adolescents who understand people's expectations but don't use them as a guide to personal behavior are called _____ or _____ . Those who deliberately react against the group's expectations are called _____ or _____ .

conformity, independent, nonconformist, rebellious, anticonformist

30. Models are more likely to be imitated if they are _____ . Hence, school _____ and older _____ are likely to be adopted as models.

powerful, leaders, adolescents

31. The group can provide an adolescent with a means of _____ _____ . This _____ when children move into adolescence.

social comparison, increases

32. _____ exist because of a mutual interest in activities, not because members are mutually attracted to each other. The members of a _____ are attracted to each other. Cliques are _____ , involve greater _____ , and have more group _____ than _____ . Coleman found that the leading crowds in high school are likely to be composed of _____ and _____ _____ .

Crowds, clique, smaller, intimacy, cohesion, crowds, athletes, popular girls

33. Crowd membership may be important in the maintenance of _____ - _____ and the development of _____ . Crowd or clique membership is seen as very _____ . _____ - _____ is higher among crowd members. However, some adolescents who realize that they are _____ but who place little importance on crowd membership are called _____ . Their self-esteem is not _____ than members of any other crowds.

self-esteem, identity, salient, Self-esteem, outsiders, independents, lower

34. The members of children's groups are often _____ . Adolescent groups are frequently more _____ than children's groups. They also are more _____ . There are more likely to be _____ and _____ in adolescent groups.

neighbors, formal, heterogeneous, rules, regulations

35. Dating appeared during the _____ . Its purpose was _____ _____ . Today, dating serves four functions: _____ , source of _____ , _____ , and _____ _____ .

1920s, mate selection, recreation, status, socialization, mate selection

36. Most girls begin to date at age _____ . Boys begin between the ages of _____ and _____ . Most adolescents have their first date between the ages of _____ and _____ . _____ _____ percent of 10th- through 12th-graders date more than once each month.

14, 14, 15, 12, 16, Eighty-five

37. The sexual motivation of _____ appears greater. Both sexes, however, show _____ sexual interest after several dates with the same person.
   boys, increased

38. _____ theorists think that the nature of past relationships with _____ influences the construction of dating relationships. Theoretically, a boy's positive relationship with his mother should result in the boy's expectation that relationships with females will be _____ . A girl from a divorced family with fighting parents might _____ males.
   Psychoanalytic, parents, rewarding, mistrust

39. Parental involvement in dating patterns is more likely for _____ than for _____ . Younger siblings seem to learn from older ones and to date at an _____ age. Large adolescent crowds are likely to be _____ . Leaders date _____ frequently than other members.
   daughters, sons, earlier, heterosexual, more

40. At various times, the function of secondary schools has been to _____ , to delay entry into the _____ _____ , to provide an environment for _____ development, and to provide _____ training. The current trend is _____-to-_____ , that is, the training of _____ skills.
   educate, work force, socialization, vocational, back, basics, intellectual

41. Lipsitz found that the most striking features of good middle schools were _____ to the needs of the students and the early creating of a _____ environment for the adolescents' social and personality development.
   adaptability, positive

42. The junior high school and sometimes the middle school were created because the students are going through _____ .
   puberty

43. _____ makes the transition to junior high school more difficult, as does the appearance of _____ _____ thought, the increase in _____ and _____ , the move to a _____ school, and an increased focus on _____ and _____ .
   Puberty, formal operational, responsibility, independence, larger, achievement, performance

44. The move from the top position in the elementary school to the lowest position in the junior high school is called the _____-_____ phenomenon. This is an additional source of _____ . The transition may be a bit easier for _____ who mature earlier.
   "top-dog," stress, girls

45. Hawkins and Berndt found that _____ classes and _____ individual attention ease the transition from elementary school. They also found that adolescents with higher scores on _____ measures had a more positive perception of themselves and of school.
   smaller, increased, friendship

46. Lipsitz blames the lack of appropriate after-school activities for adolescents on lack of _____ .
   money

Key Terms Matching Exercise

Match the Key Term on the left with the correct definition on the right.

____ 1. interactions (LO–1, p. 549)
____ 2. relationships (LO–1, p. 549)
____ 3. groups (LO–1, p. 549)
____ 4. nonconformists (LO–7, p. 561)
____ 5. anticonformists (LO–7, p. 561)
____ 6. social comparison (LO–8, p. 562)
____ 7. crowd (LO–9, p. 562)
____ 8. clique (LO–9, p. 562)
____ 9. "top-dog" phenomenon (LO–14, p. 574)

a. Individuals who know what the people around them expect but who don't use these expectations to guide their behavior
b. Patterns of communication that occur between persons who may or may not be intimates
c. Moving from the highest-status position to the lowest-status position
d. Group that meets because of mutual interest in activities, not because of mutual attraction
e. Patterns of communication that occur between people with enduring bonds to each other and that are often marked by histories of past interactions as well as commitments to the future
f. Individuals who react counter to the group's expectations and deliberately move away from the actions or beliefs the group advocates
g. Group whose members are attracted to each other on the basis of similar interests and social ideals
h. Social structures that carry with them normative expectations about acceptable and unacceptable aspects of behavior and influence interactions and relationships of members
i. Using the peer group to provide information about one's relative abilities, talents, and characteristics

Answers to Key Terms Matching Exercise

1. b	4. a	7. d
2. e	5. f	8. g
3. h	6. i	9. c

Self-Test A

Choose the best alternative.

1. Which of the following is not a distinct pattern of adolescent autonomy? (LO–1, p. 546)
   a. permissiveness in outside activities
   b. permissiveness in age-related activities
   c. parental regard for judgment
   d. permissiveness in home activities

2. Which parenting style produces the least autonomous adolescents? (LO–2, p. 547)
   a. democratic
   b. permissive
   c. authoritarian
   d. authoritative

3. Adolescents who show a healthy exploration of the environment most likely (LO–3, p. 548)
   a. were securely attached infants.
   b. were resistant infants.
   c. were avoidant infants.
   d. were insecurely attached infants.

4. Adolescents who are securely attached to their parents (LO–2, p. 548)
   a. are remote with their peers.
   b. are also securely attached to their peers.
   c. show hostility to their peers.
   d. are insecurely attached to their peers.

5. According to Hinde, what term is used for communication patterns between people who may or may not be intimate? (LO–2, p. 549)
   a. relationships
   b. interactions
   c. social comparison
   d. group membership

6. Parent-adolescent conflict escalates (LO–4, p. 553)
   a. during early adolescence.
   b. during middle adolescence.
   c. during late adolescence.
   d. throughout the whole course of adolescence.

7. Which parent-child relationship is most stressful during puberty? (LO–5, p. 554)
   a. mother-daughter
   b. father-daughter
   c. mother-son
   d. father-son

8. Cognitive changes in the adolescent contribute to conflict with parents because the adolescent (LO–5, p. 554)
   a. threatens the parents physically.
   b. questions parental reasoning.
   c. flaunts his or her sexuality.
   d. spends more time with peers.

9. According to research, how do older fathers differ from younger fathers? (LO–5, p. 556)
   a. Older fathers place more demands on their children.
   b. Younger fathers are warmer with their children.
   c. Older fathers communicate better with their children.
   d. Younger fathers encourage intellectual achievement more.

10. Adolescents who cope most effectively with parental divorce (LO–6, p. 557)
    a. side with one parent against the other.
    b. attempt to reconcile the parents.
    c. become involved in caring for younger siblings.
    d. distance themselves from parental conflict.

11. Which of the following groups of female adolescents shows the most hostility toward males? (LO–6, p. 557)
    a. daughters of divorced women
    b. daughters of widows
    c. daughters from intact homes
    d. Both a and b are correct.

12. According to research by Berndt, conformity to peers peaks in (LO–7, p. 561)
    a. 12th grade.
    b. 9th grade.
    c. 6th grade.
    d. 3rd grade.

13. Jane knows that both her parents and people at school expect her to dress neatly. However, she does not want to be controlled by others, so she always wears dirty and rumpled clothing. Jane would be described as (LO–7, p. 561)
    a. a conformist.
    b. a nonconformist.
    c. an anticonformist.
    d. a member of an in group.

14. One of the most important roles of the peer group during adolescence is (LO–8, p. 562)
    a. freedom from parents.
    b. providing a means of social comparison.
    c. forcing conformity.
    d. supporting individuality.

15. Which of the following is characterized by small size, intimacy among members, and group cohesion? (LO–9, p. 562)
    a. clique
    b. crowd
    c. club
    d. team

16. What characteristic is most likely to be found in the leading crowds in a school? (LO–10, p. 562)
    a. intelligence
    b. looks
    c. grades
    d. athletic ability

17. Alex dates because, if he doesn't, he is looked down on by the other boys in his school. The function that dating serves for him is (LO–11, p. 566)
    a. recreation.
    b. status.
    c. learning to get along with others.
    d. as a means of mate selection.

18. During the early 1970s, secondary schools were thought to be (LO–12, p. 568)
    a. alienating students.
    b. helping students to become adults.
    c. providing adequate job training.
    d. fostering the development of the whole individual.

19. According to research by Lipsitz, effective middle schools (LO–13, p. 571)
    a. have a primary emphasis on cognitive development.
    b. use the same model for all students.
    c. focus on the needs of the individual.
    d. use a standard curriculum.

20. All of the following make the transition from elementary to middle school difficult except which? (LO–14, p. 573)
    a. the onset of puberty
    b. the change to a large, impersonal structure
    c. the increased focus on achievement and performance
    d. the presence of friends

Answers to Self-Test A

1. d	5. b	9. c	13. c	17. b
2. c	6. a	10. d	14. b	18. a
3. a	7. c	11. a	15. a	19. c
4. b	8. b	12. b	16. d	20. d

Self-Test B

Choose the best alternative.

21. Autonomy connotes (LO–1, p. 546)
    a. attachment and dependence.
    b. independence and self-direction.
    c. attachment and control.
    d. identity and intimacy.

22. Which parenting style promotes the overall competence and adjustment of the adolescent? (LO–2, pp. 547–48)
    a. authoritarian
    b. permissive
    c. neglecting
    d. authoritative

23. People with enduring bonds to each other engage in (LO–3, p. 549)
    a. relationships.
    b. conflicts.
    c. interactions.
    d. messages.

24. An essential characteristic of a group is that (LO–3, p. 549)
    a. it must be single-sexed.
    b. it must be mixed-sexed.
    c. there are norms of behavior.
    d. it cannot involve individuals who are not at least adolescents.

25. Which of the following is a possible explanation for the increase in conflict with parents during adolescence? (LO–4, p. 551)
    a. the appearance of sexuality in the adolescent
    b. the aging of the parents
    c. the inability of the parents to understand what being an adolescent means
    d. sibling rivalry

26. Conflict between parents and the adolescent decreases between the ages of (LO–4, p. 553)
    a. 13 and 15.
    b. 15 and 17.
    c. 17 and 20.
    d. 19 and 22.

27. The son's pubertal transition puts a particular strain on his relationship with his mother, who is unhappy with his (LO–5, p. 554)
    a. participation in family activities.
    b. sexual activity.
    c. changing body.
    d. lack of respect for her.

28. In Hetherington's study, the husbands of the daughters of divorced women (LO–6, p. 558)
    a. were much older than their wives.
    b. were more likely to have drug problems.
    c. were more likely to be puritanical.
    d. were much younger than their wives.

29. In Hetherington's study, the husbands of the daughters of widows (LO–6, p. 558)
    a. were much older than their wives.
    b. were more likely to have drug problems.
    c. were more likely to be puritanical.
    d. were much younger than their wives.

30. An adolescent who always does the opposite of what others expect him or her to do is (LO–7, p. 561)
    a. not a member of any group.
    b. independent.
    c. an anticonformist.
    d. a nonconformist.

31. With which of the following issues would peers have more influence than parents? (LO–8, p. 561)
    a. choice of college
    b. whether to have sex with a boyfriend
    c. deciding which political candidate to work for
    d. deciding how to prepare for a career in business

32. Which of the following characteristics makes a better peer model, that is, is more likely to be imitated? (LO–8, p. 561)
    a. being unpopular
    b. being a nonconformist
    c. being in a powerful position at school
    d. being very smart

33. One distinction between a clique and a crowd is (LO–9, p. 562)
    a. size.
    b. that the members of a crowd are psychologically closer to each other.
    c. sex.
    d. age.

34. The leading crowds in many schools are composed of (LO–9, p. 562)
    a. the brightest students.
    b. the most middle-class students.
    c. the school politicians.
    d. athletes and popular girls.

35. Dating (LO–11, p. 566)
   a. has only been an important factor for about 30 years.
   b. is intended mainly for mate selection.
   c. rarely is associated with sex.
   d. is a source of recreation.

36. According to Blos, dating relationships are influenced (LO–11, p. 567)
   a. primarily by peers.
   b. by the nature of past relationships with parents.
   c. by age.
   d. by experience.

37. Secondary schools (LO–12, pp. 568–70)
   a. keep people out of the work force.
   b. teach skills.
   c. socialize.
   d. All of the above are correct.

38. According to research by Lipsitz, effective middle schools (LO–13, p. 571)
   a. emphasize intellectual development.
   b. all use the same school organization.
   c. encourage parents to take the lead in teaching morals and values.
   d. take an adaptable approach.

39. Which of the following can ease the transition from elementary to junior high school? (LO–14, p. 574)
   a. less complexity in school organization
   b. more anonymity
   c. meeting large numbers of new peers
   d. being intelligent

40. The transition to junior high school may be more difficult for boys than for girls because (LO–14, pp. 574–75)
   a. boys are not as smart as girls.
   b. boys usually have not yet gone through puberty.
   c. boys have higher expectations for success in the new school than girls do.
   d. None of the above is correct.

Answers to Self-Test B

21. b	25. a	29. c	33. a	37. d
22. d	26. c	30. c	34. d	38. d
23. a	27. a	31. b	35. d	39. a
24. c	28. b	32. c	36. b	40. b

Questions to Stimulate Thought

1. How does attachment "pave the way" for autonomy?
2. Does the style of parenting make a difference in the struggle for autonomy?
3. What are the relationships among attachment, autonomy, and identity formation?
4. What are the effects of divorce on adolescents, and is there anything that can be done about them?
5. If you were a family court judge and a married couple getting a divorce both wanted custody of the children, what would you do?
6. What is the relationship between peer pressure and autonomy and/or identity formation?
7. Compare the relationships in dating with those of attachment and other peer associations.
8. Is dating a good social development? Does it lead to better marriages?
9. What is the relationship between school and social development?
10. How can the transition to junior high school be eased?

Research Project

Use the structured interview format presented on the data sheet to interview two friends—one male and one female—about the reasons they date. Record each subject's answers on the data sheet and then answer the questions.

Data Sheet

Question	Subject 1 Age _____ Sex _____	Subject 2 Age _____ Sex _____
1. What is the most important reason you go on a date?		
2. What are two other reasons you date?		
3. How do you decide whom to date?		
4. What do you do if you are interested in someone you would like to date?		

Questions

1. What was the male's most important reason for dating? How did that differ from his other reasons for dating?
2. What was the female's most important reason for dating? How did that differ from her other reasons for dating?
3. Did the reasons for dating differ for the male and female you interviewed? Did the way they go about getting dates differ? Did they seem to follow traditional male-female roles, or were they nontraditional? How did their reasons for dating compare to the four functions of dating reported in the text?

---

14 Personality Development in Adolescence

Learning Objectives

After studying this chapter, you should be able to:

1. Define identity and present Erikson's position. (pp. 584–89)
2. Describe Marcia's four identity statuses and explain how they are related to the notion of facing a crisis and making a commitment. (pp. 590–91)
3. Explain the importance of confidence in parental support, a self-reflective perspective about the future, and a sense of industry in preparing the way for identity exploration. (pp. 591–92)

4. Explain the role of individuation and connectedness in the family context. (pp. 593, 594–95)
5. Describe the issues involved in the measurement of identity. (pp. 593, 595–96)
6. Explain how intimacy develops. (pp. 596–97)
7. Describe the five statuses of intimacy. (p. 597)
8. Describe the nature and extent of drug use among current high school seniors. (pp. 600–601)
9. Explain what distinguishes an adolescent's abuse of alcohol. (pp. 602–3)
10. Describe the effects of marijuana. (pp. 604–5)
11. Define juvenile delinquency. (p. 606)
12. Describe the factors that are thought to cause juvenile delinquency. (pp. 606, 608–10)
13. Describe the extent of adolescent suicide in the United States. (p. 609)
14. Describe the relationship between depression and suicide. (p. 612)
15. Explain how adolescent cognitive processing makes suicide prevention difficult. (p. 612)
16. Describe what to do and what not to do when you suspect that someone is considering suicide. (p. 613)
17. Describe anorexia nervosa, bulimia, and obesity. (pp. 613–16)
18. Define youth and list and explain the criteria for entering early adulthood. (pp. 617–18)

Summary

Identity is a major developmental task for adolescents. Erikson describes an identity crisis as a period during which adolescents actively seek an identity and try out many different possibilities before becoming committed to occupational choices and political, religious, moral, and sexual values and attitudes. Personality and role experimentation are thus cornerstones for the identity crisis described by Erikson. According to Bourne, there are seven components to Erikson's definition of identity: genetic, adaptive, structural, dynamic, subjective or experiential, psychosocial reciprocity, and existential status.

Marcia has identified four different statuses of adolescent identity: (1) identity achieved describes individuals who have gone through an identity crisis and made a commitment; (2) individuals in the moratorium status are in the middle of a crisis and have not yet made a commitment; (3) individuals experiencing identity foreclosure have made commitments without going through a crisis; and (4) identity diffused individuals have not experienced an identity crisis and have made no commitments. Research has shown that the frequency of identity achievement goes up with an increase in grade level, and the most significant changes occur between 18 and 21 years of age. College experiences may increase the likelihood that adolescents will enter a status of identity moratorium, and this, in turn, may promote an identity crisis. Vocational identity may be more central to identity formation in males, while affiliative needs may be more important for identity formation in females, although the social-historical context may have affected this finding. Both connectedness to parents and a family environment supportive of individuation may facilitate identity achievement.

Identity is difficult to measure. Marcia developed a structured interview technique that focuses on crisis and commitment. Grotevant has extended Marcia's interview to cover several important areas of interpersonal relationships. Constantinople has developed a questionnaire focusing on a number of conflicts from Erikson's stages. All of these measurement techniques are more rigid and formal than Erikson's own therapeutic techniques.

Erikson believes that identity is theoretically related to intimacy and that intimacy should follow the establishment of an identity. Orlofsky and Marcia have described five statuses of intimacy. The intimate person forms one or more deep and long-lasting love relationships. The preintimate person offers love without obligations or long-lasting bonds. The stereotyped individual has superficial relationships. The pseudointimate person maintains a long-lasting attachment, but the relationship has no depth. The isolated person withdraws from social contact. College students with a stable identity are more likely to achieve an intimate status than students who are less identity achieved. Women may resolve the intimacy crisis before the identity crisis.

Drug and alcohol abuse is a major problem for many adolescents. Almost two thirds of high school seniors report some incidence of illicit drug use in their lives. However, a national survey indicates that drug use has been declining since 1980. Adolescent males are more involved in drug use than adolescent females. Alcohol is the most widely used of all drugs by adolescents. Recent research has shown that adolescents at risk for alcohol abuse expect that alcohol will produce desirable "personal effects," such as increased cognitive abilities. Parental attitudes can affect adolescent drinking. Marijuana reduces short-term memory and impairs motor coordination. Extended daily use may also impair the reproductive system. Marijuana is typically used by college students because it is pleasurable. Parental use of drugs is correlated with adolescent use of marijuana. Peers also influence marijuana use.

Juvenile delinquency, a problem that is specifically defined by the legal system, can also be a problem for teenagers. Erikson describes delinquency as the formation of a negative identity. Some characteristics of the lower-class culture, such as antisocial norms in gangs and peer groups, are likely to promote delinquency. Antisocial behavior in adolescence is also related to parents' family management practices. Specifically, indifferent parental monitoring is related to delinquency.

Suicide is another major problem for adolescents and has become the second leading cause of death in adolescents today. Adolescent males are three times more likely to be successful in committing suicide than adolescent females. A long-term history of negative family experiences is often involved, as well as depression. There is usually an immediate precipitating factor, such as a relationship breakup or failure in school. Adolescents may also believe that death cannot happen to them.

Eating disorders, such as anorexia nervosa (a refusal to eat) and bulimia (where periods of heavy eating are followed by self-induced vomiting), involve a preoccupation with food and a distorted body image. They are much more frequent in adolescent females than any other population. Obesity is another eating disorder and is characterized by weighing more than 20 percent over normal skeletal and physical requirements. Genetic influences, such as basal metabolism rate, may play a role in obesity. Psychological factors, such as a distorted body image and low self-esteem, may also be causes of obesity. A research study showed that obese girls who exercise move less than normal girls, making it difficult for them to use exercise to lose weight unless given specific feedback.

Overall, adolescents do not seem to have more problems than younger children. In fact, some behavior problems may decline with age.

Youth is the transition from adolescence to adulthood. Economic independence and autonomous decision making mark the entrance into early adulthood.

Guided Review

You may want to look at the answers to the "Guided Review" statements as you read, or you may want to use the exercise as a form of self-test by covering up the answers below the statements with a sheet of paper and not consulting them until you have attempted to fill in the blanks of each statement.

1. The adolescent stage in Erikson's eight stages of the life cycle is _____ versus _____ _____ . This is the _____ stage in the life cycle.

   identity, identity confusion, fifth

2. According to Erikson, the adolescent enters a _____ _____ , during which he or she tries several _____ . Coping with this experimentation results in a new sense of _____ .

   psychological moratorium, roles, self

3. _____ _____ results when adolescents are unable to resolve the _____ _____ . They then may _____ from peers and family, or they may lose their _____ , taking on that of the _____ .

   Identity confusion, identity crisis, withdraw, identity, crowd

4. Erikson found that, in the United States, the choice of _____ is a particularly important part of identity formation. This includes the decision of whether or not to go to _____ . Identity confusion may explain the substantial number of students who _____ _____ .

   occupation, college, drop out

5. The crisis of identification or self-image is called an _____ _____ . Its definition has recently been broadened to apply to both _____ and _____ .

   identity crisis, individuals, institutions

6. Erikson viewed the _____ _____ as a _____ for a place in the world. Adolescents should be allowed _____ for this search.

   psychological moratorium, search, time

7. The _____ _____ states that anything that grows has a ground plan. Out of this ground plan _____ arise, each one having its special time of _____ .

   epigenetic principle, parts, ascendancy

8. Erikson believes that _____ formation implies a _____ relationship between the _____ and the _____ .

   identity, mutual, adolescent, community

9. In the _____ mold, the adolescent seeks the _____ to his or her life as well as the _____ of life in general.

   existentialist, meaning, meaning

10. Marcia views the identity process as beginning in _____ and ending in _____ _____ . At the time of adolescence, there is a coincidence of _____ development, _____ skills, and _____ _____ .

    infancy, old age, physical, cognitive, social expectations

11. According to Marcia's analysis of the adolescent identity crisis, those classified as _____ _____ have neither experienced a crisis nor made a commitment. Those adolescents who make a commitment without experiencing a crisis are in a status of _____ _____ . Those adolescents who are in the midst of a crisis but who have not yet made a commitment are in the _____ _____ status. The successful negotiation of this period results in a status of _____ _____ .

    identity diffused, identity foreclosure, identity moratorium, identity achieved

12. Most early adolescents are in either the identity _____ or identity _____ statuses. The frequency of identity _____ appears to go up with level in school. Meilman found that the most important changes in identity status occurred between the ages of _____ and _____ and were from identity _____ and identity _____ to identity _____ .

    diffusion, foreclosure, achievement, 18, 20, diffusion, foreclosure, achievement

13. Some argue that _____ increases the number of adolescents who enter the identity _____ status.

    college, moratorium

14. _____ identity appears to be crucial to the identity formation of midadolescent males. Their female counterparts find _____ needs more important. In college, _____ choices and _____ orientations are important factors for males, while females focus on _____ and _____ _____ . Apparently, _____ are better able to resolve an identity crisis than _____ .

    Vocational, affiliative, ideological, vocational, intimacy, interpersonal relationships, males, females

15. According to Grotevant and Cooper, both _____ and the fostering of _____ promote identity achievement. Individuation is composed of _____ and _____ - _____ . Connectedness includes _____ and _____ .

connectedness, individuation, separateness, self-assertion, mutuality, permeability

16. Separateness involves expression of how _____ the self is from others. Self-assertion is involved in the expression of a personal _____ of _____ . Mutuality is the adolescent's _____ to and _____ for other points of view. Permeability involves _____ and _____ to the views of others.

distinctive, point, view, sensitivity, respect, openness, responsiveness

17. The _____ _____ , the _____ or _____ , and the _____ - _____ task are the usual methods used for the study of identity development. The use of surveys or questionnaires for this work has been criticized because _____ _____ are believed to be necessary. Mischel believes that these assessments must include information from _____ .

semistructured interview, survey, questionnaire, sentence-completion, multiple assessments, others

18. Erikson believes that the development of intimacy must be preceded by the development of _____ . He viewed _____ versus _____ as the _____ stage in human development. It usually occurs during _____ _____ .

identity, intimacy, isolation, sixth, young adulthood

19. According to Erikson, intimacy involves both _____ relationships and _____ . Difficulties in this realm may lead adolescents to _____ themselves with a _____ .

sexual, friendships, merge, leader

20. In a study of divorced women, _____ identity and _____ were remembered to be highest during _____ _____ and _____ . Identity _____ was highest during the _____ . Identity _____ was highest after the _____ .

foreclosed, romantic intimacy, high school, marriage, moratorium, divorce, achievement, divorce

21. In the case of identity foreclosure, the position consistent with Erikson's views is that _____ may be experienced but not resolved. The individual must go back to resolve the _____ crisis before resolving the _____ crisis. The person could then move on to the _____ versus _____ crisis.

intimacy, identity, intimacy, generativity, stagnation

22. The percentage of high school seniors who report some illicit drug use is _____ . The most used illicit drug is _____ , with _____ percent of seniors reporting use. The most used licit drug is _____ , with _____ percent of seniors reporting use. _____ were the second most used licit drug, with _____ percent of seniors reporting use.

67, marijuana, 54.9, alcohol, 92.6, Cigarettes, 69.7

23. Since around 1980, adolescent drug use seems to have been _____ . This is true for _____ drugs.

decreasing, all

24. Overall, _____ take more drugs than _____ . In the case of stimulants, _____ are more likely to take _____ pills, while _____ are more likely to take _____ - _____ pills. Females are more likely to smoke _____ than males.

males, females, females, diet, males, stay-awake, cigarettes

25. In the period from 1979 to 1984, the use of alcohol by high school seniors _____ . The only personality characteristic that shows up in the makeup of adult alcoholics is _____ _____ . However, the personality of individuals who drink may result from _____ on alcohol rather than be a contributing factor to drinking.

decreased, personal maladjustment, dependence

26. One risk factor for adolescents is an expectation that alcohol will produce _____ _____ . In fact, adolescents at risk for alcohol abuse may get bigger _____ _____ benefits. Males at risk for alcohol abuse also appear to have a strong motive for _____ .

personal effects, tension reduction, power

27. Heavy drinkers are more likely to say that they have parents who _____ drinking by _____ . This is a stronger relation than the one between _____ _____ and drinking.

sanction, adolescents, peer pressure

28. Auto crashes involving alcohol decreased _____ to _____ percent after raising the _____ _____ in one state.

10, 30, drinking age

29. A school-based program, such as having students discuss alcohol-related issues with the _____ group, is an example of an _____ _____ . A one-year follow-up revealed _____ _____ _____ .

peer, environmental intervention, less alcohol abuse

30. The active ingredient in marijuana is _____ - _____ - _____ or _____ . It has effects on _____ , _____ of stimuli, and _____ coordination. It may distort _____ . Its duration of action is _____ to _____ hours.

delta-9-tetrahydrocannabinol, THC, memory, perception, motor, judgment, four, eight

31. Male users of marijuana risk reduced _____ count. Women risk reduced _____ . Animal studies link marijuana use with an increase in _____ _____ .

sperm, fertility, birth defects

32. Most college students smoke marijuana because it is _____ . The motivation for the first use seems to be _____ . Most of those who smoke marijuana (do/do not) _____ use hard drugs.

fun or enjoyable, curiosity, do not

33. Apparently, teen use of marijuana is more likely to be related to _____ use than to _____ use.

peer, parental

34. One successful antismoking campaign for junior high school students used _____ and _____ pressure to discourage smoking.

peer, parental

35. Three general approaches characterize all drug intervention attempts. _____ interventions focus on the abuse substance and use _____ to reduce use. _____ interventions emphasize the _____ where substance abuse originates and where it can be prevented. _____ interventions try to change the _____ .
Agent, laws, Environmental, settings, Host, user

36. A child or adolescent who breaks the law is called a _____ _____ . Technically, this term applies only to those _____ .
juvenile delinquent, convicted

37. During the last decade, the rate of juvenile delinquency has _____ relative to the level of adult crime. According to FBI statistics, _____ percent of all youths are involved in juvenile court cases.
increased, 2

38. Recently, the rate of juvenile delinquency among _____ has increased significantly. The rates among _____ groups are particularly high compared to the overall populations of those groups. However, these groups may not have equal access to the _____ .
girls, minority, law

39. Erikson sees delinquency as an attempt to establish an _____ . According to Blos, delinquency is caused by an increase in _____ - _____ behavior caused by sexual urges and separation pressures. Bloch and Niederhoffer see delinquency as caused by _____ _____ in a culture.
identity, acting-out, blocked opportunities

40. The norms of lower-class peer groups are more likely to be _____ than are middle-class group norms. Being _____ and _____ are high-status traits for lower-class boys. Lower-class communities are more likely to have a high _____ rate, may feel _____ toward the _____ class, and tend to have _____-quality schools.
antisocial, tough, masculine, crime, alienation, middle, poor

41. Occurrence of delinquency seems to be linked to the failure of _____ _____ skills. These skills include _____ the adolescent's whereabouts, using effective _____ for antisocial behavior, calling on effective _____ - _____ skills, and supporting the development of _____ skills.
family management, monitoring, discipline, problem-solving, prosocial

42. Of these family management practices, _____ _____ seems to be more related to delinquency than the others. The parents of delinquents generally (do/do not) _____ keep track of their children's whereabouts, and discipline is _____ .
parental monitoring, do not, inconsistent

43. The second leading cause of death among adolescents is _____ . Its current rate is _____ times the 1950 rate. Only _____ kill more adolescents. More _____ than _____ commit suicide. This difference may reflect the use of _____ efficient means for attempting suicide by _____ .
suicide, three, accidents, males, females, more, males

44. It appears that _____ is a predisposing condition in suicide, but family _____ may also be involved.
depression, instability

45. The precipitating event, as opposed to the predisposing condition, in a suicide attempt is likely to be a severe _____ . This may result from the loss of a _____ or a _____ , failure at _____ , getting _____ , or even the fear of getting _____ .

   stress, boyfriend, girlfriend, school, pregnant, pregnant

46. Elkind explains the _____ in incidence of suicide during adolescence as being related to the construction of a _____ _____ . Adolescents think that _____ cannot happen to them. They also believe that their stress and pain are _____ and that no one else can understand.

   increase, personal fable, death, unique

47. Suicide prevention efforts depend on the adolescent shifting from the feeling of _____ to a feeling of _____ with regard to death and suicide. The effectiveness of suicide hotlines is _____ . Apparently, only about _____ percent of individuals considering suicide call a hotline.

   invincibility, vulnerability, low, 2

48. About _____ percent of adolescent girls and _____ percent of adolescent boys suffer eating disorders. _____ percent of the boys and _____ percent of the girls report periodic food binges.

   12, 4, Forty, 34

49. _____ _____ is the condition of extreme, apparently voluntary starvation that afflicts many adolescent women. Its symptoms include severe _____ , _____ , and _____ . Anorexics may show obsessive _____ and an intense interest in _____ . They may not feel that they _____ their lives and may feel _____ . They complain of being _____ after a few bites and are obsessed with body _____ .

   Anorexia nervosa, malnutrition, emaciation, amenorrhea, activity, food, control, useless, full, size

50. The syndrome that involves a cycle of heavy eating followed by induced vomiting is called _____ . It is characteristic of the final stages of _____ _____ .

   bulimia, anorexia nervosa

51. _____ is weighing more that 20 percent over the normal body weight. _____ percent of all young adolescents and _____ percent of all older adolescents are obese.

   Obesity, Five, 15

52. It is possible that obesity is inherited, that is, has a _____ cause. It is also possible that the _____ _____ fixed by the _____ is too high. In addition, a particular person may simply burn less energy at rest than others, which means that he or she has a lower _____ _____ _____ . Basal metabolism _____ during adolescence.

   genetic, set point, hypothalamus, basal metabolism rate, drops

53. Obese adolescents have a distorted _____ _____ and do not feel in _____ of their lives. They are _____ with food, both _____ about it and _____ it. They sense a constant _____ and also have low _____ - _____ . They tend to blame everything on their _____ .

   body image, control, obsessed, thinking, eating, emptiness, self-esteem, weight

54. One study found that, when obese girls exercise, they (do/do not) _____ expend as much energy as nonobese girls doing the same activity.

   do not

55. Adolescents (do/do not) _____ have more problems than children. This is true both for _____ and _____ samples of adolescents and children. There actually is a tendency for the incidence of problems to _____ during adolescence.

do not, clinical, nonclinical, decline

56. The period between adolescence and full adulthood has been called _____ . It appears to involve a conflict between the newly autonomous _____ and the pressure to become _____ involved.

youth, self, socially

57. _____ _____ and _____ _____ _____ signal full adulthood. In very recent times, the former has become _____ difficult to obtain.

Economic independence, autonomous decision making, more

Key Terms Matching Exercise

Match the Key Term on the left with the correct definition on the right.

_____ 1. identity crisis (LO–1, p. 585)
_____ 2. epigenetic principle (LO–1, p. 589)
_____ 3. crisis (LO–2, p. 590)
_____ 4. commitment (LO–2, p. 590)
_____ 5. identity diffused (confused) (LO–2, p. 590)

a. Theory that states that, anything that grows has a ground plan, and out of this plan the parts arise, each one having its special time of ascendancy

b. In Marcia's theory, the extent to which an adolescent shows a personal investment in what he or she is doing or is going to do

c. Feeling of a loss of identification or self-image

d. In Marcia's theory, an adolescent who has not experienced a crisis or made a commitment

e. In Marcia's theory, a period during which an adolescent is choosing among meaningful alternatives

_____ 6. identity foreclosure (LO–2, p. 591)
_____ 7. identity moratorium (LO–2, p. 591)
_____ 8. identity achieved (LO–2, p. 591)
_____ 9. connectedness (LO–4, p. 593)
_____ 10. mutuality (LO–4, p. 593)

a. Reflected in mutuality and permeability

b. In Marcia's theory, an adolescent who has made a commitment without experiencing a crisis

c. Refers to the adolescent's sensitivity to and respect for the views of others

d. In Marcia's theory, the adolescent who has experienced a crisis and made a commitment

e. In Marcia's theory, an adolescent who has made no commitment and is currently experiencing a crisis

____ 11. permeability (LO–4, p. 593)
____ 12. individuation (LO–4, p. 593)
____ 13. separateness (LO–4, p. 593)
____ 14. self-assertiveness (LO–4, p. 593)
____ 15. intimate (LO–6, p. 597)

a. An adolescent's expression of his or her own point of view and in taking responsibility for communicating this clearly

b. Indexes openness and responsiveness to the views of others

c. Composed of separateness and self-assertion

d. Describes one who forms and maintains one or more deep and long-lasting love relationships

e. Seen in the expressions of how distinctive the self is from others

____ 16. preintimate (LO–6, p. 597)
____ 17. stereotyped (LO–6, p. 597)
____ 18. pseudointimate (LO–6, p. 597)
____ 19. isolated (LO–6, p. 597)
____ 20. delta-9-tetrahydrocannabinol (THC) (LO–10, p. 604)

a. An individual who has mixed emotions about commitment; reflected in the tendency to offer love without an obligation

b. Active ingredient in marijuana

c. Describes the individual who withdraws from social encounters and has little or no intimate attachment to same- or opposite-sex individuals

d. Describes an individual who has superficial relationships dominated by friendship ties with same-sex, rather that opposite-sex, individuals

e. Describes an individual who appears to be maintaining a long-lasting heterosexual attachment, but the relationship has little or no depth or closeness

____ 21. host interventions (LO–11, p. 607)
____ 22. environment interventions (LO–11, p. 607)
____ 23. agent interventions (LO–11, p. 607)
____ 24. juvenile delinquent (LO–11, p. 606)
____ 25. anorexia nervosa (LO–18, p. 613)

a. Type of preventive intervention in drug use in which an adolescent's cognitive and behavioral skills are strengthened so that he or she can resist substance abuse

b. Adolescent who breaks the law or engages in behavior that is considered illegal

c. Type of preventive intervention in drug use in which attempts are made to modify everyday influences on adolescents' substance abuse

d. Voluntary starvation leading to severe malnutrition and emaciation

e. Type of preventive intervention in drug abuse that makes use of legal, technical, and social controls of the target substance

____ 26. bulimia (LO–18, p. 613)

____ 27. obesity (LO–18, p. 615)

____ 28. set point (LO–18, p. 615)

____ 29. basal metabolism rate (BMR)
        (LO–18, p. 615)

____ 30. youth (LO–19, p. 617)

a. Minimum amount of energy a person uses in a state of rest

b. The weight an adolescent maintains when no effort to gain or lose weight is expended

c. Weight more than 20 percent over normal skeletal and physical requirements

d. Extended period of economic and personal "temporariness" after the teenage years but before the adult years

e. Syndrome involving bouts of uncontrolled eating followed by self-induced vomiting

Answers to Key Terms Matching Exercise

1. c	6. b	11. b	16. a	21. a	26. e
2. a	7. e	12. c	17. d	22. c	27. c
3. e	8. d	13. e	18. e	23. e	28. b
4. b	9. a	14. a	19. c	24. b	29. a
5. d	10. c	15. d	20. b	25. d	30. d

Self-Test A

Choose the best alternative.

1. The psychologist known for his theory about the development of identity in adolescence is (LO–1, p. 584)
   a. Piaget.
   b. Freud.
   c. Kohlberg.
   d. Erikson.

2. The crisis of identity versus identity confusion is which of Erikson's eight stages of the life cycle?
   (LO–1, p. 584)
   a. fourth stage
   b. fifth stage
   c. sixth stage
   d. seventh stage

3. According to Erikson, forming an identity involves examining and making commitments to all of the following except which? (LO–1, p. 589)
   a. occupation
   b. politics
   c. religion
   d. ego control

4. The view that anything that grows has a ground plan, and out of this ground plan the parts arise, each one having its special time of ascendancy, is the (LO–1, p. 589)
   a. epigenetic principle.
   b. static view of identity.
   c. cohesive aspect of identity.
   d. reciprocal view of identity.

5. John is a devout Jew. He was raised Jewish and has never questioned these beliefs. According to Marcia, what is John's identity status? (LO-2, p. 591)
   a. identity achieved
   b. identity foreclosure
   c. identity moratorium
   d. identity diffused

6. Which of the following is most likely to facilitate an identity crisis? (LO-3, p. 592)
   a. going to college
   b. getting married immediately after high school
   c. dropping out of high school to work
   d. getting pregnant as a teenager

7. Mutuality is an aspect of (LO-4, p. 593)
   a. individuation.
   b. separateness.
   c. connectedness.
   d. self-assertion.

8. Marcia's measure of identity is based on (LO-5, p. 593)
   a. a survey.
   b. a questionnaire.
   c. a structured interview.
   d. behavioral observation.

9. According to Erikson, the crisis that follows identity versus identity confusion is (LO-6, p. 596)
   a. initiative versus guilt.
   b. autonomy versus doubt.
   c. industry versus inferiority.
   d. intimacy versus isolation.

10. Will's relationship with a woman has been going on for quite a while, but it has no real closeness to it. Marcia would characterize Will as (LO-7, p. 597)
    a. intimate.
    b. preintimate.
    c. pseudointimate.
    d. stereotyped.

11. Which of the following drugs (licit or illicit) was used most widely by high school seniors in 1984? (LO-8, p. 601)
    a. alcohol
    b. cigarettes
    c. marijuana
    d. heroin

12. Adolescents who are heavy drinkers often have parents who (LO-9, p. 603)
    a. are teetotalers.
    b. sanction drinking.
    c. are authoritarian.
    d. are warm and caring.

13. Marijuana use has been found to impair (LO-10, p. 604)
    a. relaxation.
    b. self-confidence.
    c. short-term memory.
    d. creativity.

14. According to the text, attempts to prevent substance abuse in adolescents can be classified as all of the following except which? (LO–11, p. 607)
    a. agent intervention
    b. subject intervention
    c. environment intervention
    d. host intervention

15. Juvenile delinquency is primarily a _____ category. (LO–12, p. 606)
    a. legal
    b. behavioral
    c. social
    d. psychological

16. The family management practice that has been found to relate most strongly to delinquency is (LO–13, p. 609)
    a. discipline.
    b. problem solving.
    c. reinforcement.
    d. parental monitoring.

17. The national suicide rate for adolescents makes suicide the _____ major cause of death in that age group. (LO–14, p. 609)
    a. first
    b. second
    c. third
    d. fourth

18. Which of the following makes suicide prevention in the adolescent difficult? (LO–16, p. 612)
    a. formal operational thought
    b. focus on imaginary audience
    c. creation of personal fable
    d. inability to take the perspective of another

19. Which of the following should a person *not* do when he or she suspects an adolescent is contemplating suicide? (LO–17, p. 613)
    a. Be supportive and listen.
    b. Ask if the person is thinking of hurting himself or herself.
    c. Try to persuade the person to get professional help.
    d. Assure the person that everything will be all right.

20. An eating disorder that involves binging on food and then purging oneself through vomiting is called (LO–18, p. 613)
    a. anorexia nervosa.
    b. bulimia.
    c. encopresis.
    d. obesity.

Answers to Self-Test A

1. d	5. b	9. d	13. c	17. b
2. b	6. a	10. c	14. b	18. c
3. d	7. c	11. a	15. a	19. d
4. a	8. c	12. b	16. d	20. b

Self-Test B

Choose the best alternative.

21. According to Erikson, the development of an identity in adolescence requires (LO–1, p. 585)
    - a. a psychological moratorium.
    - b. good ego control.
    - c. strong ego resiliency.
    - d. authoritarian parents.

22. After much thought and experimentation with many different ideas, Anne has decided that she really wants to be a sculptor and is now taking art classes that will allow her to sharpen the skills she needs to succeed. According to Marcia's categories, Anne would be classified as (LO–2, p. 591)
    - a. identity diffused.
    - b. identity achieved.
    - c. in the identity moratorium status.
    - d. identity foreclosed.

23. Marcia's structured interview for measuring identity focuses on crisis and commitment in all of the following areas except which? (LO–5, p. 593)
    - a. occupation
    - b. religion
    - c. politics
    - d. sex roles

24. In Erikson's theoretical view, (LO–6, p. 596)
    - a. identity and intimacy develop together.
    - b. intimacy precedes identity.
    - c. identity precedes intimacy.
    - d. many different relationships between identity and intimacy are expected.

25. Margaret has many superficial relationships, mainly with other women. According to Marcia, Margaret would be classified as (LO–7, p. 597)
    - a. intimate.
    - b. preintimate.
    - c. pseudointimate.
    - d. stereotyped.

26. Research on the relation between intimacy and identity suggests that (LO–7, p. 599)
    - a. identity always precedes intimacy.
    - b. for females, intimacy may precede identity.
    - c. intimacy usually precedes identity.
    - d. identity and intimacy usually develop simultaneously.

27. In 1984, what percentage of high school seniors reported illegal use of drugs at some point in their lives? (LO–8, p. 600)
    - a. 27.9 percent
    - b. 54.9 percent
    - c. about 67 percent
    - d. 92.6 percent

28. What has been found to prevent heavy drinking by adolescents? (LO–9, p. 603)
    a. parental nurturance
    b. parental discipline
    c. parental conflict
    d. parental drinking

29. Research has found a correlation between marijuana use in adolescents and (LO–10, p. 605)
    a. authoritarian parents.
    b. parental monitoring.
    c. parental permissiveness.
    d. parental drug use.

30. Preventive health efforts described in the text have been primarily aimed at (LO–11, p. 605)
    a. heroin use.
    b. marijuana use.
    c. cigarette smoking.
    d. use of LSD.

31. When does an individual become a juvenile delinquent? (LO-12, p. 606)
    a. after committing a crime
    b. after being arrested
    c. after being convicted
    d. Both b and c are correct.

32. Who of the following is the least likely to be labeled a juvenile delinquent? (LO-13, p. 606)
    a. a black adolescent
    b. a white middle-class adolescent
    c. a Chicano adolescent
    d. a lower-class adolescent

33. What is the current attempted suicide rate for adolescents? (LO–14, p. 609)
    a. 1 out of every 500
    b. 1 out of every 1,000
    c. 1 out of every 5,100
    d. 1 out of every 10,000

34. Which of the following is *not* a sign of potential suicide? (LO–15, p. 612)
    a. talk about suicide
    b. previous suicide attempts
    c. severe family problems
    d. a close family relationship

35. What percentage of individuals who commit suicide call a hotline? (LO–16, p. 612)
    a. 2 percent
    b. 4 percent
    c. 8 percent
    d. 12 percent

36. Which of the following should you do with an adolescent suspected of thinking about suicide? (LO–17, p. 613)
    a. Ask if he or she is thinking about hurting himself or herself.
    b. Say that everything will work out fine.
    c. Show your disapproval of suicide.
    d. Say that everyone has a right to self-determination of their own lives, including taking them.

37. Which of the following is not a specific symptom of anorexia nervosa? (LO–18, p. 613)
    a. heavy eating followed by self-induced vomiting
    b. amenorrhea
    c. severe malnutrition
    d. preoccupation with food

38. Research on adolescent girls in a camp showed that (LO–18, p. 616)
    a. obese girls participated in sports less than normal girls.
    b. obese girls were less active in sports than normal girls.
    c. normal girls participated in sports less than obese girls.
    d. normal girls were less active in sports than obese girls.

39. The term *youth* is used to denote (LO–19, p. 617)
    a. the transition into adolescence.
    b. the middle portion of adolescence.
    c. the transition from adolescence to adulthood.
    d. late adolescence.

40. Entry into adulthood is characterized primarily by (LO–19, p. 618)
    a. the development of a primary pair-bond.
    b. economic independence.
    c. autonomous decision making.
    d. Both b and c are correct.

Answers to Self-Test B

21. a	25. d	29. d	33. b	37. a
22. b	26. b	30. c	34. d	38. b
23. d	27. c	31. c	35. a	39. c
24. c	28. a	32. b	36. a	40. d

Questions to Stimulate Thought

1. How are Marcia's ideas related to Erikson's?
2. What is the relationship between identity and intimacy?
3. Should anything be done to reduce the use of drugs by adolescents? If so, what?
4. What causes and what can be done about juvenile delinquency?
5. What could be done about adolescent suicide?
6. What are the differences between wanting to have a slim body and being anorexic?
7. Compare and contrast anorexia nervosa and obesity.

Research Project

In this exercise, you interview five friends about their history of alcohol use. (If you want, you can respond to the questions yourself, as one of the five individuals.) Use the interview questions on the data sheet, record each person's responses, and then answer the questions.

Data Sheet

Question	Person 1 Sex _____ Age _____	Person 2 Sex _____ Age _____	Person 3 Sex _____ Age _____	Person 4 Sex _____ Age _____	Person 5 Sex _____ Age _____
1. How often do you have a drink?					
2. At what age did you first drink?					
3. When you take a drink, how much do you drink?					
4. Do you ever get drunk?					
5. If you answered "yes" to question 4, how frequently?					

Questions

1. What is the average frequency of drinking in your subjects? What is the range among individuals? Are there large individual differences in frequency of drinking? Are there age or sex differences?
2. What is the average age at which your subjects first drank? What is the range among individuals? Are there large individual differences in the age at which they started drinking? Are there age or sex differences?
3. On the average, how much do these subjects consume when they drink? What is the range among individuals? Are there large individual differences in the amount they drink? Are there age or sex differences?
4. How often, overall, does this group get drunk? What is the range among individuals? Are there large individual differences in the frequency of drunkenness? Are there age or sex differences?
5. How do your data compare with the data on adolescent alcohol use presented in the text? Do your data support or refute the text?